THE PITTSBURGH THEOLOGICAL MONOGRAPH SERIES

General Editor
Dikran Y. Hadidian

9

SEMIOLOGY AND PARABLES
Exploration of the Possibilities
Offered by Structuralism for Exegesis

SEMIOLOGY AND PARABLES

Exploration of the Possibilities
Offered by Structuralism for Exegesis

Papers of the conference
sponsored by the Vanderbilt Interdisciplinary Project,
"Semiology and Exegesis",
and supported by a grant from
The National Endowment for the Humanities,
held at Vanderbilt University,
Nashville, Tennessee,
May 15-17, 1975

Edited by
Daniel Patte

THE PICKWICK PRESS
Pittsburgh, Pennsylvania
1976

Library of Congress Cataloging in Publication Data

Main entry under title:

Semiology and parables.

(Pittsburgh theological monograph series ; no. 9)
1. Jesus Christ--Parables--Congresses. 2. Parables--
Congresses. 3. Semiotics--Congresses. I. Patte,
Daniel. II. Vanderbilt University, Nashville.
III. Series.
BT375.2.S45   226'.8'06   76-20686
ISBN 0-915138-11-5

CONTENTS

Preface, by Daniel Patte v

Acknowledgements xix

Foreword to the Discussions. xx

I. "The Parable of the Unjust Judge: A Metaphor
      of the Unrealized Self"

    by *DAN O. VIA* (University of Virginia). 1

RESPONSES:

    Norman R. Petersen (Williams College) 33

    Edward McMahon (Vanderbilt University). 42

    James L. Crenshaw (Vanderbilt University) . . . 47

PANEL DISCUSSION, edited by Gary Phillips. 57

II. "Structural Analysis of the Parable of the
       Prodigal Son: Toward a Method"

    by *DANIEL PATTE* (Vanderbilt University) 71

RESPONSES:

    Robert C. Culley (McGill University). 151

    William G. Doty (Rutgers University). 159

PANEL DISCUSSION, edited by Gary Phillips. 169

III. "The Semiotic Endeavor: Two Responses"

    Walburga von Raffler Engel. 179
            (Vanderbilt University)

    David Roberson. 186
            (University of California, Davis)

IV. "A Parable of Pascal"

    by *LOUIS MARIN* (Johns Hopkins University) . . . 189

    RESPONSES:

        Larry S. Crist (Vanderbilt University). 221

        Robert Detweiler (Emory University) 230

        Lou H. Silberman (Vanderbilt University). . . . 236

    PANEL DISCUSSION, edited by Gary Phillips. 242

V. "Parable, Allegory, and Paradox"

    by *JOHN DOMINIC CROSSAN* 247
        (DePaul University)

    RESPONSES:

        John R. Donahue (Vanderbilt University) 282

        John R. Jones (Vanderbilt University) 291

    PANEL DISCUSSION, edited by Gary Phillips. 306

VI. "Meaning and Modes of Signification:
    Toward a Semiotic of the Parable"

    by *SUSAN WITTIG* 319
        (University of Texas, Austin)

    RESPONSES:

        John F. Plummer (Vanderbilt University) 348

        Gary A. Phillips (Vanderbilt University). . . . 357

    PANEL DISCUSSION, edited by Gary Phillips. 373

PREFACE

The Conference on "Semiology and Parables" (Vanderbilt University, May 15-17, 1975) had as its purpose the exploration of the possibilities offered by semiological and structuralist methods for biblical exegesis. This exploration was determined by the very nature of semiology as well as by the texts we chose as a testing ground: parables (the Gospel parables and parable-like texts in other literature).

The papers, responses and discussions represent several types of semiotic research at their present stage of development. One could have easily been bewildered by the diversity of approaches and of technical vocabularies. Yet, many participants made it a point to express to me their feeling that the conference had not been a series of isolated papers but rather an integrated collective research. In this preface I shall try to describe what the integrating factor was which made this conference a "meaningful whole".

When looking at this conference on "Semiology and Parables" from a semiological (or meta-semiological!) perspective we could say that it is perceived as a "meaningful whole" because of the constraints of a complete network of structures. Limiting ourselves to that which was most characteristic of this conference, i.e., its focus on semiology, we could in addition say that the conference may be perceived as a meaningful whole because all of the contributions belong to the same "system": the system of semiological quests. In this system some of the contributions manifest the "norm" (the structure of this system while other contributions are "paradoxical" like the parables themselves: i.e., revealing both the norm and its relativization at one and the same time (cf. Professor Crossan's paper and its discussion). My task in this preface is therefore an attempt at formulating a model, a theory, for the "structure of this system of semiological quests". My formulation of this model will necessarily be tributary to the symbol system in which I am immersed. The other participants would certainly present diverse and possibly even conflicting formulations of this model of the integrating factor of this conference. This truly serves as a reminder that our models are always relative as the paradoxical contributions often warned us and that there might be several equally valid models representing the same phenomenon as is the case for the several theories explaining the phenomenon electricity.

The fact that all of these contributions (including papers, responses, and discussions) have been integrated into a "meaningful whole" through three days of interaction among participants implies that each contribution received connotations that it would not have had if it had remained an isolated piece. Some of these connotations may well have not been originally intended by the authors. Yet they emerged during the conference as a result of the integrating factor which we identified as semiology. What is semiology? We do not intend to give here an abstract definition of this field-encompassing field. We shall focus our remarks instead on the few characteristics of the semiological research which appear to have been presupposed by the conference as a whole.

Semiology, the science of signs, aims at studying texts and other cultural phenomena in terms of linguistic paradigms as opposed to historical paradigms which characterize traditional exegetical methods. A sentence is meaningful because its linguistic elements are interrelated in a specific way. To begin with, a sentence would be meaningless if its words were not interrelated according to the constraints of the grammatical rules of the specific language in which the sentence is written (e.g., according to the constraints of the grammar of the English language). Yet there are other, indeed more subtle, constraints which are at work in a meaningful sentence. There are constraints--which can also be termed "structures"--which govern the interrelation of phonetic features. For example, certain sounds can be associated together while others cannot be. Others govern the interrelation of semantic features. These constraints or structures which characterize respectively the phonetic and semantic systems specific to a given language are themselves submitted to broader constraints which can be found at work in any human language.

Another aspect of sentential meaning is provided by the meaning which is attributed to each of its words. The meaning of a word is in large part determined by the specific ways in which it is interrelated with other words in the language viewed as a "system of signs" (or words). For instance, if in a specific language the word "culture" is primarily associated with "good manners", it does not have the same meaning as in a language in which it is primarily associated with "learning". Thus, the meaning of a word is also determined in part by the constraints or structures of the specific system of signs to which it belongs. These structures implicitly set this word in relation with other words.

Two conclusions may be drawn from these far-from-comprehensive remarks. First, the meaning of a word in a sentence is determined by the interaction of a series of constraints (all of those mentioned above) as well as by the intentionality of the author. Second, meaning, e.g., the meaning of a sentence, appears as something which can be deconstructed, in other words, analyzed. Following Greimas, we should speak of "meaning effect" rather than "meaning" in order to avoid thinking of meaning as an entity.

It is this interaction of series of constraints in the sentence which is studied in structural linguistics. Yet there are still other constraints at work in a meaningful text. Let us understand "text" to include narrative as one sub-type, and further, parable to be a particular kind of narrative. Narrative is not the mere succession of a series of meaningful sentences. It is a meaningful narrative only if its various linguistic elements are interrelated in a specific way, that is, according to broader constraints or structures. These include, for example, the "narrative structure" which allows the reader to apprehend this text as a meaningful narrative rather than another type of discourse; the "literary genre" which in a given culture allows the reader to apprehend another dimension of the meaning effect; the "mythical structure" which permits the reader to apprehend this text as meaningful in terms of a given mythical system; the "cultural codes", and the like. When C. Lévi-Strauss, R. Barthes, and A. J. Greimas (among others) began the investigation of the constraints at work in communicative phenomena beyond the sentence it appeared that the research in structural linguistics was only a part of a wider field, semiology, which also encompassed research in anthropology, literary criticism, fine arts, etc.

As Professor Wittig emphasizes in the first part of her paper, at the present stage of semiological research we can no longer assume that the analysis of a text in terms of a few selected structures accounts for its total meaning effect. We have to acknowledge that there is a complex network of constraints or structures at work simultaneously and at all levels of a text. For instance, the narrative structure is a constraint which partially governs both the interrelation of a series of sentences and the interrelation of linguistic elements within the sentence. It is convenient to distinguish between three types of constraints or structures at work in any text in this regard: the cultural structures--the constraints which characterize a specific culture including specifically the literary genre; the deep structures or structures of "the human mind" which characterize man qua man, including the narrative and mythical structures; and the structures of the enunciation which include the intentionality of the author, the constraints of the specific situation in which he writes or speaks and the relation of the text to the hearer/reader.

At the present stage of research, a large part of the semiological activity must be devoted to the identification of specific constraints by means of "model" building at each level of constraint ("model" in the scientific sense of the term) as well as more generally by a model or theory which can represent the structural network as a whole. Consequently, semiological research is necessarily progressing in quite different directions. Some scholars are primarily concerned with the establishment of a general semiotic theory; others study a limited number of constraints which belong to a specific level of the structural network (i.e., cultural structures, deep structures or structures of the enunciation);

still others study the interaction of several constraints belonging to various levels. Furthermore, the research takes place simultaneously in the traditionally separated fields of linguistics, anthropology, various fields of literary studies, etc. It is no wonder then that many different semiological theories, models, and methods are proposed.

The very nature of the subject matter--the whole phenomenon of human communication--demands that semiological research be a thoroughly interdisciplinary endeavor. This is the reason why this conference gathered together scholars from various fields: linguistics, English literature, French literature, as well as biblical studies. Furthermore, theories and models from the fields of psychology, philosophy, and anthropology were used by the various participants. One of our goals was to bridge the gap created by the use of various technical vocabularies so as to help in the understanding of the interrelation of various types of semiological research. In some instances, two (or more) models or theories were proposed by scholars either in different fields or in the same field for the same level of the structural network. It was then our task to evaluate whether the differences were either simply a matter of formulation, perhaps as a result of an individual's technical vocabulary, or more substantially the manifestation of two conflicting understandings of that structural level. In other instances, models or theories which were apparently conflicting were found to be dealing with different structural levels. In that case it was a matter of finding the broader semiotic theory which integrated them.

During the conference these interdisciplinary exchanges were manifested in the formal responses and in the discussions (edited by Gary Phillips from tape recordings) as well as by the juxtaposition of the papers. When dealing with a structural level which had not yet been thoroughly explored, the paper presented the quest for a semiological model: such a paper was by necessity theoretical and methodological even though it may have proposed the analysis of a given text. By contrast, when dealing with a structural level for which a model had been at least provisionally established, the paper presented a method: the model was used for the analysis of a text and in the process the model was refined.

As was emphasized by Professor Reynolds (cf. the discussion of Professor Crossan's paper) and other participants, the semiological or structuralist enterprise as a whole is built on the notion of "integration". The meaning effect of a text is the result of an integrating process. We could say then, that the integrating factor is the structural network briefly discussed above. Indeed, the ultimate goal of the semiological research is a better, fuller apprehension of the "meaning effect" as an integrated whole. Each individual piece of semiological research is disappointing in the sense that it rarely reaches this goal. It can only deal with limited aspects of the meaning effect and often with aspects which appear quite secondary. This stage of the research is nevertheless necessary. The linguistic and discourse elements have to be identified rigorously by means of an atomistic analysis so that the various constraints of the structural network might in turn be identified. It is only on this basis that the meaning *effect* will truly be apprehended as an *integrated* whole.

We are, all of us, impatient to reach this goal and our analytical patience grows thin when, as we progress in our individual research, we discover that the structural network is more complex than expected. But when scholars involved in various specific types of semiological research are gathered together and dialogue beyond their differences and incompatibilities, the complementarity of their quests is manifested. A glimpse at the structural network as a whole is possible; the integration can be envisioned. Admittedly, much work is still needed at each level before a complete model for the structural network might be soundly established. Yet it is already possible to apprehend some of its main features.

The preceding remarks suggest that the reader can apprehend the following papers, responses, and discussions as a meaningful whole by attempting to discern how they complement each other by the very fact that they deal with various features of the structural network. The following comments on the main papers suggest the principle lines of one (among other, of course) such readings. We propose to read all of these texts in terms of Professor Marin's paper which alone presents an overall semiotic theory. This theory implies and incorporates the narrower semiotic research presented in the other papers. Its place at the center of the volume suggests that it manifests itself the integrating factor of this conference and that it should be both the first and the last piece read. Indeed, it is worth a double reading!

The main focus of Professor Dan Via's paper appears to me to be his theoretical quest with respect to two constraints which belong to the deep structural level. Models for the narrative structure, for the "archetypal structure" and for their interrelation are proposed on the basis of Bremond's and Greimas' work on narratives and Jung's psychological theory. In what way can parable as narrative be viewed as a metaphor of the self? This is the fascinating question raised by his paper. The responses and discussion emphasize the promise of this pioneering research and a debate ensues which helps in the precise identification of the real issue at hand: the essential question of the relationship between metonymic structure (in this case the narrative structure) and a metaphoric structure (in this case the archetypal structure) within the structural network.

My own paper focuses upon the same question since it attempts to find a model which can represent the relation of the narrative structure (a metonymic structure) with the mythical structure (a metaphoric structure conceived on the basis of Lévi-Strauss' research). Consequently, an analytical method is proposed on the basis of this theoretical research. The correlations of this paper with Professor Via's forces us to raise the question of the relation between mythical structure as conceived by Lévi-Strauss and the Jungian archetypal theory. Should they be viewed as two models or theories which attempt to represent the same deep constraint? Further research is necessary on this point. The responses and discussions first of all emphasize the strict limits of this method: it cannot presume to account for the whole meaning effect of the text. Secondly, an important clarification emerges: the study of the semantization of deep structures (narrative, mythical, and elementary structures) is in fact a study of the way these structures have been invested by the other structural levels, namely the structures of the enunciation and the cultural structures. Even though we analyze the text in terms of deep structures, we are dealing with textual features which belong to all structural levels. It remains to identify which part of the investment of the deep structures is to be attributed to each of the other structures. This is precisely the type of research which characterizes Professor Louis Marin's paper. For instance, he proposes that the narrator manifests himself when he invests the narrative structure with modal statements, "by displaying for his reader what the actors secretly wish, know, what they are capable of doing, that is, everything which does not belong to the realm of events".

Professor Funk's paper (which unhappily is not presently available for publication) is focused on a quite different type of constraint: a structure which characterizes the form of the expression of the parables. We hope for a prompt publication of this paper which analyzes a significant part of the meaning effect of the parables that ought not be neglected. It is one of the ways in which the "limits" and the "center" of a text (as discussed by Professor Marin) can be determined. Judson F. Parker's response and the discussion of this paper would not have been meaningful without the paper. Hence, we reluctantly delete both. We include nonetheless Professor von Raffler Engel's and Professor Robertson's responses insofar as they raise general issues which are pertinent to the conference and its task as a whole.

Professor Crossan's paper is concerned first of all with the constraint which we could term the "literary genre". It belongs in the structural network to the level of the cultural structures. This is clear when the term parable is defined as "paradoxes formed into story by effecting single or double reversals of the audience's most profound expectations". In other words a parable challenges the "profound expectations" (the cultural codes?) which characterize a given society. Indeed the literary genre "myth" reinforces the cultural codes by integrating them into a mythical system. In the second part, "Jesus as Parabler", Professor Crossan emphasizes how one can recognize signs within the text itself of the constraints of the enunciation. Then by dealing with "allegory" Crossan suggests quite eloquently that "it is the structuring processes of the human imagination which is at work in *all* these levels of interpretative possibility". Could we say that "the single plot which can be read on all these variant levels" is the manifestation of a 'deep structure'? Would it be the narrative structure? The mythical structure? Or both? Crossan's conclusions emphasize that these various structural levels, especially the parable as literary genre characterized by paradox and the allegory as deep structure, are parts of the same structural network. Consequently, one is forced to speak of "allegorical parables".

Professor Susan Wittig's paper, after an introduction which emphasizes the complexity of the network of semiotic constraints, urges the critic to keep in mind that the analysis of each dimension must be followed by a synthesis. Beyond the semiotic model based on the sign theory of Peirce, Morris, and de Saussure, she proposes a model which would account for the polysemy of language in general and of the parables in particular. On this basis, she points out the essential role of what she calls "the psychological dimensions of the communications act", or "the rhetorical act", i.e., the relation of "sender/receiver", "text/reader", or in our terminology "the constraints of the enunciation". By approaching the text from the point of view of the "phenomenology of the reading act" (Wolfgang Iser, *The Implied Reader*), she stresses that the "meaning" of a text cannot be apprehended outside of this relation of "text/reader" and she warns that a structuralism limited to an analysis in terms of the deep structures and of the cultural structures cannot in any way claim completeness in the task of deconstructing the "meaning of the text".

Thus each of the papers in its own way emphasized the role of specific constraints in the meaning effect of the parables and more generally in human communication. The lecturers, the respondents and the participants in the discussion attempted each in their own way to contribute to a general theory of interpretation. Yet, Professor Marin, as the result of his many years of diversified semiotic research, was alone in the position to propose a theory of interpretation which fully integrated all of the levels of semiotic research without giving primacy to any one of them. His analysis of a parable of Pascal is a methodological demonstration showing the relationship among the constraints of the enunciation, the cultural structures, and the deep structures (both the narrative structure and the constraints which make out of the text a metaphor of the self) as well as a proposal for a semiotic theory.

Such a semiotic theory affirms that meaning is not an entity but an effect. This oft-repeated axiom of semiological research is displayed in all its disquieting power in Marin's analysis of Pascal's text. One of our "profound expectations" (Crossan's phrase), or better our "deep expectation", is that of finding "meaning" in a text, in life. Indeed most of our linguistic activities, in fact most of human communication, aims at establishing meaning as an entity, as something stable enough to provide an order in which man can live a meaningful life. The parables are narrative paradoxes which challenge our profoundest expectations by relativizing both the specific meaningful system and meaning in general. What was held as an established meaningful system or as a meaning-entity is revealed as an effect: that is, in terms of Pascal's parable, a simulation, an illusion. This simulation or illusion is indeed useful but it cannot claim any ontological status.

The semiotic analysis of a text aims at revealing the "plurality of meaning" (cf. Marin's definition of this phrase) of a text as the effect produced by the interplay of various constraints. It aims therefore at the same paradoxical effect as that of a parable. The semiotic analysis of a parable reveals its paradoxical effect as effect. It is a paradoxical discourse upon a paradox. Its conclusion cannot but be a paradox, as is indeed the case with Pascal's parable and the Gospel parables (cf. the conclusion of Marin's paper). The dimensions of meaning--the plurality of meaning-- revealed by the analysis is itself a simulation, "the constant and violent imposition of meaning", which must itself be deconstructed in an endless decoding, otherwise as meaning-entity it is opaque and therefore obscuring. Our discourse would once again be the discourse of the people. Indeed a useful and sound discourse ("the people's opinions are sound") which provides a necessary and meaningful order (the kingdom of the islanders with their pseudo-king) is but a "vain" discourse ("the people are vain") because "they do not know what they say".

Semiotic analysis cannot but be disconcerting and disquieting to the reader because it does not establish a meaning as *the* meaning of a text, i.e., as a meaning which could be part of a meaningful system upon which the reader could quietly settle down. In such a case, hermeneutic could be represented as the reader "going into" this meaning of the text. Rather, semiotic analysis, by the very fact that it shows any discourse as a simulation of a meaning-entity, reveals the dynamics of the meaning effects which demand that the reader settle for the "dynamics of the provisory" (Roger Schutz) of the text/reader relationship (cf. Wittig's paper). Hermeneutic must then be viewed as an open-ended process which reflects the open-endedness of human communication.

What are the possibilities offered by semiology to biblical exegesis? What is the relationship between historical critical methods and semiotic methods? These questions generated several indirect formulations. Is it not similar to the relationship between meaningful historical process and meaningful system, or between metonymic constraint and metaphoric constraint? The historical and the linguistic paradigms which respectively characterize traditional exegesis and semiology are models which allow the interpreter to apprehend different and complementary dimensions of the human discourse. How are they precisely related? A significant part of the conference was devoted to just this question of the relation of metonymic and metaphoric models. However we must leave this important question open for the present.

Daniel Patte
Vanderbilt University

ACKNOWLEDGEMENTS

The Conference on "Semiology and Parables" was part of the "Semiology and Exegesis Project, an interdisciplinary project at Vanderbilt University" sponsored by the National Endowment for the Humanities. The conference was also partially sponsored by SEMEIA, an experimental journal for biblical criticism, the Society of Biblical Literature, and by the Vanderbilt University Lecture Committee. It is my pleasant duty to express my gratitude to our sponsors.

My gratitude goes also to two graduate students, Brenda Hopson and Gary Phillips, who had much responsibility in gathering together the various elements of this volume. Gary Phillips had in addition the difficult task of editing the discussions.

This conference has been what it was because of its participants. To each I would like to express my gratitude for three long days of hard work. The members of my seminars went even further by taking care of many practical aspects of this conference.

D. P.

FOREWORD TO THE DISCUSSIONS

The editing of the taped discussions attempts to capture
in a clear and cogent fashion the major lines of argument,
counter-argument, and exposition generated by the presented
papers and responses. Given the diversity of participants,
their interests and points of view and the range of questions,
it was frequently necessary to excise segments of the dialogue
in order to preserve what was deemed central to the discussion
and to present it intelligibly to the reader who may not have
had the benefit of personal involvement in the conference.
The need for coherence in line of argument was a major crite-
rion in the editing process, and properly so, given the
difficult nature of ideas and models associated with "structuralism" and "semiology". Every effort was made to be faithful to the speaker's intent, but where the letter has been
altered, it is our hope that the spirit was not compromised.

Gary Phillips
Vanderbilt University

CHAPTER I

THE PARABLE OF THE UNJUST JUDGE:
A METAPHOR OF THE UNREALIZED SELF[1]

Dan O. Via, Jr.

University of Virginia

INTRODUCTION

I should like to begin by clarifying briefly the phenomenological framework within which I will place the structuralist
categories that will be used in trying to interpret this parable
taking my cue from Merleau-Ponty. For the latter the world is
always there before any reflection of mine, and the real has to
be described, not constructed. The goal of phenomenology is
to reawaken a direct and basic experience of this world.[2] But
that does not mean that Merleau-Ponty's phenomenology intends
to *describe the world as it is*. It rather wants to give a
"direct description of *our experience* as it is" (my italics).[3]
Perception (our original, unreflective experience of the world)
is always a seeing from somewhere, from an horizon which draws
together all other horizons; therefore, my experience is perspectival, and the world is the world as I experience it.[4]
The world which I distinguish from myself as the totality of
things or processes in causal connection I rediscover in myself, a world speaking to me of myself. The world is that of
which I form a representation.[5] Perception is a dialogue between subject and object which annuls the subject/object
dichotomy and which is grounded in the equivocal nature of

our own bodies as both subject and object.[6] The thing--in
our case a text--is not given in perception but is taken up
and reconstituted.[7]

To have said these things does not mean that every
aspect of the world or every "world" is equally revealing
to me of myself. It should also be recognized that there is
not just a one way movement in which I read myself into the
world--or a text--and then see myself there. The movement
is dialectical: I am also affected by the world.

It would seem that phenomenological reduction, as well
as perception, is perspectival.[8] Certain ways of seeing are
bracketed out, but the reduction is never complete, and one
must always begin again.[9] This is to recognize that when one
way of seeing is bracketed out, another is bracketed in, and
it seems to me that the interpreter's job is to be clear about
what is being bracketed in. Let me state my agreement with
Julian Marias that reality does not finally disclose itself
nakedly but rather elicits from man innumerable interpretations[10] and also my agreement with the correlative judgment
that since a literary text has no independent existence, the
critical task is to describe it as it exists in the flow of
history and in the mind of the reader.[11]

What I am bracketing in as my vantage point for reading,
which defines the mind of this reader, at least for this
paper, is certain structuralist categories and the Jungian
concept of the Self or the ego-Self relationship. The
analysis of narrative functions and actants has as its purpose the displaying of the network of relationships and
movements which are to be translated into psychological
terms, more specifically into some components and movements
of the Self as understood by Jung. The bracketing in of
Jungian categories simply means that the subject matter to

be looked for is the dynamics of the Self. It does not mean
that what the story discovers specifically about the Self is
determined in advance. That must be inferred from the interrelationships of the psychological categories as defined by
the structural arrangements of this particular story. The
use of Jungian categories at all might be defended, not only
by Jung's theory of archetypes, discussed immediately below,
but also by Heidegger's contention that the interpreter may
have to use "violence" on the text in order to "show what
does not stand in the words and is nevertheless said".[12]
Stated less provocatively this means that the interpreter of
a text is positioned at a different point in cultural history
than is the author. He has a different horizon and pre-under-
standing, therefore he will choose levels of reading and see
things--naturally, inevitably, and legitimately--that would
have been impossible for the author to have envisioned. The
interpreter has to *choose* some level of reading; there is no
neutral choice and any alternative chosen reveals something
about the interpreter[13]--including the impact which the text
itself has had upon him.

Every fairytale, according to Marie Louise von Franz,[14]
wants to describe the same complex psychic phenomenon--the
Self. We might make the same claim for parables, or at least
some parables, and then we can begin to test the validity of
this claim by determining whether the dynamics of the Self
can actually be seen to be operative in the parables. That
a story may be so treated I will ground here in a provisional
way on Jung's theory of archetypes or primordial images,
which are ultimately unknowable and indescribable, and which
project and express themselves in what we might call secondary images or symbols. And one medium into which these
secondary images are projected is stories of various types.

4

Here in the secondary images the archetypes receive a specific stamp and determinable form, but obviously the archetype is altered in the process of projection.[15] By determining the relationships between the images in a given story and amplifying these by comparison with similar images in other stories we approach a definition of the archetypes themselves and thus gain access to a deeper level of psychic reality than appears in the textual manifestation.

Every archetype has its positive, negative, and neutral aspects or images, and the symbolic process is the experience of the alternating rhythm of these different images.[16] Thus we could say that the temporal plot movement in stories is grounded in this plural nature of archetypes. An upward moving plot reflects the shift from the negative to the positive aspects of one or more archetypes, and a downward moving plot reflects the reverse shift. This could provide a theoretical warrant for the structuralist claim that behind the chronological movement of a narrative there is a nontemporal logic.[17]

Traditionally critical interpretations of the Unjust Judge (Luke 18:2-5) (based on the one point approach) have seen the point to be either an exhortation to pray or an assurance that God is trustworthy or especially that he answers prayer. The judge is consistently taken to be an image of God and often the "how much more" argument is invoked. If an unjust judge can be prevailed upon, how much more God?[18] Such an interpretation probably grows out of the assumption that the God image in a parable should be an authority figure, and this assumption is encouraged by the fact that in most of the narrative parables it is probably true. But I will try to show that in this parable the judge is not an image of God. We might begin by observing that this is one of the very rare instances in the parables of

Jesus where the word God is mentioned, and it is mentioned
twice in this rather short narrative. This is undoubtedly
a source of chagrin for us modern secular New Testament
scholars who have taken such delight in the fact that Jesus
consistently used non-religious language in his parables,
but I think that we can still be comforted by the realization
that he so seldom lapsed into explicit God-talk. Nevertheless, since God is mentioned here we should probably pay
attention to that fact as one of the clues to the parable's
meaning. I will try to show that the overall theme is not
God's trustworthiness or an exhortation to pray but rather
the various aspects of human estrangement or alienation.

FUNCTIONAL ANALYSIS

In determining the unit for analysis we might keep in
mind the distinction between the two basic levels of narrative:
story (a self-contained fictional world constituted by the use
of third person narration, past tenses, etc.) and discourse
(the I-you dialogue between the narrator and the reader or
hearer, presenting evaluations, interpretations, etc.). Our
unit is a narrative (more story than discourse, as we shall
see below) told by a *character* (Jesus) and enclosed between
two parallel story statements made by the Lukan narrator.
The narrator's preceding story statement is "And he [Jesus]
told them a parable...saying", and his succeeding story statement is "And the Lord [Jesus] said...." But it must be noted
that the preceding story statement also contains an element of
the narrator's discourse--a brief, anticipatory interpretation
of the parable. Moreover, the succeeding story statement introduces a discourse of Jesus which is also an interpretation

of the parable, and since it is confluent with the narrator's prior interpretation, it becomes a part of the narrator's discourse as well as being a character's (Jesus') discourse.

I should also like to observe that the parable itself exercises the poetic linguistic function. It has an internally organized plot which attracts attention intransitively to itself. On the other hand, the two interpretations which surround the parable exercise the metalinguistic function: they are texts about a text. In summary: the parabolic unit clearly distinguishes itself from its context in that it is a narrative (primarily story) exercising the poetic function and told by a character. It is enclosed between two story statements of the narrator, one of which contains and the other of which generates interpretative discourse which exercises the metalinguistic function.

Because the Unjust Judge begins by describing a state which is a potentiality, the parable naturally attracts Claude Bremond's description of the functions of what he calls an elementary sequence. In his view the elementary narrative sequence is composed of three functions: (1) potentiality; (2) the actualization of a process; (3) the attainment of a goal or result. It is also possible that once the story is begun no process will be actualized or no goal will be reached. Let us observe as the analysis becomes more concrete that the initial potentiality is defined as a state which may be one of deficiency or satisfaction, that the process may be one of improvement or degradation, and that the goal or result may be an improved or deficient state. It may also be that the process of improvement is countered by opposition or setbacks of various kinds which the process of degradation is interrupted by interventions designed to help the hero. The two simplest and most general narrative movements are:

(1)   state of deficiency → process of improvement → improved state

(2)   satisfactory state → process of degradation → state of deficiency[19]

It should be noted that Bremond's position entails the view that the initial state of deficiency = a potentiality for improvement, and the initial state of satisfaction = a potentiality for degradation. The Unjust Judge fits this scheme very nicely or, more exactly, shows itself to be an actualization of this structure.

Our parable begins with a state of deficiency, which is followed by a process of improvement which meets with opposition, but the goal of an improved state is apparently reached (see figure 1). The initial deficient state as described suggests that a lack of justice prevails because a judge in a certain city neither fears God nor regards man. In the next function a widow initiates a process of improvement by persistently coming to the judge and asking that he vindicate her against her opponent. She is seeking justice and in doing so is offering him the opportunity to institute justice, but he refuses to hear her case (opposition). Her goal finally appears to be reached when the judge decides to vindicate her in order to be free of her nagging presence.

The first two functions are primarily at the story level although in the second one there is a discourse statement by the widow: "Vindicate me...." The third function begins at the story level, "but after this he said...", however, this function is primarily a discourse which the judge speaks to himself in the first person. In it he recapitulates the earliest part of the narrative but also a new move occurs. Having refused in the past to hear her case, he now decides that he *will* vindicate her and gives his reason. In this

third function we are inside the judge's head and inside the
future tense. Therefore, the widow's vindication is only
suggested, not described as having happened. But the judge's
decision is represented as having occurred, reversing the
stance which he took in the second function. Thus, we have
in the third function a psychic event in the life of the
judge which is certain--his decision--and a probable inter-
personal event, the widow's vindication by him. In any case
the widow's vindication is in the narrative as a possibility.
The final function then is a fusion of the story and discourse
levels; the two are not mutually exclusive.[20] If the judge's
discourse with himself is more prominent than the story level,
that poses no problem for my interpretation, for I see the
judge to be the central character anyway, and I am aiming
ultimately at an intra-psychic reading of the parable.

However contradictory it may sound, I would now like to
tighten this analysis up a little bit by using some of
Greimas' categories in a more or less imprecise way. According to Greimas the text sequence, which is a syntagmatic
scheme composed of five functions, is the irreducible diachronic element of a story. The five functions (which I
will call component functions in order to distinguish them
from Bremond's elementary functions) are: contract [(1) mandate or injunction vs. (2) acceptance], struggle [(3) confrontation vs. (4) success] and (5) consequence [which may
be the reception of a helper, the liquidation of the lack,
or the recognition of the hero; or two or all three of these
may appear].[21]

In the first elementary function the very fact that a
character is introduced as a judge implies that a mandate
had been given, for in Israel a judge is regarded as appointed
to carry out God's own justice among the people, and he is

specifically enjoined to fear the Lord (II Chr. 19:5-7). But our judge has not accepted but has rather refused this mandate, thereby creating a lack of justice and order. In the process function we have an ongoing confrontation between the widow and the judge. In the goal function the judge's statement that he will vindicate the woman seems to syncretize three component functions: the widow's success in her struggle following confrontation, the final acceptance by the judge of his original mandate to dispense justice, and the consequence constituted by the liquidation of the original lack of justice. But we shall see, especially in the light of an actantial analysis, that while the widow is vindicated and achieves a kind of success (this "success" is given an unexpected twist in the psychological interpretation), the judge's acceptance of the mandate is ambiguous, and there is no certainty that there will be a general restoration of justice. This is because the judge acted, not with conviction, but in order to avoid the woman's continual coming. This motive makes the story in the end more the judge's story than the widow's, and the end is not happy.

The Unjust Judge: *In a certain city there was a judge who neither feared God nor regarded man; and there was a widow in that city who kept coming to him and saying, "Vindicate me against my adversary." For a while he refused; but afterward he said to himself, "Though I neither fear God nor regard man, yet because this widow bothers me, I will vindicate her, or she will wear me out by her continual coming."*

FIGURE 1 (Functional)

Elementary Functions

State of deficiency: lack of justice; alienation

Process of improvement: the widow seeks vindication (justice)

Opposition: the judge refuses

Goal or result: improved state-- the widow is vindicated

Result: state of deficiency for the judge--his continued alienation

Component Functions

Mandate and refusal

Confrontation

Success of widow

Acceptance by judge of the original mandate

Consequence: the liquidation of the original deficiency

FIGURE 2 (Actantial)

Ordainer ——— Object ———→ Recipient

Helper ——→ Subject ←—— Opponent

FIGURE 3

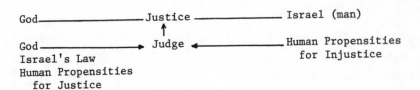

FIGURE 4

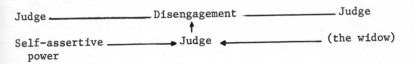

FIGURE 5

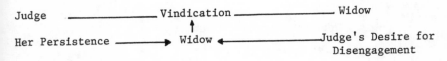

FIGURE 6

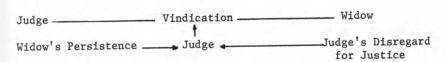

FIGURE 7

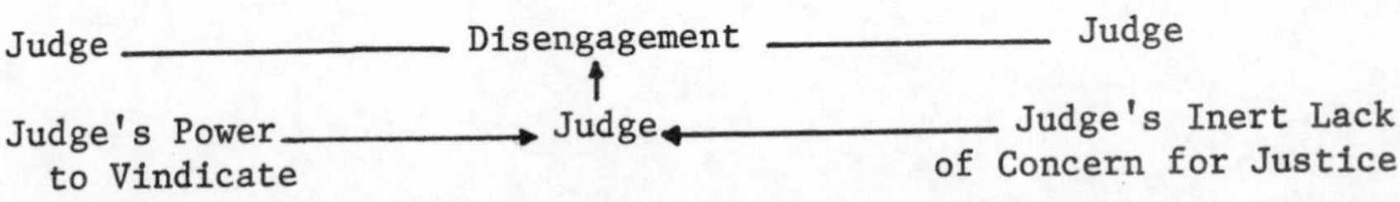

Judge ———————— Disengagement ———————— Judge

Judge's Power ——→ Judge ←——— Judge's Inert Lack
to Vindicate   of Concern for Justice

ACTANTIAL ANALYSIS

The actantial model[22] is a semantic construct composed
of six actants, or spheres of constant action. These six
actants are a constellation of forces positioned on three
axes and acting upon one another. On the axis of communication an Ordainer seeks to communicate an Object to a Recipient.
On the axis of volition the Subject, who has been mandated by
the Ordainer, exercises his will toward the Object--to possess
it or to communicate it, for the Ordainer. On the axis of
power the Helper and the Opponent struggle, respectively, for
and against the Subject as he pursues his quest. An actant
or actantial slot may be filled by more than one character
(or other element) during the course of the story, and a
given character may occupy more than one actantial slot (see
figure 2).

Here it might be helpful to mention Heidegger's three
hermeneutical principles.[23]

(1) The first phase of interpretation is to set forth
the essential meaning of the whole text which sustains it
and "towers above it". This suggests that the whole casts
light on the parts.

(2) The second phase is to pass through the parts observing how the main theme unfolds itself.

(3) The third phase is to find that center-point in
the text where it can be discovered what is said, though not
directly in the words.

Grasping the meaning of the whole may be helpful or
necessary in identifying what actors or other elements, at
least by implication, fill the actantial slots in the early
part of the narrative.

The initial elementary sequence, which we have seen to display a deficiency, lack of justice, presupposes as the normative and proper situation that which can be rendered actantially in figure 3. God, as Ordainer, has put the judge in the position of Subject to communicate justice to Israel. The legal and moral indices referring to the Old Testament enable us to say that the judge would be helped by God, the law, and any human propensities toward justice while he would be opposed by an human tendencies toward injustice. But the situation actually reflected in the first sequence is represented actantially in figure 4. The judge, refusing God's mandate, has made himself Ordainer and Recipient as well as Subject. We must consider the whole story in order to discover that what the judge really desires—in his contempt for both God and man—is not to be bothered. The Object of his will, what he wants to communicate to himself, is tranquil disengagement, which I refer to henceforth simply as disengagement. He is helped by his own self-assertive powers, which seem not to be opposed by conscience or any sense of duty to his office. But he will be opposed by the widow later in the story.

In the second function (processes in conflict, confrontation) the widow is the Subject who seeks vindication for herself (see figure 5). The judge's office gives her the right to expect him to be the Ordainer of justice, but he refuses to fulfill this actantial role. She is helped by her persistence, but that is not yet sufficiently powerful to overcome the judge's desire for disengagement.

One could suppose that in the goal or result function the judge has finally assumed the role of Ordainer and that he communicates justice to the widow, for she does become the recipient of vindication, at least by implication. This

situation is seen actantially in figure 6. Her persistence
would have overcome his lack of concern for God or man. But
if we consider with care the axes of communication, volition,
and power, the real situation actantially turns out to be the
one displayed in figure 7. What the judge wills is not her
vindication but to be rid of her. As Ordainer, Subject, and
Recipient, he communicates to himself the disengagement which
he has consistently desired, and her vindication is the means
to this end. On the power axis his power to vindicate, in the
service of his desire for disengagement, has overcome his inert lack of concern for justice.

The actantial models for the first and third functions
are alike except for the occupiers of the positions of Helper
and Opponent. The Helper in the first function is the judge's
general self-assertiveness, his contempt for God and man,
while the Helper in the third function is his power to vindicate. As a means of attaining the self-assertive end of
avoiding all religious and moral entanglements he has used
his power to enact justice for another—a good means for a
questionable end. We will note later the consequence—or at
least concomitant—of this.

THE SIGNIFICANCE OF
THE IRREDUCIBLE DIACHRONIC ELEMENT IN NARRATIVE

According to the analysis of Greimas[24] the initial sequence
in a folktale is qualified by the breaking of a contract, the
rupture of order, the reversal of values, alienation. Yet, this
situation also expresses and affirms the freedom of the individual to act, even if to create disorder. The final sequence is
qualified by reintegration and the restoration of order, but

this must be paid for by the renunciation of individual freedom. It is the struggle (confrontation and success) which
enables the transformation of the initial situation into the
final one. But all of this leaves us without freedom. The
real significance of the folktale then is seen to be the
presentation and mediation of this opposition. How does the
folktale mediate between freedom and order? It does so by
affirming both at the same time but in such a way that the
contradition is not visible to the naked eye. The narrative
gives the impression of balance and of neutralized contradictions.

One may want to ask, however, what is happening beneath
that impression. What does it mean for self-understanding
or psychic reality that freedom and order are mediated?
That is a question which I will address later. At this
point I want to consider our parable in the light of Greimas'
view of the folktale's significance.

The initial situation is one qualified by disorder, a
lack of justice, and also by the freedom of the judge
actualized in his rejection of his mandate and his disregard
for the claims of God or man. As a result of the widow's
struggle there is in the end a restoration of law--even if,
as we have seen, an ambiguous one--in that the widow is
vindicated. And to make this possible the judge had to re-
linquish some of his freedom. Perhaps the conflict between
freedom and order in the judge's life is mediated by the new
freedom of the widow from the oppression by her adversary.
But the judge is the central figure in the story, so we must
consider more carefully what happens with his freedom. He
surrenders momentarily his freedom to be indifferent to the
law for the sake of what he takes to be a greater freedom--
the freedom to be disengaged, to be rid of the woman. But

freedom for disengagement is isolation. The widow moves in
the story from deficiency through conflict to vindication.
But the judge moves from alienation to alienation between
his action and his intention. He acted to vindicate the
widow but not because of concern about her, God, or justice,
but because he intended to maintain his disengagement. In
the judge we have a protagonist who obtained his object,
but because his object was mischosen, his success was a
catastrophe.

SOME JUNGIAN CONCEPTS

At this point I should like to discuss briefly just those
Jungian categories which will be pertinent for the intra-
psychic interpretation of the parable.

I begin with Jung's complex concept of the Self. The
Self is an archetype of wholeness or totality which embraces
all of the components of the individual personality (conscious or unconscious) and which is ultimately indefinable
and unknowable and exceeds the consciousness of the individual
by an indeterminable extent. But not only is it the totality
and center it is the source of life which is there from the
beginning and which confronts the individual independently
of his conscious will. It is in addition the process of becoming what one always was as well as the goal of the total
man.[26] Within the Self all of the opposites are contained,
and the Self as an archetype of totality cannot be empirically
distinguished from the image of God.[27] The dynamic process by
which the Self is realized (which is identical with the process of individuation) can best be described after a discussion of some of the component aspects of the Self, to which
I now turn.

Consciousness develops out of the unconscious and exists as the awareness of opposites, manifesting itself in the exercise of exclusion, selection, and discrimination.[28] The center of consciousness is the ego, which is the subject of all personal acts and of all successful attempts at adaptation in so far as they are achieved by the will.[29]

The personal unconscious is comprised of lost memories, repressed ideas and other elements which could just as well be conscious. That from the personal unconscious which can be summoned up into consciousness should be kept there and assimilated into one's conscious outlook.[30]

"Beneath" the personal unconscious is the collective unconscious, which is the realm of the archetypes. The latter are the inherited deposits of the ever repeated experiences of the race and are universal and identical in all persons, the identity of mental functioning being based on the universal similarity of the brain.[31] The archetypes are the foundation stones of the psychic structure which make knowledge of objects possible. They are not inherited ideas or patterns of thought but are inherited *empty forms* or *possibilities* of certain types of actions, perceptions, or ideas. Because the archetypes are the forms through which we think and therefore cannot be fully got out of in order to be thought about, and because they are empty, they can never be fully known or described.[32] The concept of archetypes simply means that imagination, perception, and thinking, like the instincts are influenced by inborn, formal elements.[33]

While the archetypes are ultimately unknowable, they can be circumscribed and something can be said about them on the basis of the multiplicity of images and parables which each of them generates and on the basis of the psychic contents which they attach to themselves through empirical experience.[34]

There are as many archetypes as there are typical life situations,[35] and although an archetype is indescribable and expresses itself in many different images, it nevertheless must
have a character because Jung states that an archetype is
recognizable[36] and is the possibility of a *certain* kind of
action or perception. Thus each archetype must be the
possibility of a *particular* kind of experience, however
varied its manifestations, and its numerous images would
have to have a recognizable relationship to each other. But
when all is said and done, any interpretation of an archetype
remains an "as if".[37]

While Jung recognizes that the unconscious possesses a
certain inert tendency to remain unconscious, at the same time
it wants to become conscious; and the latter seems to be the
emphasis of Jungian psychology. The unconscious wants to
communicate itself and break into consciousness.[38] The proper
response to this on the part of the ego is to accept and integrate the *contents* of the archetype into consciousness and
to become conscious of the archetype itself as something which
the ego is *not* and should not identify itself with.[39]

Before leaving the concept of the archetypes as such we
might observe the paradox that the Self is one archetype, the
archetype of wholeness, but as the totality of the psyche it
also embraces all the other archetypes.

The most important archetype for our purposes, other than
the Self, is the anima. The latter is the archetype of the
woman in a man's unconscious, which receives its content from
the feminine traits in the man's personality and from his
experience with women. It projects images of the mother,
daughter, sister, beloved, heavenly goddess, etc., and man
experiences the anima as the feminine not-I in himself.[40] The
anima may be regarded as the archetype of life itself. It

corresponds to female consciousness in man and is characterized by eros, the function of relationship.[41]

The anima, like any other archetype, may take the
initiative to act upon consciousness. She cannot solve her
own problems, but she and the ego are in mutual need of each
other for self-understanding. In the interest of this she
may pursue a long quest.[42] If the male ego listens and the
contents of the anima are integrated into consciousness, then
the anima becomes the representation of the man's emotional
and feeling life, his capacity for relatedness, and his pattern
of behavior toward women.[43] A further consequence of making
the contents of the anima conscious is that she then becomes
a bridge between the ego and the collective unconscious,[44]
thus enhancing the possibility of realizing the Self.

I turn now to a consideration of the relationship of the
ego to the Self, a relationship which is subject to two
problematical distortions. The first of these is inflation.
This is the identification of the ego (something small) with
the Self (something large) so that the ego is blown up *be-*
yond its proper limits. This is the situation into which
one is born, and it may occur also later in life, but always
with some kind of suffering because the ego will have appro-
priated for itself energies that are too great for it.[45]

In order for consciousness and proper psychological
development to take place, the ego must separate from the
Self. But the consequence of separation is that disidenti-
fication becomes disconnection: the alienation of the ego
from the Self is the second distortion of the relationship.[46]
What is desired is neither inflation nor alienation but a
relationship between ego and Self constituted by a conscious
axis or line of communication between the two. Thus the ego

will neither be filled beyond capacity nor separated from its origins and foundations.[47]

The problem with E. F. Edinger's discussion of this situation is that he defines the emergence of the ego or consciousness as a *separation* from the Self,[48] but he has also said that this separation involves *inflation*, which he has defined as *identification* with the Self.[49] He has then implied that identification and separation, inflation and alienation, are simultaneous. But he has not really noticed this paradoxical implication or tried to explain it. He rather tends to say that the individual gets stuck in one or the other or alternates between them.[50] Our reconsideration of the Unjust Judge will hopefully shed some light on the simultaneity of these two states.

Finally in this section I should like to present the Jungian view of the process through which the Self is realized --as a psychological interpretation and substantiation of Greimas' contention that the diachronic essence of the folk-tale is a movement from disorder and freedom (alienation) through struggle to order without freedom (reintegration) and that the folktale mediates between order and freedom. In Jungian terms, the ego, in order to act in freedom (become conscious), breaks a contract with the Self, and, becoming the effective center of the psyche, causes the alienation of consciousness from the unconscious. Therefore, the Self does not develop as a totality. A crisis (tests, the pain of alienation, suffering like that of Job)[51] may cause a breach in the wall between consciousness and the unconscious, and the Self as wholeness or totality begins to emerge because of the reintegration of conscious and unconscious. Con-comitantly, the ego loses its position as power center, and the center of power moves from the ego to that ineffable

position on the boundary between consciousness and the unconscious;[52] but the ego is now part of a much larger and
richer whole and is supported by the depths of the Self.
Thus the whole movement shows the initial act of free rebellion to have been a fraudulent one. Or, more paradoxically if more accurately, the ego's free act of separation in order to find consciousness is desirable, but the
alienation which this produces is undesirable if inevitable.[53]
Therefore, the loss of freedom in the end is the loss of an
ambiguous freedom and the gaining of a greater scope. The
mediation between the ego's freedom--its central position--
and the reestablishment of order--the reign of the Self--
shows that the initial freedom was really alienation (and
inflation) and *is* the restoration of order as a larger and
richer totality in which the ego has more freedom, i.e.,
more scope. In being divested of its initial mistaken sense
of being the center, the ego is given a larger field of
action and a deeper reservoir of resources.

This is not what happens in the Unjust Judge, but the
opposite, which does happen, may be understood against this
background.

THE UNJUST JUDGE: A JUNGIAN INTERPRETATION

In general terms, I am treating this parable as a representation of a problem in male psychology. The male ego refuses to respond in any significant way to the anima. But it
should be recalled that for Jungian psychology a woman contains within her collective unconscious an archetype of the
male, the animus, with which she must come to terms. The anima
and animus "collect" different types of experiences and create

different kinds of specific problems. For example, the anima
may cause a man to have shadowy feminine-like moods, while
the animus may cause a woman to have unfounded masculine-like
opinions.[54] But the male and female psyches are in principle
formally analogous.

Or the parable could be taken as displaying the problematic relationship between consciousness and the unconscious
as such, whether male or female. James Hillman treats the
Greek story *Eros and Psyche* as relevant for a new psychology
and as equally applicable for men and women. The story has
to do with the emergence of psyche as such and not just with
the problem of the development of the feminine, despite the
fact that in the story Psyche is a female character.[55] The
specifics of the Unjust Judge have led me to treat it, as indicated, as the representation of a male problem, but the
larger possibilities should be kept in mind while reading my
interpretation.

Beginning with the first narrative function, it may be
noted that a judge, as one who must discriminate and make
choices between opposing claims, is an apt image of the ego.
Awareness of opposites is the essence of consciousness. We
should also observe that God, an image indistinguishable from
the image of the Self, is also mentioned. If women are
relatively absent at the beginning of a story but abundantly
present at the end, then the story will probably be about
the redemption of the female principle.[56] In our parable
there is no woman present at the beginning and the one
woman in the story is being got rid of at the end, so we may
expect that this is not going to be a story about the redeem-
ing of the female principle. The judge's lack of regard for
God and man is typical of the assertiveness of that male ego
which recognizes no female component within itself.[57]

Recall from our actantial analysis that the judge has assumed the Ordainer's position, properly occupied by God (Self), as well as the positions of Subject and Recipient. This displays the inflationary identification of the ego with the Self, and the fact that his object is disengagement manifests the ego's alienation. The judge acknowledges God's existence but does not consider God existentially viable (alienation). Therefore, he identifies himself with God for practical purposes, recognizing no theoretical limitations upon himself; but he does not consciously identify himself with God because he theoretically acknowledges his existence. In psychological terms, the ego's alienation from the Self involves a simultaneous unconscious identification (inflation). The separated ego functionally identifies with the Self by operating as the center of the world (or psyche). The un-consciousness of the identification prevents the emergence of a conscious ego-Self axis, a conscious relationship which entails neither inflation nor alienation, neither identifica-tion nor separation. That is, because the ego unconsciously identifies with the Self, it is not conscious that there even is such a dimension as the Self with which it is not really identical.

Now, as we move to the second narrative function, how might the alienation between ego and Self be overcome? The anima, like any archetype, may try to attract the attention of consciousness and break into it. The widow, a secondary image of the anima, seeks a hearing from the judge, but he refuses to listen to her pleas: the anima wants to be heard by the ego, but the latter in typical ego fashion wants to shut out the unconscious (the anima is an archetype of the collective unconscious) as much as possible.[58] The anima to

be sure can be the chaotic urge to life, and she may entice
a man into foolish relationships. She intensifies, falsifies,
and exaggerates a man's relationships to his work and to
people of both sexes, but when she is seriously heard she may
lead one to a higher sense of life.[59] The ego (judge) in our
parable perhaps intuits her threatening role and refuses to
listen; therefore, he does not experience her as eros and
relatedness, and that bridge between consciousness and the
unconscious, which enables the emergence of the Self, is not
formed.

My reflection in the previous paragraph on *why* the ego-
judge resists the anima-widow--he intuits her potentially
dangerous aspects--may be thought to be reading more into
the story than it can bear. Perhaps it is, but I hope and
think not. It is the aim of Jungian analysis of narrative to
translate every motif in the story into strictly psychological
language.[60] Since the story at the most obvious level deals
with *why* the judge refuses to hear the widow, a Jungian reading must explain--or suggest--*why* in psychological terms the
ego might resist the anima.

In my earlier discussion of the third function I
suggested that the judge vindicates the woman only for the
sake of maintaining his disengagement and that her success
is given a surprising twist. What is meant by this suggestion? It is necessary for cultural achievements that consciousness should be directed by acts of judgment. The dis-
advantage of this is that directedness excludes elements that
seem incompatible with the conscious intention, and consciousness becomes one-sided and dissociated from the unconscious. In response, the unconscious seeks to compensate
the one-sidedness by breaking through into consciousness.
But if the directedness is so great that the unconscious

cannot get through, then the energy of the unconscious is added to the conscious direction.[61]

In the Unjust Judge, because the ego has not listened to the anima and finally has vindicated her, not for her sake, but for the sake of his continued disengagement (the ego separated from the Self), her vindication turns out to be negative, and not positive, at least in relation to the ego. The judge is in the same position of estrangement at the end that he was in at the beginning: he neither fears God nor regards man. The psychological considerations have led us to see that the final alienation is even more intense than the initial. The anima is not heard: her qualities are not assimilated into ego-consciousness. But she exacts a price for being refused. She *is* vindicated in that her power is expressed by being added to the ego's directedness toward alienation. And the judge-ego turns out to be a hidden adversary against whom the widow-anima is vindicated. The ego (judge) loses by winning. The opposites--consciousness and unconscious, ego and anima--are not united: the Self is not realized.

Let us observe explicitly that the woman is a widow. It is ironical that a person of such helplessness in her society should turn out to be a figure of power. The widow, as the "parted one", has been shown by Jung to be an important image in the individuation process of realizing the Self. Widowhood is a stage through which one must pass if the ego-Self axis is to emerge consciously. The ego must be parted from that on which it is dependent but which it is not--the Self.[62] In the parable, the widow-anima wants to be assimilated by the ego thus creating a bridge between consciousness and the unconscious and making possible the conscious ego-Self axis. Had this happened the ego would have

been parted from its unconscious identification with the
Self, and, simultaneously, its alienation from the Self
would have been annulled. But the ego would not.

The moral, existential, psychological, and theological
levels of the story reinforce one another. There is moral
dissonance in that the judge does perform an act that is
beneficial for another, but as a means to his own self-
assertive end. Existentially, there is estrangement of the
Self from the Self because act and intention are divided, and
the judge remains estranged from other men. Psychologically,
the ego is alienated from the Self. Theologically, man is
estranged from God. Reflective theology will have to consider whether each or any of these levels is reducible to
any or all of the others or whether the relationship of man
to himself, his neighbor, and God is such that the four levels
are inseparably co-implicated with one another, but that each
is irreducible to any other.

PARABLE AND METAPHOR

In Jesus' narrative parables in general, the story itself is a concrete vehicle for a mysterious tenor, God's
reign. The tenor is usually represented within the parable
by an authority figure such as a king, father, or employer;
but the divine is not explicitly mentioned. And man, en-
countering the divine and having the issues of his existence
decided, is represented by a subordinate figure--a son or an
employee. A new metaphorical vision of the reign or kingdom
of God emerges from the dramatic interactions of these two
figures (this is somewhat oversimplified) in a realistic story

in which the unexpected and surprising nevertheless happen. The new vision is that the kingdom of God is not a cosmic apocalypse, or the eternal world beyond, or the rule of theocratic law, but human existence as a realistic narrative in which the everyday is transected by the unexpected (God is the Unexpected)--and the narrative may move upward or downward.

In the Unjust Judge the situation is globally the same although there are differences of detail. The realistic narrative is the vehicle for a mysterious tenor--God's reign, or the Self. But the dramatic encounter is not between a figure representing man and a figure representing God (although it is between an authority figure and a subordinate figure, who, as we have seen, ironically exercises power) but between two human figures, and God is explicitly mentioned. If the judge had acted differently, he might have overcome his moral and existential estrangement, and thereby his religious alienation. But he acted as we have seen him act, and God is kept in the margin as one who does not have to be revered. Or, ego and anima are not joined, and the Self remains unrealized.

NOTES

1. I am grateful to the respondents to this paper at Syracuse University and Vanderbilt University for their helpful suggestions. The paper has been changed somewhat in the light of their criticisms but probably not improved as much as they would have liked. I would also like to acknowledge the stimulation received from a paper by a graduate student at the University of Virginia, Ms. Jenny James.

2. M. Merleau-Ponty, *Phenomenology of Perception*, trans. C. Smith (London: Routledge and Kegan Paul [New York: The Humanities Press], 1967), pp. vii, viii, x.

3. *Ibid.*, p. vii.

4. *Ibid.*, pp. 68-69, 70-71; *The Visible and the Invisible*, trans. A. Lingis (Evanston: Northwestern University Press, 1968), p. 41.

5. *Perception*, pp. xii, xiii, 132.

6. *Perception*, pp. 91, 92, 95, 132; *Visible*, pp. 131-139.

7. *Perception*, pp. 9, 214, 326.

8. *Ibid.*, p. 61.

9. *Ibid.*, pp. vii, xiii, xiv.

10. Julián Marías, "Philosophic Truth and the Metaphoric System," *Interpretation: The Poetry of Meaning*, edit. S. Hopper and D. Miller (New York: Harcourt, Brace, and World, 1967), pp. 47-48.

11. See Neal Oxenhandler, "Ontological Criticism in America and France," *Modern Language Review* 55 (1960): 19-21.

12. Martin Heidegger, *An Introduction to Metaphysics*, trans. R. Manheim (Garden City, N.Y.: Doubleday and Co., 1961), p. 136.

13. Roland Barthes, *On Racine*, trans. R. Howard (New York: Hill and Wang, 1964), pp. 164-167, 171-172.

14. *Interpretation of Fairytales* (Zurich: Spring Publications, 1973), p. 2.

15. C. G. Jung, *Two Essays on Analytical Psychology*, trans. R. Hull (New York: Meridian Books, 1959), p. 230; *The Archetypes and the Collective Unconscious*, trans. R. Hull (New York: Pantheon Books, 1959), pp. 5, 70.

16. C. G. Jung, *Psyche and Symbol*, edit. V. de Laszlo (Garden City, N.Y.: Doubleday, 1958), p. 82; *Archetypes*, pp. 38-39.

17. See Roland Barthes, "Introduction à l'analyse structurale des récits," *Communications* 8 (1966): 12.

18. See T. W. Manson, *The Sayings of Jesus* (London: SCM Press, 1950), pp. 305-308; Rudolf Bultmann, *Jesus and the Word*, trans. L. Smith and E. Lantero (New York: Scribner's, 1958), pp. 185-189; Günther Bornkamm, *Jesus of Nazareth*, trans. I. and F. McLuskey, J. Robinson (London: Hodder and Stoughton, 1960), pp. 134-136; Joachim Jeremias, *The Parables of Jesus*, trans. S. Hooke (New York: Scribner's, 1963), pp. 153-156; Eta Linnemann, *Parables of Jesus*, trans. J. Sturdy (London: SPCK, 1966), pp. 119-123; Norman Perrin, *Rediscovering the Teaching of Jesus* (New York and Evanston: Harper and Row, 1967), pp. 129-130.

19. Claude Bremond, "Morphology of the French Folktale," *Semiotica* 2 (1970): 248, 249, 251, 252, 261, 267.

20. See Gérard Genette, "Frontières du récit," *Communications* 8 (1966): 161.

21. A. J. Greimas, *Sémantique Structurale* (Paris: Librairie Larousse, 1966), pp. 195-197, 202-205.

22. See *Ibid.*, pp. 173-174, 176-177, 178, 180, 186, 187, 206.

23. Heidegger, *Metaphysics*, pp. 125, 129, 136.

24. Greimas, *Sémantique*, pp. 200, 202, 207-208, 210-213.

25.   Jung, *Two Essays*, pp. 234, 242-252; "Commentary" in *The Secret of the Golden Flower*, trans. R. Wilhelm (New York: Harcourt, Brace and World, 1962), p. 124; *Psyche*, p. 4; *Aion*, trans. R. Hull (New York: Pantheon Books, 1959), pp. 195-196; von Franz, *Fairytales*, p. 43.

26.   Von Franz, *Fairytales*, p. 43; Edward F. Edinger, *Ego and Archetype* (Baltimore: Penguin Books, 1973), p. 4; Jung, *Aion*, p. 260; *Archetypes*, p. 40; *Answer to Job*, trans. R. Hull (Princeton: Princeton University Press, 1973), pp. 97, 106.

27.   Jung, *Job*, pp. 54-55, 106, 107; *Psyche*, pp. 30-31.

28.   Jung, *Archetypes*, pp. 276, 281, 288; *Golden Flower*, p. 88; *Aion*, p. 204.

29.   Jung, *Two Essays*, p. 234; *Psyche*, pp. 1-2, 5; von Franz, *Fairytales*, p. 41.

30.   Jung, *Two Essays*, pp. 76, 90, 137, 145.

31.   Jung, *Archetypes*, p. 43; *Two Essays*, pp. 79, 157; *Psyche*, pp. 115, 117.

32.   Jung, *Psyche*, pp. xvi, 19, 61, 118-119, 123; *Archetypes*, pp. 38, 48, 57, 66.

33.   Jung, *Archetypes*, p. 44.

34.   Jung, *Two Essays*, p. 200; *Psyche*, pp. 118-119, 123; *Archetypes*, p. 38.

35.   Jung, *Archetypes*, p. 48.

36.   *Ibid.*, p. 38.

37.   Jung, *Psyche*, pp. 118-119, 123.

38.   Jung, *Job*, p. 94; *Two Essays*, p. 194; von Franz, *Fairytales*, pp. 1, 116, 123.

39.   Jung, *Psyche*, pp. 19-20; *Two Essays*, pp. 83, 108, 159-162.

40.   Jung, *Two Essays*, pp. 198-201; *Psyche*, p. 11; *Archetypes*, pp. 26-28.

41. Jung, *Golden Flower*, p. 118; *Psyche*, p. 13; *Archetypes*, p. 32.

42. Jung, *Two Essays*, pp. 193-194, 217; von Franz, *Fairytales*, p. 108; *A Psychological Interpretation of The Golden Ass of Apuleius* (Zurich: Spring Publications, 1974), Lecture VI, p. 5.

43. Jung, *Psyche*, p. 15; von Franz, *Golden Ass*, Lecture V, pp. 14-15.

44. Jung, *Two Essays*, pp. 222, 239; *Golden Flower*, p. 119; Edinger, *Ego*, p. 100.

45. See Edinger, *Ego*, pp. 7, 35.

46. *Ibid.*, pp. 12, 37, 42.

47. *Ibid.*, pp. 6, 38, 41.

48. *Ibid.*, pp. 6, 17-18, 25, 96, 121.

49. *Ibid.*, pp. 7, 18.

50. *Ibid.*, pp. 5, 62.

51. See *Ibid.*, pp. 62, 88, 91, 93, 96.

52. Jung, *Two Essays*, pp. 234, 242-252; *Golden Flower*, p. 124.

53. See Edinger, *Ego*, pp. 42-43.

54. Jung, *Two Essays*, pp. 205-210, 218; *Psyche*, pp. 12-15.

55. James Hillman, *The Myth of Analysis* (Evanston: Northwestern University Press, 1972), pp. 57-60.

56. Von Franz, *Fairytales*, pp. 27-28.

57. See Jung, *Two Essays*, pp. 199, 205.

58. See Jung, *Archetypes*, p. 281.

59. *Ibid.*, pp. 30, 70.

60. Von Franz, *Fairytales*, p. 31.

61. C. G. Jung, *The Structure and Dynamics of the Psyche* (New York: Pantheon Books, 1960), pp. 70-71, 79, 80.

62. See Edinger, *Ego*, p. 162.

RESPONSE TO DAN O. VIA

Norman R. Petersen

Williams College

I cannot imagine many more important contributions than the one Dan Via has tried to make in his paper. Whereas so-called "structuralists" have thus far attempted to show that verbal texts and media are ultimately generated by or grounded in structurational operations of the mind, Via has gone a step further by arguing that one medium, the parable, like another, the fairytale, is a medium which represents metaphorically that complex psychic phenomenon, the Self or personality. Via has thereby moved from the semantic effects of logical mental operations to the semantics of psychic investment in the *relata* which the mind structures. [N.B. For a more Freudian sketch of a similar program, see C. Lévi-Strauss, "The Effectiveness of Symbols", in his *Structural Anthropology*.]

Because of the importance of the issues raised by Via, it is imperative that we understand them, and it is even more imperative that we earn any conclusions we may arrive at about them. The question I am concerned with is basically this: has Via earned his conclusion that parables, or at least some parables, or maybe only the Parable of the Unjust Judge, are metaphors of the Self? Since I will be critical of Via's argument, let me insist now that I am not rejecting Via's enterprise, only the way he has carried it out. My goal is merely to ask for a saner methodological policy.

My questions about Via's approach to the problem of parable as metaphor of the Self arise already in connection

with his introductory remarks. I find myself asking: What
is he trying to buy with his references to Merleau-Ponty's
theory of perception? Remembering that the title of his
paper refers to *a* parable as *a* metaphor of the unrealized
Self, the first answer I come up with is that Via is using
Merleau-Ponty to shift our focus from the text to our mental
reconstitution of it. Thus Via observes that texts are "not
given in perception", but are taken up and reconstituted.
"A literary text," he says, "has no independent existence."
Further, in shifting our focus from a now non-objective text
to a subjective reconstitution of it, he leads us to the
point where we can begin to see how a text may be a metaphor
of the Self. Thus Via says that in the process of reconsti-
tuting texts in our minds, we rediscover in ourselves a world
which speaks to us of ourselves. *The text-in-our-minds is a
representation of something about our selves.*

In this way, Via introduces a phenomenological premise
which, if it is correct, requires that we see *all* texts as
speaking to us about our selves. To some extent, therefore,
all texts are metaphors of the Self. For the sake of discussion, let me suggest that this premise is in fact the
primary *thesis* or proposition of Via's paper, whether he intended it or not. Also, let me remind you that a thesis is
to be accepted without proof; it is a position from which
one argues.

Having arrived at one answer to my question about what
Via is trying to purchase with Merleau-Ponty's theory of
perception, I find that the answer produces another question:
If I accept this theory of textual perception, am I not forced
to ask how a text represents in my perception the dynamics of
perhaps my personality, not *if* it represents such dynamics?

That is to say, if I begin with the *thesis* that the text *is* such a subjective representation, I cannot find in an objective text evidence which will contradict my thesis--a thesis which also to some extent denies the objectivity of texts. In yet other words, to ask *if* the text represents such and such would be to transform my thesis into an *hypothesis*, for unlike theses hypotheses are subject to verification and proof--or so my dictionary would have it.

It is with these issues in mind that I come to Via's assertion that he wants "to *test the validity*" of the claim, namely of his *hypothesis*, that parables describe the complex psychic phenomenon of the Self, a claim which von Franz originally made for fairytales, but also a claim implicitly made for all texts in Via's thesis. Now when Via explains the ground-rules for his text, I find him contradicting the answers to my first questions. Seemingly consistent with those answers, he does say that he will use the analysis of narrative functions and actants *to display* the relationships of some components of the Self as understood by Jungian psychology. However, he is now no longer asking *how* the mentally reconstituted text represents the dynamics of self-hood, which would be consistent with his thesis, but he is also saying that elements in the text itself, narrative functions and actants, display psychic phenomena. Thus he has shifted from a self talking to itself as a result of a textual stimulus, to a textual stimulus which contains in it representations of psychic phenomena. *The representations are not only in the mind, they are in the text as well.*

Via has therefore now shifted from a thesis orientation to an hypothesis orientation. Accordingly, he speaks about a *test* which will determine "*whether* the dynamics of the Self

can actually be seen to be operative in parables". Apart from
leading to confusion about exactly what his purpose is, this
shift from thesis to hypothesis entails both a tautology and
a contradiction. It is a tautology when seen from the perspective of his thesis, for if all texts are metaphors of the
Self, so are parables, by definition. When seen from the
perspective of his hypothesis, however, the shift entails a
contradiction--having said that all texts do represent the
Self, he contradicts himself by asking whether some texts *do*
represent the Self. Moreover, his hypothesis contradicts a
corollary to his thesis, namely that texts have no independent
existence.

To conclude my first and somewhat sophistic point, I
find that Via's paper contains a confusion of purpose which
precludes a systematic and bona fide test of a worthwhile
hypothesis, namely that parables are metaphors of the Self.
I would like to go further, now, and show why his test is
also a failure, at least in terms of his hypothesis. I want
to show that he has neither verified nor proven the hypothesis
that parables are metaphors of the Self, or that the parable
of the Unjust Judge is a metaphor of the unrealized Self.

Regardless of his phenomenology of perception, Via has
made statements about things outside of his personal per-
ceiving-set. He has talked about parables and metaphors,
about narrative functions and actants, and about a text called
the Parable of the Unjust Judge. Indeed, he has talked *to* us
about them in such a way as to suggest that there are textual
limits or constraints as to what one might say about them.
From among these constraints I want to focus on several
classificatory categories that Via uses in his argument--
parable, metaphor, fairytale and/or folktale, and narrative
or story.

Presumably, these categories refer to different kinds of texts or to different aspects of texts. Presumably, that is to say, they are not all synonyms for one and the same textual phenomenon. Accordingly, the problems surrounding these categories, and Via's use of them, may be divided into three groups: first, narrative and/or story; second, parable and metaphor; and third, parable and fairytale or folktale. I will lead into the question of narrative through a consideration of the other two groups. For the moment, let us bracket out of consideration the thesis that all texts are in effect metaphors of the Self. We are now concerned with the categories Via uses in testing his hypothesis that parables are metaphors of the Self.

The first problem concerns the relationship between parable and metaphor. Here we find Via arguing that what is formally or structurally a parable is functionally a metaphor. The word "functionally" is not Via's. I use it in order to show that he does not treat metaphor as a formal or structural phenomenon. Indeed, he does not say much at all about the nature of metaphor. Nevertheless, the question appropriate to the relationship between parable and metaphor has to do with how one thing can also be something else. One possibility is to say that one category, parable, refers to form or structure, and the other, metaphor, to function. Another possibility is to say that both are formal or structural, or that both are functional. But if we say this, then we have no reason to use separate categories, unless one category is a sub-class of the other--which is a third and legitimate possibility, but one which Via does not explore. He says that parables, or at least some of them, are metaphors.

My point in this regard is that our theoretical and methodological problem now becomes one of finding criteria and evidence that will enable us to verify or falsify the hypothesis that a parable is a metaphor, or that all parables are metaphors. I consider this a problem worthy of, indeed requiring, full and careful consideration. But I find neither the problem nor the consideration in Via's paper. To the contrary, his *thesis* that all texts are in effect metaphors of and for the perceiving Self swallows up the issues posed in his hypothesis. I consider this methodological defect failure number one in the text of his hypothesis. *His test lacks controls for speaking about parable(s) as metaphor(s).*

The second problem related to categories concerns parables and folktales or fairytales. In introducing his hypothesis, Via says that Marie Louise von Franz sees fairytales as describing the complex psychic phenomenon of the Self, and that *he* wants to see if parables, or some parables, describe the same thing. Because Via does not introduce the notion of metaphor here, but does so in his title, we may recast his hypothesis as follows:

Fairytales are metaphors of the Self.

Parables are metaphors of the Self.

The constants are "the Self" and "metaphors", and the variables are "fairytales" and "parables". The question is, how from these constants and variables are we to conclude that parables are metaphors of the Self? As we have seen, Via answers: by showing that the dynamics of the Self can be seen to be operative in parables. Now just as the question of how parables are metaphors can be treated separately, so can we treat separately the question of whether the dynamics of the Self are operative in parables. If we were to do so, however, the controls for our test would have to come from an answer to the question: How *are* the dynamics of the Self to be discerned in parables? Then, in order to find controls for saying that parables are *metaphors* of the Self we would have to ask: How do the dynamics of the Self seen in parables render parables metaphorical? Via does not systematically ask these questions and therefore he does not answer them. Thus the question is, how *does* he arrive at his conclusion that parables are metaphors of the Self?

The strongest part of his answer is his focus on the Self and his use of Jung to define the dynamics of the Self, presuming, of course, the adequacy of Jung's theories, which is another issue that Via does not consider. Be this as it may, the weakest part of his answer is his reference to fairy-tales or folktales, and his use of structuralist narrative criticism. Let us begin with the matter of tales, because it is related to structuralist narrative criticism, in his argument.

Via's reference to tales only obscures the methodological issues I have been describing. While we can perhaps be thankful that he did not continue the logic entailed in my reformulation of his hypothesis, and conclude that because both tales and parables are metaphors of the Self, tales are parables and vice versa, we *are* nevertheless left to wonder about the relationship between tales and parables on the one hand, and about the relationship between them and metaphor on the other. Here I find failure number two in Via's test. The failure consists of the fact that although he makes distinctions, *generic* distinctions, between tales and parables by using these genre names, the distinctions are irrelevant both for his test and for his conclusion. The generic issue never arises. Thus we must conclude either that his use of generic names is an obfuscation of his point, or that his failure to consider the textual bases for the distinctions renders his conclusions

incomplete--and therefore ill-founded. In fact, both alternatives are true. I think the generic distinctions are obfusca-
tions because his point is to argue a *thesis which transcends
generic distinctions*, and because his method is based on
theories and models which also transcend generic distinctions.
This is evident both in his use of Merleau-Ponty, from whose
theory of perception he concludes that all texts are in effect
metaphors, and in his use of Bremond and Greimas, from whom
he implicitly concludes that the *narrative* common denominator
of tales and parables transcends generic differences. Thus
*Via argues about parables on the level of narrativity and not
on the level of genre.*

From these observations I conclude that his test is incomplete because he has not considered generic issues, and
that it is invalidated because he says nothing about parables
or metaphors, the terms of his hypothesis. All he has done
is talk about narrativity and the psyche. And in this connection I must confess that I find his thesis, that all texts, or
at least all narratives, are metaphors of the Self, an absurd
position.

Neither time nor my abilities permit me to explore
further Via's use of the actantial model which "display the
relationships of some components of the Self as understood by
Jungian psychology". By indicating how Via's notion of genre-
transcendent narrativity affects his argument about parables
and metaphors, I hope to have pointed to his actantial analysis
as the ultimate locus of his contribution. *The critical center
of his whole argument is the notion that actantial analysis
reveals the dynamics of the Self to be operative in the
Parable of the Unjust Judge.* Perhaps someone more adept than
I at the arcane discipline of actantial analysis will be able

to document my own suspicion that Via's analyses too con-
veniently fit the Jungian categories which he hoped analysis
would reveal. If so, we are back to square one--to the
suggestion that the dynamics of the Self are operative in the
Parable of the Unjust Judge, and to the methodological problem
of how this suggestion might become a verifiable conclusion.
While I am unpersuaded by Via's argument in these and other
respects (e.g., why metaphor and not allegory, and how
legitimate is his delimitation of Luke 18:2-5 as a text?),
I remain fascinated by his suggestion, and even more so by
the methodological issues his paper has raised.

RESPONSE TO DAN O. VIA

Edward McMahon
Vanderbilt University

In Dan Via's paper on the Unjust Judge we have a highly suggestive synthesis of French structural narrative analysis and Jungian literary criticism. With this last feature he has again moved to the frontiers in New Testament research while avoiding both the dangers of "psychologizing" Jesus and of making the parables nothing more than objects provoking our own psychological reflections.

My own questions about this piece in many ways complement those already so aptly raised by Norman Petersen. Although I want to spend most of my alloted time referring to Via's narrative analyses, I do have some questions about his Jungian interpretation. After reading Via's discussion of selected Jungian concepts and then reading the sources listed in his notes, I have come to appreciate his skill in capturing and expressing the essence of Jung's thought on these matters. I do wonder, though, just how Via decided that the categories he chose to treat were those "pertinent for the intra-psychic interpretation of the parable". Surely it is more than seeing that since we are talking about a judge, the *ego* must be involved; a widow, so the *anima* must be involved. Since neither of us are Jungian scholars in the technical sense and most others who choose to pick up on this new approach (new for American biblical studies) will not be either, this question is of some import. The very nature of the material we are dealing with would seem to further compound the difficulties. We are, after all, dealing not with a myth or a fairytale which is closer to the archetypes and hence should be more revealing of them but with polished literary pieces which might obscure the identification.

In addition to a lack of criteria for judging the correctness of an analysis, I find lacking in Via's paper a theory of how these archetypes relate to the other structures involved in the production of meaning. Do we proceed in our analyses directly from the level of the narrative structures to that of the deepest structures of the mind as Via seems to suggest? Or must we visualize a more complex interplay of structures:

narrative structures
mythical structures   intermediate structures
elementary structures   deep structures   logical ordering
archetypal structures   "story" ordering

If we turn our attention briefly to the specific interpretation of the parable which Via offers, one question immediately suggests itself. Has Via made the correct assessment of the psychological dynamics of the situation described in the text? Does not the twice repeated description of the judge as a man who "neither feared God nor regarded man" show that the ego is not in such a state that it is "not conscious that there even is such a dimension as the Self with which it is not really identical". If so, perhaps an alternative Jungian interpretation is needed. Possibly the text could be read as the story of the psyche with the Hero archetype in conflict with the Great Mother archetype (cf. James Hillman, *Re-Visioning Psychology*, Harper & Row, 1975, xiii-xiv).

Turning now our attention to his efforts to deal with the narrative structure of the text, we find him at first using the scheme of analysis proposed by Claude Bremond in his article "Morphology of the French Folktale". With respect to his use of these models, I have two questions: 1. What is the significance of describing Bremond's functions as "elementary functions" and those of Greimas as "secondary functions"? Does this imply that for him the latter are less important in some way, or function at a different level in the narrative? (I see Bremond and Greimas operating at the same level at this point.); 2. I am not clear how Via has used Bremond's diagram 5 in constructing his figure 1. Does the Bremond diagram describe basic transformations or the flow of the narrative? If the former is the case, then Via's diagram should be corrected by removing "Opposition: the Judge refuses". If the latter, then in addition to "Accomplished improvement" (Via's goal or result) you could include "Missed improvement" in Via's diagram--the judge is further alienated. This latter choice further suggests that the diagram could be read equally well with the widow as main character.

Via's use of the Greimas models for narrative analysis presents a number of theoretical and practical questions. A major theoretical question is involved in Via's movement from text to sequence to actantial model. Can one do a rigorous narrative analysis without giving attention to the syntagmatic analysis and the distinction of the Contract Syntagm (Mandation CS1 and Communication CS2), the Disjunction Syntagm (DS), and the Performance Syntagm (Confrontation PS1, Domination/Submission PS2, and the Attribution PS3). Our own work at Vanderbilt on the structural analysis of the parables has shown how important these elements are to discern.

Four questions about his procedures may be asked in
relation to Via's figures 3-7. 1. On the level of the
actantial analysis, how much should we "fill-in" the
diagrams with elements that do not appear in the text?
For example, in Via's figure 3, "God" and "Israel's Law"
appear. These may be involved in the context (though what
about the parable is specifically Jewish?) but they don't
appear in the text. Our experience has been that it is
better to stay close to the text. This would mean not
putting in such items. Furthermore it would mean that we
would respect the diachronic element in narrativity and not
include items in the model which do not appear until later
in the text. 2. If we adopt the meaning of Subject-
Ordainer-Recipient, as proposed by Patte, following Greimas
(*Semia* II, 8) can we do as Via does in figures 4 and 7 and
identify the judge as holding three positions in the
actantial model? The communicator of the mandate in our
text is not necessarily the judge. 3. In figure 4, should
we read with Via that the judge is trying to transmit disengagement to himself or rather read it as an interrupted
PS2 with the judge failing to communicate religious fear
to God and regard to man? 4. While the judge ultimately
is the agent of vindication as sender in the text, don't we
have the woman as mandator to the judge? Instead of Via's
figure 5 we would see something like this:

Widow	Vindication	Widow
	Judge	

These questions about the details of Via's analysis are important; for if we do not make a correct analysis of the text in its diachronic state we will be unable to describe the text paradigmatically with due attention being paid to the hierarchial structure of the text. This last element is important if we wish to elucidate the mythical structure and elementary structures which produce the "meaning effect" of this text.

RESPONSE TO DAN O. VIA

James L. Crenshaw
Vanderbilt University

My introduction to Professor Via's work in structural-ism came in July of '73. Traveling home on the S. S. France from a sabbatical in Europe, I met a close relative of Jean Starobinski, noted Geneva physician and literary critic, to whom the latter had given a copy of a structural analysis of the story of the Gerasene demoniac which he had written and which Dan Via translated into English for the *New Literary History*.[1] My newly acquired friend confessed an inability to comprehend the essay, and gave it to me on the assumption that I would appreciate its particular style and content. Between ping pong matches, endless dining, and evening con-versations I managed to find time to read Starobinski's venture into alien territory. To these untutored eyes the essay was an exercise in stating the obvious, and I was curious why Via would take the trouble to translate such a work. Subsequent acquaintance with structuralism and with Via's pioneer efforts in this area has convinced me that my judgment was affected by the French wines that flowed so freely during those five days on the high seas. But I con-fess that I am still "at sea" where structural analysis is concerned!

Via's study of the parable of the Unjust Judge does not belabor self-evident truths. On the contrary, it opens up a wholly new way of looking at the story. The essay is clear and forceful, and the insights into structural analysis

and Jungian thought demonstrate the workings of a highly
original mind. His discussion of the Self's emergence
sparkles with insights, as does the actantial analysis of
the parable. My inclination is to devote the time allotted
me to praising the essay. But the purpose of the group will
be better served, I think, by a different tack. In brief,
setting aside my deep appreciation for Via's essay, I wish
to raise four fundamental objections, and to pose a fifth
question for reflection.

I.

My first objection to Via's analysis arises from his
ignoring the framework within which the parable appears.
If I understand him, Via wishes to offer *his own reading*
of the story rather than its original meaning. Indeed, at
no time in the text's rich history has it ever meant what
it does in Via's analysis. Caution compels me to avoid
name-calling, but Via's interpretation strikes me as *reading into* rather than a *drawing out of*. Stated another way,
Via uses the text as a medium of comprehending his own self-
hood, thus reversing traditional approaches that see the
text as an end and not a means. While I have no objection
to such an approach to biblical texts, I would insist that
it follow upon a rigorous attempt to discover what the text
meant originally.

In my view, the interpreter must keep two foci in mind
at all times, specifically settings ancient and modern.
Failure to ask what the text said in earlier generations *as
a way toward* discovering its contemporary meaning constitutes,

in my judgment, a serious flaw in Via's treatment of the parable. Structural analysis cannot dispense with literary, form, and redaction history and remain true to its conviction about a text's "flow of history".

The parable of the Unjust Judge once spoke to a vital issue within the lives of those who compiled Christian traditions. Ancient response to the story, embedded within the framework of the parable, becomes an integral part of the story's meaning. With each response the parable takes on richer--or poorer--dimensions, retaining its vital quality. Clues to such interpretation, tantalizingly obscure, permeate the narrative, particularly in the frame.

Significant features of the framework, which one ought to explore thoroughly, include: (1) the identification of the literary genre as a parable; (2) the specification of the audience; (3) the statement of the story's intended purpose; (4) the summons to take note; (5) the rhetorical question about divine compassion for the elect; (6) the affirmation of divine providence; and (7) the enigmatic question concerning the possible paucity of trustworthy people on earth when the Son of Man returns. It may even be possible to move backwards to an earlier stage in the parable's history. In any event, clarification of the meaning of key words and phrases cannot be avoided if one intends to discover an ancient meaning of the story. Chief candidates for such exploration are the semantic field of the word widow, the usage of the expression "neither feared God nor regarded man", and the concept of vindication.

A few remarks about the last point may be helpful. The description of the judge as one who neither fears God nor regards man may not be derogatory at all. Rather, the Semitic

background of these ideas suggests to me that the judge cannot be forced into precipitous decisions by a religious oath
aimed at him or by efforts at bribery. Such an interpretation of this phrase leads me to question Via's casual remarks about the secular character of Jesus' parables, a
feature Via finds most desirable. I wish to point out the
fact that God-talk may be implicit within the most secular
sounding story imaginable. Furthermore, the canonical
setting tempers all biblical stories, regardless of their
former character. Let me illustrate this point from my
own area of study, wisdom literature. In Egypt sapiential
literature appears to be remarkably secular and pragmatic.
For years scholars either rejoiced in this feature, or
lamented such humanism, until the discovery of the literature's deeply religious presuppositions. To return to the
parable of the Unjust Judge, one cannot fail to discern the
theological tenor of the attempted response to an agonizing
delay in divine retribution. The choice of a widow as the
supplicant poses the problem in its sharpest form, for
Israelite hymnody lauds God as vindicator of the oppressed,
champion of widows.

II.

My second objection relates to the first in that it
takes up the vexing question of perspective. Via specifies
the phenomenological position from which he works, largely
that of Merleau-Ponty. I wish to amend some of his observations and to elaborate upon the matter of perspectival perception. Via writes that perception is a dialogue between

subject and object. I would add that a text becomes the occasion for dialogue between subjects past and present, and the conversation transcends my own self at least to that extent. Via also thinks the text is taken up and reconstituted in perception. It seems to me that too much emphasis upon a mythic constituting of the universe or something like that shines through such a statement. I would prefer to lay emphasis upon the power the text wields over the reader. In short, the text takes me up and *reconstitutes me*. Coming fresh from a structural analysis of Genesis 22, God's monstrous test of Abraham, I bear witness to a text's transforming power.[2]

I should like to remark further that perspectival analysis has been around a long time, millennia before Merleau-Ponty got around to articulating it. The ancient sage knew that contexts demand different responses; he placed back-to-back the following proverbs:

> Answer not a fool according to his folly
> lest you be like him yourself. Answer a
> fool according to his folly lest he be
> wise in his own eyes (Pr. 26:4-5).

"Good" was not always good, nor was "evil" in every circumstance evil. To combat this problem the sage developed rhetorical devices expressive of gradation and antitheses. Similarly the redactors of Old Testament narratives juxtaposed complementary viewpoints. The biblical idea of creation best illustrates my point. Three competing perspectives are proffered: creation by battle, by procreation, and by divine fiat. I shall refrain from claiming that ancients intuited what modern scientists surmise, but the similarity cries for

comment. If we were to use language comparable to the
ancient Israelite, we would speak of modern theories as
the "Big Bang" hypothesis, the "Bang, Bang, Bang" hypothesis, and the "No Bang" hypothesis. The first, the catas-
trophic theory, corresponds to the myth of a battle; the
second, the Pulsating Universe theory, resembles the pro-
creational view of ancients; and the third, the Steady
State theory, strangely and ironically recalls theories
of creation by an eternally existent Being. I shudder to
think what Jung would have made of such an insight into the
mind of ancient Near Easterners.

The tendency of the ancient redactor to view a problem
from various angles has always enriched biblical exegesis.
I refer to Kierkegaard's masterful vignettes about the
offering of Isaac, and to Rembrandt's four attempts to interpret the same text.[3] For the latter the story probed
(1) intention versus deed, (2) the Oedipal impulse, and (3)
parental love versus fear of the gods. Regrettably, none
of us possesses God's ability to view the flow of history
as present knowledge; we must, therefore, content ourselves
with one perspective at a time.

In short, Via is absolutely right in calling attention
to the necessity of recognizing the perspective from which
one views a text. However, I think unconscious perspectives
lurk beneath the surface, picking up the inactive pen and
filling in empty spaces each time the reader's mind wanders.
That little enemy (or friend!) can scarcely be caught in
the act.

III.

My third major objection amounts to something like a
footnote on Via's superb discussion of the emergence of the
Self. Extensive reading in Hermann Hesse, and moderate
reading of Brecht and Jung, have familiarized me with the
idea of a female principle of completion. Jung's use of
the biblical concept of *ḥokhmah* in providing an answer to
Job is a powerful, if subjective, response. My own explanation for hypostasis differs little from his in fundamentals,
for I would also relate the emergence of personified wisdom
to the problem of divine justice. Dame Wisdom assures God's
presence when history appears to refute such a claim, and
her love for God's creatures expresses itself in discipline,
which molds character. Growth through conflict has been
known from time immemorial.

A question comes to mind, perhaps as a result of the
times. Is there an animus, a male alien self that is lacking in all females? If the query appears ludicrous, it is
certainly not so intended. Instead, it asks whether we
should continue to use such assumptions as male = perfec-
tion, female = completion.

Via's description of self-realization and alienation
illuminates the biblical narrative of the fall, and indeed
the ever present conflict between order and chaos. Biblical writers perceived the necessity of an impulse toward
chaos, or freedom; consequently, Behemoth is allowed to
cavort in the ocean where he (or she) can cause little harm.
Flirting with freedom runs the risk of exposure; nakedness
induces efforts at concealment, whether by fig leaves or by
forgetting one's heritage. The Southerner who turns his

back upon his tradition differs little from ancient cover-ups; both proclaim alienation, the child of exercised freedom.

IV.

My fourth objection to Via's essay strikes at the heart of his thesis. I would contend that the story in its present form holds up the actions of the *widow* as exemplary. Perhaps our differences are minimal, but I want to mention some specifics. The customary analysis of narrative sequence in terms of a disturbance of an original state and a restoration of that desired situation has always struck me as too broad to say very much, although I freely admit that the finest interpretation I know of, the little book of Ruth, employs the rubrics emptiness-fullness.[4] Still I wonder whether Via's astute analysis of actantial roles contributes anything substantial to our understanding of the story. I confess further uneasiness over the lack of objective criteria in the assignment of actantial roles.

Another point of disagreement between us concerns the pilgrimage of the judge. In my view he moves through inner conflict from ease to dis-ease, and back again. By way of contrast, the widow goes from dis-ease to ease, making dis-engagement a possibility for her. Via writes that the story does not have a happy ending. I would contend that it has a jubilant ending, a confirmation of order, and of divine goodness and sovereignty. The difference lies in the perspective; the widow is ecstatic and the judge can bask in the certainty that his services cannot be constrained. Or can he?

Via recognizes the dissonance inherent within the story, and makes some suggestive observations. But once we move into the area of motivation, the possibility always exists that actions do not transcend self interest. Moreover, human intention does not necessarily assure a desired result. The ancient proverb, "Man proposes but God disposes", reminds us that every human deed must reckon with an intangible quality, the will of God or blind Fate. Existential dissonance characterizes human decisions, for every decision is ambivalent. Via moves beyond the evidence, I think, when attributing to the judge contempt for God and man.

V.

I would like to pose a final question, half humorously. Via spoke of *the total man*, a creature as elusive as Dame Wisdom. I wish to know whether the total man is comparable to "The Total Woman" some of us have been reading about recently.

To sum up. Via describes what he sees in the story of the Unjust Judge. I would like to see his interpretation come into dialogue with an ancient one. Perhaps the result would be a *bath qol*: Both Crenshaw's reading of the text and Via's are correct, but for the purposes of this conference we shall follow Via. If such a voice shatters the silence, I shall gladly submit to its ruling.

NOTES

1. "The Struggle with Legion: A Literary Analysis of Mark 5:1-20," *New Literary History*, 4 (1972-1973), 331-356.

2. "Journey into Oblivion (A Structural Analysis of Gen. 22:1-19)," *Soundings*, 58 (1975).

3. See Gerhard von Rad, *Das Opfer des Abraham* (München: Chr. Kaiser Verlag), 1971, for excerpts from Kierkegaard and for reproduction and discussion of Rembrandt's paintings inspired by Genesis 22.

4. D. F. Rauber, "Literary Values in the Bible. The Book of Ruth," *JBL*, 89 (1970), 27-37.

DISCUSSION

VIA: First of all, one of the easier questions to respond to
is Jim Crenshaw's point about the secularity or religiousness
of language. I was being completely ironical in that statement
and was sure everybody would understand that I was poking fun
at New Testament scholars, myself included. Second, with respect to the anima-animus, yes that certainly is a Jungian
thought-concept of the animus and the female. This is a
whole other matter which could be gone into in a parallel way
but I don't think it is in the story. That certainly is an
important part of Jungian psychology. I think that one of
the problems with this whole thing is that I have been criticized on the one hand for getting out of the text and on the
other hand for not accounting for the context. I don't know
how I could have done both of these things adequately at all.
Third, on the business about figures #5 and #6 where Ed
McMahon adjusted some actantial schemes that would be different from mine, I still feel that the way I did it is much
closer to what is in the text and much less speculative than
his. I think I have said what is in the text. Finally, in
answer to Norm Petersen, I don't know where I say that *all*
texts are metaphors of the Self, unless you see that implied
in what I said earlier about Merleau-Ponty and I suppose it
perhaps is implied there. Rather, I see the same sort of
spectrum here in psychological terms that Bultmann sees when
he applies his existential hermeneutic. Bultmann makes the
value judgment that the most significant question asked by
the test is what does it say about the meaning of existence,

but he recognizes that not all texts answer that question:
some answer it in a very rich way, some in a moderate way, and
some hardly at all. I would say that the very same thing is
true at the psychological level: some texts have a great deal
to say about one's psychic reality and some may have very
little. It is reasonably clear that I see interpretation,
along with Merleau-Ponty, as interaction between Self and
text, Self and world. The Self does learn and is changed by
this confrontation with the world. In this particular text
something is said about how the Self is realized.

DOTY: Maria Louise von Franz who is the Jungian interpreter
to whom he refers, makes a claim that would raise Norm Petersen's hackles: all fairytales are about the Self.

VIA: Yes, I virtually quoted or at least paraphrased her.
She says all fairytales.

DOTY: But the important thing is what she then does with the
fairytale. She shows that each fairytale in some way sheds
light on the archetype of the Self.

VIA: She doesn't say though that they say exactly the *same*
thing about the Self.

CROSSAN: Looking at the text on the first page I would brack
et out the Lucan frame and the title "The Unjust Judge" becaus
I see nothing in the text that says the judge was unjust. He
simply neither feared God nor regarded man. As I would read
it, there is a judge with absolute power; there is no sanction
of fear. And I read the judge as a metonym and not as a metaphor for absolute power. And I look at the widow and I don't

consider her right or good. Maybe her adversary is right, but more polite. I want to bracket morality when I see this metonym for absolute power and this metonym for absolute powerlessness: the judge and the widow.

VIA: I didn't say she was good, did I?

CROSSAN: No. I am not disagreeing with you on this point. But then as I read the story apart from any question of morality, it is one of victory of absolute powerlessness over absolute power. That is how the story tells it. Now if that paradoxical message is in the story and if I were turning to Jung I would want to know in effect if Jung says anything like "the Self is constituted by the victory of powerlessness over power". If he says that then I see the same structure in this as in Jung's psychology.

VIA: Well, Jung says that the Self is constituted when there is at least the beginning of the breakdown of the separation of ego-consciousness with unconsciousness. And there are at least points in Jung where the unconscious tries to compensate for a one-sided consciousness--a consciousness too intellectual, too romantic or too anything. The other side tries to get through. Now there is a sense in which the unconscious is powerless if the conscious is so directed that the unconscious when trying to get through into consciousness, fails to get through and so to be assimilated into one's conscious self understanding. There is no broadening of that conscious understanding and no bridge between the conscious and the unconscious. But, he says, if that is the case the power which the unconscious has is added to that unhealthy, one-sided conscious direction. No, Jung does not say that Self is constituted by the powerless unconscious having a victory over the conscious. He says the Self, by implication, fails to be achieved if the unconscious can't get through to the conscious and to be assimilated into the consciousness. Hence the center of the Self drops down from ego-consciousness to a point somewhere between conscious and unconscious. That is the point of the whole title--the "Metaphor of the Unrealized Self". If this can be taken as a narrative of the failure of the Self to be realized it is because of the anima as a representative of the unconscious never gets through to the conscious; it simply never gets a hearing.

HARRELSON: So this is quite different from Dom's [Crossan's] reading.

MARIN: To carry on our dialogue begun at Syracuse University, I have two questions. My first question concerns the analysis of the narrative part of the parable itself. When I read this narrative I immediately observe that there are two levels of discourse: one which is properly speaking narrative and a second level of discourse which is constituted by a dialogue of the judge with himself. Now I observe a very interesting thing: the judge repeats the story. He repeats the three episodes of the narrative part of the parable, but each time he repeats the story in a different way. I think the whole problem of this parable is to discern exactly the way in which the judge repeats what is stated as fact at the beginning of the narrative. Note that he repeats the story by modalizing the sequences: "*Though* I neither fear God...", "*yet* because this widow bothers me...I will vindicate her". And I observe

finally, that the narrative has no conclusion. The parable
ends with the intention of the judge to vindicate the widow,
whether for good or bad reasons--that is not the point. Now,
if this analysis is correct, it seems to me very important to
relate this non-closure of the story with the series of
rhetorical questions [found in Lk. 18:1-8] which are very
important as part of the parable itself. They are a sort of
decoding or interpretation of the parable. I think part of
your analysis is in a certain sense weakened by the fact that
you did not consider the two levels of the story and the kind
of shift the rhetorical questions create within the story.
That is my first comment.

My second question is more general. It has to do with
the degree of epistemological consistency between phenomenology, structural analysis and psychoanalysis, and especially
that you are using psychoanalysis in its Jungian interpretation. In your paper you make an observation about the Jungian
approach that I did not understand. Are the Jungian archetypes and their various manifestations a kind of particular
surface investment of the logical patterns that your structural analysis provides for you? Or are the Jungian archetypes prior to the structural analysis and hence a kind of
ontological ground of your structural analysis? At first, I
disagreed fundamentally with your use of Jungian archetypes,
but after a second thought I said if the Jungian archetypes
were a particular investment of the logical or semantic
patterns provided by structural analysis, why could we not
think of the archetypes in this way? We have on the one hand
the parables, the surface projection of these basic patterns,
and on the other hand another story, another tale, perhaps
another parable which is the Jungian narrative.

VIA: I think that I assume for the purposes of this paper at any case that the Jungian categories are ontologically significant and hence prior to the telling or interpreting of the parable. I suggested only tentatively that one could at least account in one way for plot movement by saying that it is determined by the shift from positive to negative secondary images to archetypes. In saying that I was presupposing that there are such things as archetypes and that they do operate upon the human psyche. I don't see any a priori reason for not thinking that Jung's psychological categories have as much ontological status as any philosopher's more explicit ontological categories. Secondly, Jungian archetypes do project and Jung says this quite explicitly. That doesn't mean it is right because I work within a Jungian framework. I do think, rightly or wrongly, that the Jungian categories have a significant ontological status and that these things occur in the story because the archetypes are operating in the psyche of the narrator. Therefore, I am not allegorizing the story because I say the archetypes have put the images there any more than Bultmann thinks he is allegorizing when he finds existential significance in all sorts of myths.

MARIN: I understand. But if so, why do you need the structural analysis?

VIA: Because it gives me a way of relating the dynamics and the tensions, that is of defining the relationships between, on the one level, characters in the story and, at another level, the aspects of the Self into which they can be translated. I am also assuming von Franz's position here that in the psychological interpretation of a story the goal is to

reduce every single thing in the story to a psychological
category. I hope I make some improvement on what she does
in that she and I and most Jungian interpreters of stories
don't make any attempt at all to give a hermeneutical significance to doing this. She raises the question quite explicitly
in her book on interpretation of the fairy story. Why do we
interpret fairy stories this way now? Just because it works
now! That is all she has to say. It worked at one time to
tell the stories; it works now to interpret them in this way.
I regard this as a tentative beginning at trying to introduce
some systematization into this kind of interpretive process,
and I must say it is a whole lot more systematic than what
she is doing. I do use the structuralist categories and I
think I can show in detail if I were to go back through the
paper again that I have related these aspects of the Self in
the same way that I related the elements of the actantial
analysis.

CRIST: It seems we are dealing here with the text as pre-
text. This, I suppose is not ultimately wrong. It is a
question of whether you are doing interpretative analysis or
religious studies or psychology. I was bothered by what
Professor Marin referred to as the gap between the story and
the psychological allegorization of it. Rosemond in a very
nice book called *Allegorical Imagery* uses the term "imposed
allegory" to refer to a late medieval allegory in which the
pre-existing terms are put on the points of a system and then
another system is worked into that. We use Greimas, we use
Marin because these people are working out of a linguistic
model and we are all somewhat familiar with that because we
use language. But then once we get into psychology the only

way we get into psychology is through language, and I think
that is what really bothers me. Texts are in language.
Structural analysis is based on a linguistic model which is
based on language. Psychological analysis is a using of
words to talk about a thing which does not take place in words

VIA: What is the "psychological thing" that is non-linguisti

CRIST: I suppose this is non-behaviorist, but some things
take place inside our skull--connections are made, etc. Then
we verbalize them and so we do psychology. In other words,
we talk about it. We might call it anima. That is an allegorical figure and we define it in a particular way. We may
give it a mythical definition but the phenomena take place
inside our skull and the only way to get that out into the
open is by talking about it. This puts us one degree away
from these phenomena.

VIA: But, I don't think we really have anything until we
have it in language.

CRIST: That is my problem! If we have a linguistic model,
I can follow this because a linguistic model is metalinguistic
it is talking about talking. But when you are talking about
thinking you have changed a category.

VIA: I didn't realize I was talking about thinking. I
thought I was talking about talking.

CRIST: You are talking about a phenomenon in the psyche whic
is not a linguistic phenomenon that we can put into words.
For Jung the archetypes are not linguistic.

VIA: Yes, but they constitute a limit. That is one way of finding the limit of either our thinking or language. You can't define the archetype. All you can do is circumscribe it with certain other language. You can't get to the archetype itself. You can only get some representations of it. I was arguing that the judge and the widow are representations of certain aspects of the Self. Now, I can't say any more than I already have said about how to bridge this gap that bothers you. I am simply resting on the Jungian view that the Self and its components project certain images of themselves in myth and folktales. I think that the way these characters in the story operate in relationship to each other reflects either by correspondence or opposition the dynamics of Jung's psychology.

WITTIG: It seems to me that the problem here is not to know which model is qualitatively more valuable than another model but rather the fact is that we are all working from models, every single one of us. Models are deductive models which are derived by a variety of methods. Nevertheless we possess them and we all allegorize. Every single statement is an allegory. Some of them are metonymic allegories which are chronologically based and much more analytic than others. Dan Via I think is working out of a metaphoric model. One of the problems he has faced in this paper is putting together that metaphorical Jungian model with an analytical, chronological, syntagmatic model that is Greimasian. What we have heard from the respondents though are efforts to force the metaphoric model into the metonymic mode and they don't fit. All I am suggesting is that we recognize the differences between the two models which are being used here and that just for the moment we stop and listen to how one can be used to shed light on the other. That is my answer to Larry Crist's comment about allegorizing.

A further comment. I want to say to Jim Crenshaw that reading is always a reading into something from out of whatever model you happen to be working out of. There is no way to stick to a text without filling in the gaps. You cannot do it. You are always filling in the gaps. As I am going to argue on Saturday, texts are always indeterminate in one way or another. They always have holes in them and our whole business of reading and understanding is to fill in those holes. Finally, picking up Jim's point that the text takes up and reconstitutes the reader, I really disagree with Dan Via on this question of the text annulling the subject-object distinction in literature. I think that the function of a text is to cause us as readers to examine the process of reconstruction. What happens at that point is that instead of a subject-object dichotomy, I have a subject-object over here totally integrated and totally engaged, and a subject over there watching the engagement. So I have a subject-object-subject dichotomy. The inter-relationship of the two gives the text its dynamic.

PATTE: What I found quite fascinating in the use of Jungian categories is that everything that is said by Dan Via about the Self could be translated without difficulty into Lévi-Strauss' terminology. Instead of the Self you could say the mythical system; you have a unity of elements within the Self. All of the oppositions are contained within the Self and the Self is an archetype of totality and so forth. For example, the anima and animus are mythemes in opposition, etc.

Now I recognize the problem of passing from the metonymic model of Greimas to the metaphorical model of Lévi-Strauss. This is a major problem as long as you confuse the two; that is when you don't realize that you are trying to pass from one to the other, when you identify the narrative transformation with the mythical oppositions. But where one realizes that the two modes are closely interrelated, one must conclude, as I shall argue in my paper, that narratives can be understood to be metaphors of the Self. My question is this: I am not sure of your position; would you agree that all folktales are metaphors of the Self?

VIA: In the paper I said that Maria von Franz says that all folktales are metaphors of the Self; I said I would test the hypothesis whether this parable could be considered as a metaphor of the Self. I don't think I have committed myself any further.

PETERSEN: You said "some" parables and not just one.

VIA: Well yes, I guess I did say some; however, I haven't said *all* parables, though I suspect I would be prepared to say it.

DONAHUE: I am still not clear on this question of the move from the structural analysis to the metaphorical analysis of the Self in terms of the content of the story and the character of the story as being really significant. Is it only the formal things that happen in a story that are significant? For example, suppose you had different Old Testament models or different images used in a story. Suppose it was a parable

of one of the rich widows of Basham who would not hear the
complaint of the oppressed alien in the land, which formally
would be the same story as this parable. Would it then provide the same ability to make the transfer to the Jungian
analysis that you made?

VIA: Yes, I think you can make the transfer but you would
have a different story: that is, you would have depicted a
different psychological situation. Since you have mentioned
the women, the animus can project secondary images of all
sorts of women, positively or negatively.

DONAHUE: Yes, but does that make any difference on the
structural level of the analysis of the story?

VIA: Yes, I think it would. If I understood myself at the
simplest I was trying to do a very simple functional, actantial
analysis. It certainly was simple. I really find the
elaborate Greimasian system very burdensome and very unpro-
ductive and the results as far as I am concerned never justify
the effort. That is a hard thing to say in this group. There
is tremendous effort but very little fruit. All I attempted
to do was to show how the characters were related by this
simple, functional actantial analysis and then to try and reduce all of the elements in the story to psychological categories.

SUNDBERG: In this regard, I have a question about universalizing our western psychological construction. The blacks
on our faculty at Garrett Evangelical tell us that our white
psychological systems don't fit them. I don't know whether

it is that they don't know these systems well enough, but
they know other things well enough to make me think that I
can't accuse them on that count. This leads me to raise
the question, how universalistically should we treat our
western upper-middle and upper-class psychology? I know
there is a great deal that is said about it being univer-
salistic, but it is said by people I've just described.

VIA: I think that is a good point. We can commit a lot
of errors by not being cognizant of it and I may have
committed some of these errors.

HARRELSON: Your undertaking would not be vitiated however
if it is parochial, would it, if Jung's view is deemed a
parochial one?

VIA: No, I don't think so. It is Jung's view that the
archetypes are universal. But it is also his view that they
are culturally modified when they express themselves in the
symbols of any given culture. Jung's own studies are not
parochial because he has done a lot of work on Chinese texts,
and so on. When he finds his psychology there it may be that
he is allegorizing visciously, but not purposefully. In
short, there are two things to be said about Jung's scheme:
first, Jung does regard the archetypes as universal but at
the same time he regards them as culturally modified and
therefore not identical from one culture to the next;
secondly, he has immersed himself in non-western materials.

ROTH: What do you think is operative when we choose a model
or when a model chooses us? Is it an accident of birth,

accident of schooling or do we play with models as a child plays, almost aimlessly, or with an aim?

VIA: I think all of those things happen. I would go right to the old Roland Barthes of *On Racine* in which he says you always choose a reading and no one is innocent; the choice reveals the situation of the interpreter. So I am revealed. Make of me what you will from this interpretation of the parable.

CHAPTER II

STRUCTURAL ANALYSIS OF THE PARABLE OF THE PRODIGAL SON: TOWARDS A METHOD

Daniel Patte

Vanderbilt University

This paper proposes a structural analysis of the Parable of the Prodigal Son. It follows the methodology that we developed in the context of the Vanderbilt project "Semiology and Exegesis" both in the Vanderbilt seminars and in the three-week long workshop in Annecy, France (July 1974, among the participants in this workshop: Professors Jean Delorme, Jean Calloud, Jacques Geninasca, and A. J. Greimas' assistant Michael Rengstorf). This methodology, which is primarily derived from Greimas' and Lévi-Strauss' work, is outlined in my two articles: "A Structural Analysis of Narrative," *Semeia* 2 (October 1974), and "Structural Network in Narrative," *Soundings* (June 1975), and further discussed in my book, *What is Structural Exegesis?* (Fortress Press, spring 1976). The present paper does not intend to be methodological: it will *not* deal with structuralist or semiotic theories. Rather, it is an attempt to develop a method for the analysis of narratives in terms of the narrative structure, the mythical structure, and the elementary structure. This method is built on four theoretical models:

1. a model of the *narrative structure* as network of "narrative sequences" which themselves include six "narrative functions" and the "actantial model".

2. a model of the *mythical structure* represented by Lévi-Strauss' formula:

$$F_x(a) : F_y(b) :: F_x(b) : F_{\bar{a}}(y)$$

3. a model of the *elementary structure* represented by the semiotic square.

4. a model of the *interrelation among the narrative, mythical, and elementary structures*.

These four theoretical models should not be construed as anything else than *models*. That is, they are constructs which, in our view, best account for a part of the "meaning effect" of narratives...in the same way that scientific models may be viewed by the scientist as what, at the present stage of research, best represent a natural phenomenon. The validity of a model is then verified and eventually established by means of experiments. The first three models have been extensively verified by various scholars in Greimas' and Lévi-Strauss' schools. By contrast, the fourth model of the interaction among the three structures above has only been verified through a few analyses. We are presently involved in the first stages of its verification by proceeding to as many analyses as possible. Eight graduate students are presently involved with me in the analysis of the main New Testament parables; each of them is contributing to the development of the method presented in this paper. They are: Brenda Hopson, David N. Jones, John R. Jones, Edward McMahon, Sung Sang Pahk, Judson Parker, Gary Phillips, and Larry Vigen.

In this analysis in terms of these four models, we are always ready to modify the models. When in the course of the analysis we find that part of the model does not account adequately for a part of the meaning effect, we have progressed, for we can then propose a revision of the model and thus progressively elaborate a more adequate model. If I dare to present this as yet incomplete analysis in terms of the four models to such a distinguished group, it is in hopes that the critique of my analysis and of these models will help us progress in our research aimed at establishing these models.

1. Delimitation of the Text to be Analyzed

We intend to study the parable of the Prodigal Son (Luke 15:11-32) in terms of four *deep* structures. Since we do not intend to study it in terms of the "structure of the enunciation" we can ignore its context in the Gospel of Luke as well as its eventual *Sitz im Leben* in Jesus' ministry. These are strict limits and under these constraints our analysis cannot pretend to be complete.

The specific methods which we propose to use suggest how the text should be delimited. Our analysis is first an analysis in terms of the narrative structure and on this basis unfolds itself into an analysis in terms of the mythical structure and of the elementary structure. An analysis in terms of the narrative structure is possible only if the text to be analyzed is a narrative unit. The Gospel of Luke as a whole is a complex narrative in which are embedded multiple sub-narratives. A parable is one of those sub-narratives which in itself is a complete narrative. As sub-narrative it contributes to the overall meaning effect of the Gospel. Conversely, the fact that it is embedded in the Gospel contributes to the meaning effect of the parable. Obviously we are not ready to deal with the relation of this sub-narrative with the rest of the Gospel--the study of this relation would demand the structural analysis of the whole

Gospel. Consequently, we shall limit our analysis to the sub-narrative Parable of the Prodigal Son in itself and in so doing bracket out what links the parable with the rest of the Gospel.

In the case of this specific parable this first procedure is relatively simple: it is enough to bracket out the first words of verse 11, "And he said". Verses 11b-32 form a complete sub-narrative without any "extraneous material" (that is, without material which refers to the broader Gospel narrative or to the enunciation). In so doing we have isolated a sub-narrative of the narrative "Gospel of Luke".[1]

2. Analysis in Terms of the Narrative Structure

A. Tentative Analysis in Terms of the Broad Characteristics of the Narrative Structure

In a first reading we attempt to determine the main narrative transformations taking place in this delimited text. The transformation can be written (according to the formula used in Greimas' seminars):

$$S \cap 0 \quad \rightarrow \quad S \cup 0$$

Reading: the transformation from a situation in which a subject (S) is in a state of disjunction ($\cap$) from an object (0) to a situation in which this subject (S) is in a state of conjunction ($\cup$) with this object (0).

$S \cap 0$ can also be termed the "situation of lack" (the subject is lacking an object). It can also be viewed as an interrupted narrative sequence; because he is lacking some-

thing, an adequate helper, a subject cannot carry out his
narrative program. He cannot act according to his status
of subject as defined by his relation to his sender and his
helpers. This "situation of lack" is brought about by the
villainy (another narrative program). The transformation
is brought about by the performance of the hero which is to
overcome the situation of lack. Thus this narrative transformation can be written as follows:

> -Initial situation. Cor. Seq. 1. First form of the
>   correlated sequence.
>
> -Villainy
>
> -Situation of lack (S $\cap$ 0)
>
> -Performance of the Hero (topical sequence or T. Seq.)
>
> -Reestablished initial situation (S $\cup$ 0). Second form
>   of the correlated sequence. Cor. Seq. 2.[2]

In this first stage of the analysis, we tentatively
identify the main transformation. For this purpose we need
to determine the five narrative elements mentioned above:
Cor. Seq. 1, villainy, situation of lack, topical sequence,
and Cor. Seq. 2, keeping in mind the following. 1) This
broad narrative structure is not necessarily fully actualized
in a given narrative because it is a deep structure which can
be evoked by a few of its features. For instance, the reestablished initial situation is not necessarily actualized,
as in the case of tragedies. 2) The order of the textual
surface does not necessarily follow the structural order.
3) A narrative can potentially be read as the story of each
of the personages. A narrative can be viewed as the intersection of several narratives. For instance, the personage
which appears from a given perspective as the villain is the
hero from another perspective, and so on. In most instances,

the narrator chose to tell the story in a specific way even though he might reveal it only at the very end of the story (of course he can also choose to tell an ambiguous narrative).[3]

In the Parable of the Prodigal Son, what are the main narrative elements? If we consider the story as a whole, we have to conclude that the situation of lack is the disjunction of a father from his sons. In the initial situation "a man had two sons"--man $\cup$ two sons. This harmonious family life (the performance of the man, S^i, with the help of his two sons, H^i) is disrupted by the departure of the younger son. This is a first form of the situation of lack: man $\cap$ two sons = man $\cup$ one son. When the younger son has returned, a second form of the situation of lack appears when the elder son refuses to come home.

We have, therefore, two successive villainies. The younger son is the first villain: his villainy is not primarily what he is doing while he is away (although this performance qualifies the villainy) but rather his very departure. The elder son is the second villain in that he refuses to come home.

Who is the hero? In the case of the overcoming of the first villainy there are two possibilities: the younger son or the father. The younger son does come back to his father's house, yet not as a son but rather as a servant. Following the younger son's original plan of return then the situation of lack would not have been overcome: the father would still have only one son. The father, finally, is the one who transforms the situation by reestablishing the young man in position of son. The father is therefore the hero.

In the case of the second villainy, the hero is quite clearly the father who goes out in order to try to convince

the elder son to come back home. Of course, we do not know
if he is successful or not.

This first analysis suggests that the title of the
parable should be in Jeremias' term "the Father's Love"
rather than the Prodigal Son since titles of narratives
usually refer to the hero.

This first analysis is tentative and must be verified
by a comprehensive narrative analysis which must now account
for all the details of the text and show their interrelation.

B.   Detailed Narrative Analysis

The purpose of this analysis is to deconstruct the
narrative into its basic narrative elements and to show how
they are interrelated by constructing a narrative hierarchy.
The basic narrative elements are what we term "narrative
sequences" (they could also be termed "narrative programs")
which can be represented by the following "grid". (See next
page.)

In most instances the sequences are only partially
actualized: because the narrative sequence is part of a deep
structure the mention of a few of its features are sufficient
to evoke the whole sequence. It "makes sense" for the reader.
An extreme instance is that of the "qualifications" which
simply express that an object (e.g., the quality "good") is
attributed to a receiver (e.g., Peter). A qualification can
be viewed as the conclusion of a narrative sequence even
though the narrator did not deem it necessary to express how
the attribution took place (that is, what the performance is
which led to this attribution and how the other actantial
positions were actualized for this performance).

NARRATIVE NO. _____   TITLE _____

SEQUENCE NO. IN THE TEXT _____

☐ CORRELATED SEQUENCE NO. _____   OR ☐ TOPICAL SEQUENCE NO. _____

☐ SUB-SEQUENCE ⎫
☐ -OR-   ⎬ - OF _____ ; FROM _____ ; _____
☐ QUALIFICATION ⎭   (ACTANT)   (SEQUENCE)   (STATEMENT)

CONTRACT SYNTAGM

LEXIE NO. _____

CS1   MANDATING

SUB-SEQUENCE OR QUALIFICATION?
☐ VOLITION NOT ESTABLISHED
☐ VOLITION ESTABLISHED
☐ SEQUENCE INTERRUPTED
☐ TO CS2

LEXIE NO. _____

CS2   COMMUNICATION

SUB-SEQUENCE OR QUALIFICATION?
☐ POWER AND/OR COGNITION NOT RECEIVED
☐ POWER AND/OR COGNITION RECEIVED
☐ SEQUENCE INTERRUPTED
☐ TO DS

DISJUNCTION/CONJUNCTION SYNTAGM

LEXIE NO. _____

DS   MOVEMENT

FROM PERSON _____   TO PERSON _____
PLACE _____   PLACE _____
THING _____   THING _____

SUB-SEQUENCE OR QUALIFICATION?
☐ MOVEMENT NOT COMPLETED
☐ MOVEMENT COMPLETED
☐ SEQUENCE INTERRUPTED
☐ TO PS1

PERFORMANCE SYNTAGM

LEXIE NO. _____

PS1   CONFRONTATION

SUB-SEQUENCE OR QUALIFICATION?
☐ CONFRONTATION REFUSED
☐ CONFRONTATION ACCEPTED
☐ SEQUENCE INTERRUPTED
☐ TO PS2

LEXIE NO. _____

PS2   DOMINATION/SUBMISSION

SUB-SEQUENCE OR QUALIFICATION?
☐ SUBMISSION
☐ DOMINATION
☐ SEQUENCE INTERRUPTED
☐ TO PS3

LEXIE NO. _____

PS3   ATTRIBUTION

SUB-SEQUENCE OR QUALIFICATION?
☐ NOT COMPLETED
☐ COMPLETED
☐ SEQUENCE INTERRUPTED
☐ END OF SEQUENCE

This understanding of the qualifications as completed attributions (completed PS3) is a cornerstone of our method. For, indeed, when it is understood furthermore that any kind of object can be transmitted, it is possible to account for *all* the elements of the text in terms of narrative sequences. Consequently, a narrative text appears as a network of narrative sequences.

This network of sequences is organized according to a narrative hierarchy. Because the very purpose of the narrative is to express how the interrupted program of the initial sequence, Cor. Seq. 1, can eventually be carried out, Cor. Seq. 2, all the other sequences can be viewed as explanations of how this narrative process can take place. We shall term *subsequence* a sequence expressing a performance (or a qualification) which explains why the performance of another sequence takes place in a specific way. Thus all the other sequences are directly or indirectly subsequences of the correlated sequence (in either of its forms). The topical sequence is a special subsequence which explains how the interrupted correlated sequence is eventually reestablished by a hero. All the sequences explaining how the hero is able (or not able) to carry out his task are subsequences of the topical sequence. The villainy which is a sequence explaining how the correlated sequence is interrupted is a subsequence of the correlated sequence, etc. ...

In order to further express what the relationship is between a sequence A and its subsequence B, we could say that the subsequence tells the story of one of the actants of the sequence A. For instance, the subsequence B might tell the story of the opponent in sequence A, Op^A. In this case the subject of the subsequence B, S^B, is Op^A and the subsequence B can be termed "subsequence of the opponent" of sequence A.

Since each of the actants can have a subsequence there are six types of subsequence that we shall term subsequences of the sender, object, receiver, helper, subject, and opponent. It is to be noted that subsequences of the subject exist also: such a subsequence expresses the secondary performance of a given subject which allows him to carry out another performance. What Propp terms the "qualifying test" of the hero is therefore a subsequence of the subject of the topical sequence.

By telling the story of one of the actants of a sequence, a subsequence defines this actant by revealing how he acts (how he transmits a specific object to a receiver) and how he is related with other personages--his helper, opponent, and sender. Similarly, a qualification defines further the actant in position of receiver by attributing to him an object.[5]

Through the detailed narrative analysis we shall therefore identify the various sequences by following closely the text and showing how they are interrelated in a narrative hierarchy. The verbs of the category of "doing" express narrative programs and performances. The verbs of the category of "being/having" express attributions of objects to receivers and therefore qualifications. The modalities, which modify both categories of verbs, express if the *volition* of the subject has been established or not (CS1); if *cognition*, or know how, and *power* have or have not been received by the subject (CS2); if the various stages of the performance have been performed successfully or not; if the performance is in process, has been completed or is still to be carried out in the future, and so on.

We can now proceed with the detailed analysis of the Parable of the Father's Love keeping in mind the narrative transformation that we have tentatively identified above. Following the text we record each sequence in the grid. We shall designate each sequence according to the order of the text. For instance "(1)" should be read "sequence number 1 in the text". A new grid is necessary each time we are confronted with a new subject or with a new narrative program. A narrative program is defined by the relations among a sender, subject, object, and receiver: if any of the four actants changes we are confronted with a new program. Since the actantial model is actualized in the same way throughout a sequence, we shall summarize a grid by noting the narrative functions which are manifested among CS1, CS2, DS, PS1, PS2, and PS3 (see the grid above for definitions), and how the actantial model is invested.[6]

There was a man who had two sons (v. 11b)

This can be recorded on the grid as a qualification (Q) since we have here a verb of the category "being/having": two sons (object = O) have been attributed to a man (receiver = R). We record it as a performance of attribution (PS3) which is completed. The notation Q(1) expresses that the sequence is a qualification.

Q(1) v. 11b PS3

	two sons	man
sender	object	receiver
helper	subject	opponent

And the younger of them said to his father (v. 12a)

"Saying" is a verb of the category of "doing". We have therefore a performance and not a qualification. The subject (S) is the younger son. What is the object (O) that the younger son transmits? A message, or more precisely, a mandate as the rest of the verse shows. The father is the receiver (R). What are the narrative functions? Only one is actualized: an attribution which is completed (PS3).

(2) v. 12a   PS3

	mandate	father
	father	

Father, give me the share of property that falls to me (v. 12b.

This is a mandating, CS1, by the younger son as sender (Se) of the father who will become subject if he accepts, i.e. if his volition is established. According to the proposed program the father (S) should transmit a "share of property" (O) to the younger son as receiver (R). A helper (H) is implied in the phrase "that falls to me"; the custom according to which a share of property falls to the younger son is suggested as what should help the father to carry out this mandate if he accepts it.

(3) v. 12b   CS1

younger son	share	younger son
custom	father	

And he divided his living between them (v. 12c)

From the standpoint of the younger son the father carries out his mandate. Thus his volition has been established--CS1 is established--and a share of property is attributed to the younger son (PS3). The performance itself--domination of an opponent, PS2--is alluded to by the verb "dividing". Yet the opponent itself is not mentioned.

(3) v. 12b,c |___CS1___|_ _ _|_PS2_|_PS3_|

younger son	share of property	younger son
custom	father	

It should be noted that the performance of the father is in fact broader than what the younger son proposed. Indeed, the father carried out the younger son's mandate, but he did more: he divided his living between his two sons. In fact he carried a different narrative program: S:father; O:his living; R:two sons. The other actants are not manifested. Two functions are manifested: PS2 and PS3.[7]

(4) v. 12c _ _ _|_PS2_|_PS3_|

	his living	two sons
	father	

*Not many days later, gathering all he had, the younger son
took his journey into a far country and there he squandered
his property in loose living (v. 13)*

"Gathering all he had" is the PS3 of a sequence. The
younger son (S) attributes to himself (R) all he has--his
share of the property (O). The father is an implicit helper.[8]

(5) v. 13b _ _ |‾‾PS3‾|

| _____ | ____share____ | ___younger son___ |
| __(father)__ | __younger son__ | _____ |

The journey actualizes a disjunction from the father and conjunction to a "far country", a DS. The "far country" is an
additional helper necessary for the performance. The "father"
appears as an opponent of this performance. Squandering his
property in loose living is the successful performance: he
(S) attributes to himself as (R) a prodigal life (O) with the
help of his share of property (H).

(6) v. 13c,d _ _ _ |‾‾DS‾| _ _ _ |‾‾PS2‾|‾PS3‾|

| _____ | __prodigal life__ | __younger son__ |
| share
__far country__ | __younger son__ | _____ |

We have not yet accounted for the phrase "not many days
later". Such temporal notations are often used to manifest
the relationship between two sequences. In the present case
it indicates that the previous performance of the younger son

in (2) was directly related to this new performance in (5) and (6): it makes clear that it is in order to have a prodigal life that the younger son asks from his father his share of property. (6) is first of all possible because (5) takes place. Thus (5) is a subsequence of (6). (5) is possible because the father gave him his share in (3). Thus (3) is a subsequence of (5). Furthermore, (2) explains how (3) took place, thus (2) is a subsequence of (3).

We have therefore the following hierarchy among these four sequences. (We use the symbol SS to denote a subsequence. Thus SS(5) indicates that sequence number five is a subsequence.) (See note #12 for explanations of the symbols.)

```
:       :   QSS-R=SEQ(S6)
:       :      DS=STMT
:       :      PS2=STMT
:       :      :  QSS-S=SEQ(S5)
:       :      :     PS3=STMT
:       :      :     :  QSS-H=SEQ(S3)
:       :      :     :     CS1=STMT
:       :      :     :     PS2=STMT
:       :      :     :     :  QSS-SE=SEQ(S2)
:       :      :     :     :     PS3=STMT
:       :      :     :     PS3=STMT
:       :      PS3=STMT
```

If our preliminary analysis is correct, (6) qualified
by the SS's (5), (3) and (2) is the villainy. The villainy
is indeed the fact that the younger son had a prodigal life
(6), but the text emphasizes by means of SS(5) that the villainy is a reflexive action: the younger son is both subject
and receiver in both (6) and (5). In other words, he does
not want any longer to be the helper of his father; he wants
to strike out on his own. Because it is directly related to
(6) and because it is a subsequence of the *subject*, SS(5)
directly emphasizes that which characterizes the villainy as
action: the fact that the younger son uses for his own endeavor and by himself the father's property. This is possible
because the father gives him his share of the property: SS(3)
participates therefore in the villainy, yet this action of the
father is only indirectly participating in the villainy (as
the hierarchy shows). We can also note that the father apparently saw no harm in his son's request in SS(2).

When he had spent everything (v. 14a)

This is the *result* of the performance in (6), which can
be expressed in terms of the verbs of the category "being/
having": he has no money left. Thus it is a *qualification*
in the negative form. The attribution is interrupted:
younger son ∩ share.

Q(7) v. 14a ⎸PS3 //*

	share	younger son

---

*[Note: The symbol "//" indicates an interrupted sequence.]

a great famine arose in that country (v. 14b)

Q(8) v. 14b ,PS3,

_____	great famine	far country
_____	_____	_____

and he began to be in want (v. 14c)

This phrase expresses that the younger son is lacking an undefined object that the following verses will show to be "food". The modality "beginning" is expressing that this is a new situation and thus belongs to a new sequence. Younger son ∩ food (O). This is a negative qualification. From v. 14a and 14b it appears that the younger son (S) expected to transmit food (O) to himself (R) with the help of both his share of property and the far country.

Q(9) v. 14c ,PS3 //

_____	(food)	younger son
(share) (far country)	(younger son)	_____

So he went and joined himself to one of the citizens of that country (v. 15a)

This is a disjunction/conjunction narrative function (DS): we are therefore in another sequence with the younger son as subject. As the following verses show, it is no longer a matter of carrying out a prodigal life but simply of getting food, that is, of fulfilling the lack expressed in (9). This

DS shows that the younger son acquires a new helper for this program: "one of the citizens of that country" in order to overcome the opponent "famine"--cf. (8). As the rest of the text shows, the younger son attempts to carry out this program, yet he fails. The establishment of the volition (CS1) is manifested by another sequence.

(10) v. 15a   (CS1) _ _ DS   PS1   PS2 //

	(food)	younger son
citizen	younger son	(famine)

who sent him into his fields to feed swine (v. 15b)

Se:citizen; S:younger son; H:fields; O:food; R:swine. Only a mandating CS1 is manifested here, yet the following verse implies that the younger son carried out this mandate.

(11) v. 15b CS1 _ (DS) _ (PS2) (PS3)

citizen	food	swine
fields	younger son	

And he would gladly have fed on the pods that the swine ate; and no one gave him anything (v. 16)

This is a new program which remains potential (as the modalities "would gladly" and the negation indicate). S:younger son; O:pods of the swine; R:younger son. Yet this program is not established because of lack of "sender": no one established him as subject of this program. Thus the sequence aborts at CS1.

(12) v. 16 ___CS1_//

(no sender)	carob	younger son
	younger son	

But coming to himself he said (v. 17a)

In this abstract statement, we find two verbs of the
category of "doing": "coming", a movement, indicates a dis-
junction/conjunction function (DS), the younger son is brought
in conjunction with himself, thus he has as helper himself;
"saying" indicates the transmission of an object message (O)
by the younger son (S) to himself (R). This message is, as
v. 17b expresses it, a reflection on the situation of his
father's servants--which he compares with his own situation.

(13) v. 17a _ _ |—DS—| _ _ |—PS3—|

	reflection about father's servants	younger son
	younger son	

DS expresses either the conjunction with a new helper or the
conjunction with the receiver. In this case the DS expresses
the conjunction with the receiver.

*How many of my father's hired servants have bread enough and
to spare (v. 17b)*

This is a qualification. O:abundant bread; R:many hired
servants of his father.

Q(14) v. 17b |—PS3—|

	abundant bread	many hired ser- vants of father

but I perish here with hunger! (v. 17c)

The Greek text, despite the middle voice of the verb,
can be rendered, even though awkwardly, by a passive form--
"here I am killed by famine". Turning this passive phrase
into an active form, we can render this phrase: "famine is
killing me". We have therefore a performance in progress,
PS2, by famine (S), transmitting death (O) to the younger son.
We can see this sequence as a subsequence of the opponent of
(11).

(15) v. 17c _ _ |—PS2—|

	death	younger son
	famine	

I will arise and go to my father, and I will say to him
(v. 18a)

Two narrative functions: DS--movement of the son to
his father; and PS3--transmission of a message. The future
tense modality makes this text a proposed program rather than
a performance and thus a contractual syntagm, CS1 and CS2.
It expresses what the younger son hopes to do.

(16) v. 18a |_CS1_|_CS2_|

	message	father
	younger son	

'Father, I have sinned against heaven and before you (v. 18b)
The verb "sinning" expresses a performance which is defined simply by the relationship between the subject and the opponent. The text could be rendered: I, as subject, have performed against the opponent, "heaven and...you". The past tense indicates that the performance has been completed, and thus a PS2 and PS3.

(17) v. 18b _ _ _ _|_PS2_|_PS3_|

	younger son	heaven & father

This performance is clearly the performance expressed in the villainy defined by (6), (5), (3), and (2).

I am no longer worthy to be called your son (v. 19a)
A negative qualification: O:sonship; R:younger son.

Q(18) v. 19a |_PS3_//

	sonship	younger son

The temporal modality, no longer, indicates that (17) is
the cause of this negative qualification. Thus (17) is a
subsequence of the receiver of Q(18).

Treat me as one of your hired servants' (v. 19b)

This is a mandate, CS1, by the younger son (Se) to the
father (S) to attribute "servanthood" (O) to the younger son
(R). This program will never be established. The younger
son will not even have the opportunity to express this part
of the message to his father. Thus the sequence aborts at
CS1.

(19) v. 19b   CS1 //

younger son	servanthood	younger son
	father	

And he arose and came to his father (v. 20a)

This is the movement, DS, of the proposed narrative
program described earlier. We have the manifestation of
another function of sequence (16) which now includes:

(16) v. 18a, 20a   CS1 , CS2 , DS

	message	father
	younger son	

But while he was yet at a distance, his father saw him and
had compassion, and ran and embraced him and kissed him
(v. 20b)

The verb "seeing" and similar verbs of perception
express that a message has been transmitted—either a
mandate or some type of knowledge (cognition, i.e., helper
for a narrative program). In the present case, "seeing the
young man" is mandating the father to act in a specific way:
the sender is the young son in the act of coming back. The
phrase "he had compassion" expresses the acceptance of the
mandate. "He ran" indicates conjunction with the receiver,
DS. "He embraced him and kissed him" is the performance
itself—the transmission of the object "father" to the young
man as receiver.

(20) v. 20b $\underset{\text{younger son}}{\underline{\text{CS1}}} - \underset{\text{father}}{\underline{\text{DS}}} - \underset{\text{younger son}}{\underline{\text{PS2} \quad \text{PS3}}}$

	father	

The modality of the sequence is expressed in the phrase "But
while he was yet at a distance". It emphasizes the eagerness
that the father had to carry out this program. This new
program interrupts the program of the son.

And the son said to him (v. 21a)

This is the performance (PS2, PS3) of (16) which now
includes:

(16) v. 18a, 20a, 21a | CS1 | CS2 | DS | _ _ | PS2 | PS3 |

| _____ | message | father |

| _____ | younger son | _____ |

'Father, I have sinned against heaven and before you (v. 21b)

This is a repetition of a part of the message expressed in (17). Earlier, this message was explaining the *proposed* performance of (19) and qualified CS2. Now this message explains the performance, PS1, of (19). It is therefore another subsequence.

(21) v. 21b _ _ | PS2 | PS3 |

| _____ | _____ | _____ |

| _____ | younger son | heaven & father |

I am no longer worthy to be called your son' (v. 21c)

For similar reasons we record this negative qualification as a new sequence.

Q(22) v. 21c | PS3 //

| _____ | sonship | younger son |

| _____ | _____ | _____ |

But the father said to his servants (v. 22a)

(23) v. 22a ⌞ PS3 ⌟

	mandate	servants
eagerness	father	

"Quickly" in the following lexie qualifies the "eagerness" (H) of the father.

Bring quickly the best robe and put it on him; and put a ring on his hand, and shoes on his feet (v. 22b)

This is the mandate, CS1, which is implicitly carried out.

(24) v. 22b ⌞ CS1 ⌟ _ _ ⌞ (PS3) ⌟

father	robe, ring, shoes	younger son
	servants	

and bring the fatted calf (v. 23a)

This is a separate mandate. The fatted calf is to be attributed to the father so that he might make a feast. It is implicitly performed.

(25) v. 23a ⌞ CS1 ⌟ _ _ ⌞ (PS3) ⌟

	fatted calf	father
	servants	

kill it (v. 23b)

(26) v. 23b ⌐CS1⌐ — ⌐(PS3)⌐

_____	death	fatted calf
_____	servants	_____

and let us eat and make merry (v. 23c)

In the Greek text this is a single sequence--"let us who are eating make merry".

(27) v. 23c ⌐CS1⌐

_____	food & feast	younger son & father
servants & younger son	father	_____

for this my son was dead ... he was lost (v. 24a)

Q(28) v. 24a ⌐PS3⌐

_____	dead, lost	younger son
_____	_____	_____

and is alive ... and is found' (v. 24b)

Q(29) v. 24b $\llcorner$ PS3 $\lrcorner$

	alive, found	younger son

And they began to make merry (v. 24c)

This is the performance, PS2, PS3, of (27).

(27) v. 23c, 24c $\llcorner$ CS1 $\lrcorner$ _ _ $\llcorner$ PS2 $\llcorner$ PS3 $\lrcorner$

	food & feast	father & younger son
younger son fatted calf servants	father	

This last sequence indicates that the first villainy has been overcome: even though in a superlative way, this sequence expresses that the initial situation has been at least partially reestablished. (27) is therefore the Cor. Seq. 2. The modality "beginning" expresses that the performance is not yet complete. Before analyzing the last part of the parable, we can now propose the hierarchy since we now have the Cor. Seq. 2.

It should be noted that the Cor. Seq. 2 includes necessarily some new elements as compared with Cor. Seq. 1, the initial sequence. In our case, the narrative program is expressed in a superlative way: festivity is added to

the normal family life. We could say that the initial
situation is that of a father sharing food and other goods,
in other words "his belongings", with his two sons. For
this he needs the helpful presence of his two sons. Thus
we can write the Cor. Seq. 1 as a simplified (27).

(27A) $\_\_$ $\mid$ PS2 $\mid$ PS3 $\mid$

	his belongings	father & two sons
two sons	father	

Using a shortened notation to indicate actants, e.g.,
Se^{27}, Op^5, etc., we can summarize our analysis of this much
of the text as follows:

Q(1) as qualification of the father is a subsequence (SS)
of the subject of (27A) or S^{27A}. (4) expresses one of the
ways in which the father carries out his program—by dividing
his belongings between his two sons. (4) is a SS of S^{27A}.
The program of (4) is not in contradiction with (27A) as long
as the two sons remain with the father and allow him to make
use of these belongings with them.

The performance of the correlated sequence is interrupted
at PS2 by the villainy. This is the situation of lack: the
father, S^{27A}, lacks the younger son, H^{27A}. A qualification
explains this state of affairs: SS(28) qualifies H^{27A} (the
younger son) as dead and lost. The villainy (6), (5), (3),
(2), explains how this state of affairs has been brought
about, therefore this sub-narrative is subordinated to (29),
and is a sub-narrative of R^{28}, the younger son as villain.

So far the hierarchy includes the *correlated content 1*, father and sons before the villainy, and the *villainy content*, the younger son's life in a far country. This is displayed in the appendix.

These eight sequences represent the correlated sequence, the situation of lack, and the villainy. Are there other sequences that we should consider as subsequences of these three narrative units?

Several sequences, primarily (7) through (19), refer to the younger son--that is, to the personage who is in position of villain. In the hierarchy should they be considered as directly related to the villainy? According to our tentative analysis in terms of the broad characteristics of the narrative structure we have to consider the bulk of verses 14 through 24 as the *topical content* (i.e., the topical sequence and its subsequences) which brings about a first reestablishment of the initial situation. In such a case, (7) through (19) should not be viewed as subsequences of the villainy, but as subsequences of the topical sequence --a sequence with the father as subject, which is, as we shall see, (20).

This observation suggests that the deep narrative structure is at odds with the surface structure. In the textual surface, verses 13 and 14 are closely related by the fact that the same personage is subject in both verses. Indeed, (7) through (19) have the same central personage as the villainy: they are parts of the story of the younger son. We are witnessing here the intersection of two narratives: the narrative of the father's love and the narrative of the prodigal son. In broad outline, this second narrative could be summarized as follows:

Initial sequence: with the help of his father (H), the young son (S) lives in abundance; he has food (O) for himself (R).

	food	younger son
father	younger son	

Villainy: the younger son separates himself from his father, his helper, in order to live his prodigal life. Thus the villainy of the prodigal son's story is very similar to the villainy of the father's story.

Situation of lack: because he lacks his helper, the younger son (S) cannot feed himself.

Topical content: (the topical sequence and its subsequences) the repenting younger son returns to his father in order to reestablish some type of relationship with him, so that his father might once more be his helper.

Reestablished initial situation: because of the father's help, the young man has food for himself.

It is to be noted that in this case (7) through (19) would manifest both the situation of lack and the topical content. The villainy (which would be very similar to the one described above) would be a sub-narrative of this situation of lack, while the topical content would be directly related to the correlated sequence (as what allows the reestablishment of the initial situation). Thus, there would also be a narrative shift with the introduction of (7) in verse 14.

Yet this narrative of the prodigal son is embedded in the narrative of the father: the elements of the prodigal

son's story are viewed from the perspective of the father's
story. The father is indeed functioning at times as helper
of the younger son as in (5). Yet, it is emphasized that
he is doing it on his own terms and not on the terms suggested by the younger son. This appears already in verse
12c, which can be viewed as the fulfillment of the younger
son's request (3), although it is in fact a new narrative
program, (4). Similarly, in verses 20 and 22ff. the father
can be viewed as functioning as helper of the younger son
(in the prodigal son story), yet, in fact, he is carrying
out a quite different narrative program. This is to say
that our text is considering the prodigal son's narrative
as a sub-narrative of the father's narrative. In other
words, the elements of the prodigal son's narrative have
to be viewed as subordinated to the elements of the father's
narrative. Consequently, the narrative elements which are
related to the younger son in verses 14ff. have to be viewed
as subordinated to the topical sequence which has the father
as subject. What is expressed in verses 14ff. no longer defines the villainy--that is, how the father lost one of his
helpers--but rather is part of what will allow the father
to recover his helper, the younger son. In the Greek text
the fact that verse 14 is a narrative watershed is indicated by the particle δὲ which once more appears as a
shifter.

What is the topical sequence, that is, the sequence
which expresses that the younger son ($O^t = H^i$ in the formula
for the main narrative transformation) is communicated to
the father ($S^i = R^t$) so that the disjunction between S^i and
O^t might be overcome? (20) expresses the conjunction of the
father as object to the younger son as receiver. We have
here a situation similar to Q(1) in which the attribution of

two sons as (0) to a man (R) expressed that the man was a "father". Similarly here the attribution of the father (0^{20}) to the young man (R^{20}) establish (or better, re-establish) him in his position of son....Of course, this sequence implies that the younger son (0) is attributed to the father (R). Thus (20) implies a sequence (20A):

(20) v. 20b |—CS1—| – |—DS—| – |—PS2—,—PS3—|

younger son	father	younger son
	father	

(20A) |—PS3—|

younger son	younger son	father
	father	

(20A) is the topical sequence. (20) is a subsequence of the subject, S^{20A}, which directly defines the action of the hero. (23) is a subsequence of the subject of (20) which expresses how the father mandates his servants so that they might in his name further manifest the conjunction between the father and the younger son. (24), the attribution of the objects, "robe", "ring", and "shoes" to the younger son, expresses the meaning of PS3 of (23) and qualifies the younger son as receiver of the father. (24) is a subsequence of the receiver of PS3 of (23): or, in short, SS R^{23} at PS3.

Now we need to ask how (20) has been made possible. What are the subsequences which express the narrative features necessary for the performance of (20)? As we noted above

while analyzing verse 20b, the performance of (20) would not
have been possible without the return of the younger son.
The sight of the younger son is perceived by the father as a
mandate: the returning younger son (Se^{20}) is therefore the
sender of the father. This return of the younger son has as
its purpose the transmission of a message to the father: this
is (16) which is therefore a subsequence of the subject of
CS1 of (20), SS S^{20} at CS1.

The sequence which expresses the content of this message
and explains why it must be delivered is a subsequence of
(16): this is SS(19) which is SS R^{16} at CS2. I say that it
is a subsequence of (16) at CS2 because the content of the
message is a helper that S^{16} must have in order to carry his
program. (19) expresses that "cognition" has been received.
The father, S^{19}, is mandated by the younger son, Se^{19}, to
attribute the quality "servanthood", O^{19}, to the younger son,
R^{19}. Yet this mandate is never proposed to the father.

The reason for (19) is expressed in Q(18) which is a
negative qualification of R^{19}: the younger son is no longer
worthy to be called son; this is why he asks only to be a
servant of his father. Thus Q(18) is SS R^{19} at CS1.

(19), (18), and (17) express the content of the message
that the younger son as S^{16} wanted to deliver to his father,
R^{16}. ((17) is SS R^{18} and explains how the younger son lost
his sonship: he acted vis-à-vis God and his father as if
they were opponents.) In actuality, the younger son delivers
only part of this message. This performance, PS3 of (16) is
expressed in (22) and (21). (22), which expresses that he
is not worthy to be called son, is SS S^{16} at PS3. (21),
which expresses that he is not worthy to be called son, is
SS S^{16} at PS3. (21), which explains why, is SS R^{22} at PS2
and PS3.

(19), (18), (17), (22), and (21) express the content of
the message, O^{16}, that the younger son, S^{16}, transmits to
the father, R^{16}. Another series of subsequences express why
the younger son, S^{16}, wanted to transmit this message, that
is, how the volition has been established. This series of
subsequences is therefore SS of (16) at CS1. Consequently,
they have to be placed higher in the hierarchy.

(13) expresses that the younger son is thinking about
the situation of his father's servants is SS S^{16} at CS1.

(13) is defined by two qualifications. Q(14) is a
qualification of O^{13}: the servants have bread in abundance--
SS O^{13} at PS3. Q(15) is a qualification of S^{13}: the younger
son perishes with hunger--SS S^{13} at PS3.

Q(15) is explained by the fact that the younger son's
association with a citizen of that country fails to provide
the necessary food for the younger son. This is (10) which
is therefore a subsequence of R^{15}. (10) = SS R^{15}.

The association of the younger son with the citizen is
expressed in (11): the citizen, Se^{11}, mandates the younger
son, S^{11}, to feed the swine, R^{11}, and the younger son performs this mandate. (11) = SS S^{10} at PS2.

The situation of S^{11} is further expressed in (12):
he wished to eat the carobs. Thus (12) = SS S^{11} at PS2.

It remains a series of sequences which express why the
younger son associated himself with a citizen of that country;
these are therefore subsequences of (10). Q(9), "he began to
be in want", is a negative qualification. The younger son,
R^{9}, lacks food, O^{9}. Q(9) = SS S^{3} at CS1. From the sequences
included in the villainy, we can deduce that the younger son,
S^{9}, hoped to communicate food, O^{9}, to himself, R^{9}, with the
help of his share of property and of the far country, both

H^9. Two qualifications express that this performance was not possible because of inadequate helpers. $Q(7)$, a negative qualification, expresses that the younger son no longer has the share of property as helper. Thus, $(7) =$ SS S^9. Simultaneously the other helper, the far country, H^9, is qualified by a great famine in $Q(8)$. $Q(8) =$ SS H^9.

With $Q(8)$ we reach, at last, the end of the series of the subsequences of the topical sequence. This topical content explains how the correlated sequence has been re-established. Consequently, it has to be viewed as sub-ordinated to Cor. Seq. 2, that is, to (27): the father gives a feast and food for the younger son and himself-- and also for the elder son as the Cor. Seq. 1 requires us to expect--with the help of the younger son, for were he not present this program could not be carried out, and of the servants. The topical content expresses how the younger son has been reestablished in position of helper, H^{27}, of his father, S^{27}. This topical content is summarized in $Q(29)$: the younger son is alive and found. Thus $Q(29) =$ SS H^{27}. (25) expresses the role of the servant as H^{27}-- the fatted calf is provided by the father. $(25) =$ SS H^{27}. Yet, in order to do so they must kill the fatted calf: $(26) =$ SS S^{25}.

We now have the complete narrative hierarchy of the first part of the parable as displayed in the appendix. *Correlated content 1*--father and sons before the villainy; *villainy content*--younger son's prodigal life in far country; *correlated content 1* partially restored--the feast; *topical content 1*--the father welcoming younger son home.

Now his elder son was in the field (v. 25a)

"Now" is the translation of the shifter "δὲ". We find two qualifications: 1) elder son (O) is attributed to the father (R),

Q(30) v. 25a ▪PS3▪

	elder son	father

2) a location, field (O), is attributed to the elder son (R). This attribution of a location implies a performance—the elder son was working in the field.

Q(31) v. 25a ▪PS3▪

field	elder son	

And as he came and drew near to the house, he heard music and dancing (v. 25b)

Movement of the elder son from the field to the house of his father. This is the manifestation of a narrative program of the elder son as (S). This movement is in process, thus not (yet) completed. As is clear from the following verses, "music and dancing" confront the elder son as opponent which interrupts the sequence at DS (see v. 28b below). The very fact that we have two verbs of movement suggests that the nature of the narrative program is to perform this movement—

that is, the elder son as (S) was in the process of communicating himself as (O). The hierarchy suggests that the receiver is the father. The location, home, is functioning as helper for this communication.

(32) v. 25b ˌDS //

_____	elder son	(father)
(servant, house)	elder son	music, dancing

And he called one of the servants and asked what this meant (vv. 26, 27a)

The elder son as Se mandates, CS1, one of the servants as S to transmit to him (R) an explanation of the feast, the object (O). "And he said to him" is the performance, PS3, of this program.

(33) v. 26, 27a ˌCS1ˌ _ _ ˌPS3ˌ

elder son	explanation of feast	elder son
_____	servant	_____

Your brother has come (v. 27b)

The younger son has completed a movement.

(34) v. 27b ˌDSˌ

	younger son	

And your father has killed the fatted calf (v. 27c)

From the preceding verses we know that this phrase should not be taken literally—the servants killed the fatted calf. It means that the father (S) uses the fatted calf (H) to make a feast (O), and that the performance of this program has begun. This is in effect (27). Yet we must record it again for the repetition suggests that this sequence has here a different narrative function.

(35) v. 27c PS2

	feast	
fatted calf	father	

This verse also includes a qualification: "your father" is the attribution of father (O) to the elder son (R).

Q(35A) v. 27c PS3

	father	elder son

because he has received him safe and sound (v. 27d)

"Because" expresses that this sequence is an SS of (35). The father (R) received the younger son (O). In addition, there is a qualification of a younger son (R) as "safe and sound" (O).

(36) v. 27d |‾PS3‾|

	younger son	father
‾‾‾‾‾‾‾‾‾	‾‾‾‾‾‾‾‾‾	‾‾‾‾‾‾‾‾‾

Q(37) v. 27d |‾PS3‾|

	safe & sound	younger son
‾‾‾‾‾‾‾‾‾	‾‾‾‾‾‾‾‾‾	‾‾‾‾‾‾‾‾‾

But he was angry (v. 28a)

The verb is of the category being/having, thus this is a qualification. R:elder son; O:anger.

Q(38) v. 28a |‾PS3‾|

	anger	elder son
‾‾‾‾‾‾‾‾‾	‾‾‾‾‾‾‾‾‾	‾‾‾‾‾‾‾‾‾

and refused to come in (v. 28b)

(32) is interrupted. Now that he is qualified as angry (i.e., with anger as the opponent of his original program) he cannot, and does not want to, fulfill his original program.

His father came out and entreated him (v. 28c)

Here we have in fact two sequences: the father (S) performs a movement (DS) in order to bring the elder son as (O) back home, i.e., to the father as (R). This performance is in process, PS2.

(39) v. 28c ⌐DS¬ _ _ ⌐PS2¬

_____	elder son	father
_____	_____	_____
(message)	father	elder son

For this purpose he uses as helper a message in order to overcome the elder son as opponent. Verse 28c expresses that this message or invitation is communicated by the father as (S) to the elder son as (R).

(39A) v. 28c ⌐PS3¬

_____	message	elder son
_____	_____	_____
_____	father	_____

But he answered his father (v. 29a)

(40) v. 29a ⌐PS3¬

_____	message	father
_____	_____	_____
_____	elder son	_____

'Lo, these many years I have served you, and I never disobeyed your command (v. 29b)

The elder son as (S) has carried out, PS2, PS3, the mandate given to him by the father as (Se). This narrative program is modified in two ways: 1) "I never disobeyed your command" is in effect a qualification of the subject—loyalty (O) is attributed to the elder son (R). 2) "these many years" can be viewed as a qualification of the loyalty of the elder son. He had many years (O) of loyalty (R). Thus verse 29b can be represented by three interrelated sequences:

(41) v. 29b ⊢ PS2 ⊢ PS3 ⊣

father		
	elder son	

Q(42) v. 29b ⊢ PS3 ⊣

	loyalty	elder son

Q(43) v. 29b ⊢ PS3 ⊣

	many years	loyalty

(43) is SS of (42); and (42) an SS of (41).

Yet you never gave me a kid (v. 29c)

This is a performance which did not take place. In effect, the father (S) never felt that he was mandated to give a kid (O) to the elder son (R). The volition has never been established. The sequence is interrupted at CS1.

(44) v. 29c ⌐CS1 //

	kid	elder son
	father	

that I might make merry with my friends (v. 29d)

The elder son (S) wants to enjoy himself, to attribute "joy" or "feast" as (O) to himself (R) with the help of his friends (H) and of the kid. But this program is interrupted because the proper helper, the kid, is not communicated. The program is interrupted at CS2. "That" (ἵνα) shows that (44) is a subsequence of this new sequence (45).

(45) v. 29d ⌐CS2 //

	feast	elder son
friends	elder son	

But when this son of yours came (v. 30a)

(46) v. 30a ⎣ DS ⎦

	younger son	

who has devoured your living with harlots (v. 30b)

S:younger son; O:father's property; R:younger son; H:
harlots.

(47) v. 30b ⎣ PS3 ⎦

	father's property	younger son
harlots	younger son	

you kill for him the fatted calf (v. 30c)

Opposed and related to verse 29c, this phrase must be
understood as meaning that the father (S) gave, PS3, the
fatted calf (O) to the younger son (R).

(48) v. 30c ⎣ PS3 ⎦

	fatted calf	younger son
	father	

And he said to him (v. 31a)

(49) v. 31a |PS3|

| _____ | message | elder son |
| _____ | father | _____ |

'Son, you are always with me (v. 31b)

"Being with the father" is a qualification of the son
as one to whom the father (O) is attributed.

Q(50) v. 31b |PS3|

| _____ | father | elder son |
| _____ | _____ | _____ |

and all that is mine is yours (v. 31c)

Another qualification of the elder son:

Q(51) v. 31c |PS3|

| _____ | father's property | elder son |
| _____ | _____ | _____ |

It was fitting to make merry and be glad (v. 32a)

It is to be noted here that we have an impersonal form
instead of the personal (reflexive) form found in verse 29d.
The father is not saying that he enjoys himself, i.e., that
he (S) attributes joy or feast (O) to himself (R). The feast

here is to be attributed to the father and the younger son, both receivers, as we noted in (27) about verse 23c.

It expresses also that the volition of the father has been established by a compelling sender: the return of the younger son as described in the last part of the verse.

(52) v. 32a ⌊CS1⌋

(younger son)	feast	father & younger son
	father	

for this your brother was dead, ... he was lost (v. 32b)

Q(53) v. 32b ⌊PS3⌋

	dead, lost	younger son

and (he) is alive ... and is found' (v. 32c)

Q(54) v. 32c ⌊PS3⌋

	alive, found	younger son

It remains to establish the narrative hierarchy of this last part of the parable. In view of the main narrative transformation that we identified above, we can easily recognize in this passage a second villainy and a second topical sequence.

The refusal of the elder son to come home is the second villainy. The attempt by the father to bring his elder son home is the second topical sequence.

In verse 25a and b, we find three sequences which are in effect subsequences of the Cor. Seq. 1. Q(30) qualifies the father as having an elder son. Q(30) is a subsequence of the subject of the Cor. Seq. 1, (27A). (3) = SS S^{27A} at PS2.

Q(31) qualifies the elder son as being in the field and is a subsequence which qualifies the object of (30). Q(31) = SS O^{30} at PS3.

(32) is another SS of O^{30}, which expresses the performance of the elder son as son of the father. This performance is interrupted at DS by the music and dancing, the feast. Because of the interruption of (32) the elder son does not any longer function as helper of his father. Consequently, the father is deprived of the elder son: this is the situation of lack. (32) = SS O^{30} at PS3.

This second situation of lack is brought about by *the villainy* which interrupts (32). The villainy is expressed in summary form in Q(38): the elder son (R) is angry (O). Q(38) is therefore an SS of S^{32} and explains why (32) is interrupted. (38) = SS S^{32} at DS.

This situation is brought about by (33), the performance of the "servant", helper of the elder son in (32). The servant (S) gives to the elder son (R) an explanation of the feast (O). (33) = SS H^{32} at DS.

This explanation of the feast concerns the elder son, R^{33}, because it refers to the father of the elder son; it indeed begins with a qualification of the elder son (R) as having a father (O). (35A) = SS R^{33} at PS3.

The action of the father is expressed in (35): he gives a feast (O) with the help of the fatted calf (H). (35) = SS O^{35A} at PS3.

The father's motivation to do so, i.e., his sender, is expressed in a qualification: the father (R) has received the younger son (O). $Q(36) = SS\ S^{35}$ at PS2.

The younger son (S) came back (DS): (34) = SS O^{36} at PS3.

The younger son (R) was "safe and sound" (O) when he came back. $Q(37) = SS\ S^{34}$ at DS.

Thus, the villainy is expressed in (38), (33), (35A), (35), (36), (34) and (37).

The topical sequence is the action of the father (S) who, as discussed above, invites the elder son (O) to join the father (R) in the house with the help of a message (H); the elder son is the opponent. (39) = topical sequence.

The father (S) transmits a message (O) to the elder son (R). (39A) = SS Op^{39} at PS2.

The elder son (S) as opponent of the father in (39) manifests himself by transmitting a message (O) to the father (R). (40) = SS Op^{39} at PS2.

The elder son (S) was not able to have a feast (O) for himself (R) with his friends (H) because of lack of a necessary helper, the kid. Indeed he would like to have a feast for himself--thus CS1, or volition, is established --but the sequence must abort at CS2 because he will not receive "power" or a necessary helper. This aborted sequence is a subsequence of S^{40}. (45) = SS S^{40} at PS3.

The sequence of the feast for the elder son aborted even though the elder son (S) carried out, PS2, PS3, what the father (Se) commanded him to do. In Propp's terms this would be, for the elder son, the qualifying test if (45) were considered the main test. (41) = SS S^{45} at CS2.

The elder son (R) as subject of (41) is qualified as loyal (0). Q(42) = SS S^{41} at PS2 and PS3.

Loyalty (R) is further qualified by a temporal notation --many years (0). Q(43) = SS 0^{42} at PS3.

The father (S) as sender of (41) did not wish (CS1) to give a kid (0) to the elder son (R). (44) = SS Se^{41} at PS3.

The father, S^{44}, is also the one who kills a fatted calf (0) for the younger son (R). (48) = SS S^{44} at CS1.

The younger son, R^{48}, is defined by his action: he came back (DS). (46) = SS R^{48} at PS3.

The returning younger son is further defined as the one (S) who used the father's property (0) for himself (R) with harlots (H). (47) = SS S^{46} at DS.

The father as subject of the topical sequence (39) is further defined as the one (S) who delivers a message (0), the second message, to the elder son (R). (49) = SS S^{39} at PS2.

In the message there is the qualification of the elder son as the one to whom is attributed the father (0)--"son, you are always with me". Q(50) = SS R^{49} at PS3.

The elder son (R) is further qualified as the one to whom is attributed the father's property (0). Q(51) = SS R^{49} at PS3.

The father, as S^{49}, expresses further that his (S) volition has been established, CS1, to give a feast (0) to himself (R) and the younger son (R); the sender is the younger son as the following sequence manifests it: (52) = SS S^{49} at PS3.

The younger son, as Se^{52}, is first qualified as dead and lost (0). Q(53) = SS Se^{52} at CS1.

The younger son is later qualified as alive and found (0). Q(54) = SS Se^{52} at CS1.

We have now the complete narrative hierarchy which is displayed in the appendix.

3. Analysis in Terms of the Mythical Structure and Elementary Structure

A. The Model and the Method

On the basis of this detailed analysis in terms of the narrative structure we can now proceed to the analysis in terms of the mythical structure so as to point out the semantic categories which together form the "mythical" part of the meaning effect of the parable. We term "mythical part of the meaning effect", the system of convictional values, or religious or ethical values, manifested by the narrative.

I will make use of three models for this analysis: 1. the model proposed by Lévi-Strauss for the mythical structure as interpreted in my essay "Structural Network in Narrative"; 2. the semiotic square for the elementary structure; 3. and a model for the interrelation of the narrative structure, mythical structure, and elementary structure.

In the introduction of this paper I suggested the main characteristics of this last model. Further explanations of this model are in order.

Let me simply say here that because the mythical structure is a paradigmatic structure (a structure allowing the
apprehension of a static system), and the narrative structure
is a syntagmatic structure (allowing the apprehension of
processes) we cannot identify the narrative opposition between
the situation of lack, disorder, and the restored situation,
order, with the mythical oppositions of the mythical system.

After many different attempts, we have reached the
following model discussed in my essay "Structural Network
of Narrative".

The "situation of lack" corresponds to $F_{\overline{a}}(y)$ in the
mythical structure and the topical content corresponds to
$F_x(b)$ in the mythical structure. I also suggested that the
mythical content is organized in eight semantic categories:
the square of the "mythical functions" and the square of the
"mythical states". We can now be more specific.

The semantic value that we have termed "mythical state"
(that we shall simply call "state") is manifested in the
narrative structure in the relation between "sender", "subject", "helper", and "opponent" and secondarily between
"receiver" and "object". In the narrative, the semantic
components of the state of a subject is positively defined
as his helper(s), and negatively as his opponent(s). For
instance, if in a narrative a king (S) is shown as using his
authority (H), the state of the king in this narrative is
defined as "someone with authority". This "authority" is
further defined by the opponents that he overcomes. The
opponents manifest the negative value of the state, thus
$(\frac{-}{a})$ or $(\frac{-}{b})$. In most instances, the narrative manifests that
helpers are attributed to a given personage by means of
qualifications--attributions of a helper--and of subsequences.

In these subsequences, or qualifications, the state of a personage in position of receiver is the object which is attributed to him. To keep the same example we could imagine that the object "authority" was attributed to the king at his enthronement described in a subsequence.

The state is also defined by the sender--the subject is established by the sender. As we shall see, in terms of its function, the subject is a metonymic figure of the sender. In terms of its state, the subject is defined as "associated with the sender". Keeping the same example, if the sender of the king is the bishop, who enthrones him, the state of the king as subject includes a religious semantic feature.

The semantic value which we termed as "mythical function" or "function" is manifested in the narrative structure by the action of a *subject* which attributes an *object* to a *receiver*. The function of a subject is primarily characterized by the object: e.g., the function "killing" is manifested when somebody attributes the object "death" to somebody else. In the case of such a broad function, the function is exclusively defined by the semantic value of the object--and not by the subject and the receiver. More specific functions are also defined by the semantic values of the subject and the receiver. For instance, the function "executing"--putting to death a criminal-- is defined by the subject, the executioner, the object, death, and the receiver, the criminal.

The sender also defines the function in that the narrative program originates with him and he establishes the subject. Yet, the semantic value of the function does not appear to be directly defined by the sender (yet, as suggested below, knowing the sender is often essential in order to identify where a function is manifested in the narrative).

A given function is manifested both in a given sequence by the relation among the subject, object, and receiver, and also in the subsequences of the subject of this given sequence. Furthermore, it is also defined in the sub-sequences, which have as sender the subject of this given sequence: in this case the subject of the subsequence acts in the name of the sender. Since the subject acts in the name of the sender, the subject can be viewed as a metonymic figure of the sender.

The topical content which corresponds to $F_x(b)$ in the mythical structure includes a function x and a state (b). [Note: we shall write the states between parentheses to distinguish them from the functions.] The function x is the function of the hero, that is, the function of the sub-ject of the topical sequence. It is further defined by the following:

1. *the subsequences of the subject of the topical sequence:* the relation among the subject, object, and re-ceiver in these subsequences are other manifestations of the function x. These subsequences need to be directly related in the narrative hierarchy to the topical sequence: other subsequences even though they might have the same personage as subject are *not* manifesting the semantic value of x;

2. *the subsequences in which the sender is the subject of the topical sequence* in so far as these subsequences are hierarchically related to the topical sequence (they can be

subsequences of a subsequence of the subject of the topical sequence).

Similarly, the state (b) is the state of the hero as defined by his sender, helpers, and opponents. It is further defined by:

1. *the sender, helpers, and opponents of the subject of all the subsequences of the subject of the topical sequence;*

2. *all the qualifications of the subject of the topical sequence* and by the qualifications of the subjects of all the *subsequences of the subject* of the topical sequence (yet *not* by other qualifications of the same personage elsewhere in the narrative hierarchy). In these qualifications the state is defined by the object attributed to the receiver (who is also the hero, i.e., the subject of the topical sequence);

3. *the object attributed (PS3) to the subject of the topical sequence as receiver* in the subsequences which are hierarchically related to the topical sequence--except for those subsequences which are hierarchically related to the opponents of the topical sequence or to the opponents of subsequences of the subject of the topical sequence.

The above remarks help illustrate why a detailed and rigorous analysis in terms of the narrative structure is necessary before attempting an analysis in terms of the mythical and elementary structures.

The situation of lack which corresponds in the mythical structure to $F_{\bar{a}}(y)$ includes a function $\bar{a}$ and a state (y). In the formula for the mythical structure, the terms "x" and "y" designate functions and the terms "a" and "b" designate states. Yet, as Lévi-Strauss pointed out, the mythical structure includes a complex inversion: $F_{\bar{a}}(y)$. In the situation of lack this inversion is clear. First, the state of the subject of the correlated sequence is transformed as a result of the action of the villain. In fact, the state of the subject of the interrupted correlated sequence is nothing other than the result of the function of the villain: the state (y). For instance, in the parable of the Good Samaritan, the state of the man is "wounded", i.e., the result of the action of the robbers, the villains. The function of the personage in such a state has to be defined negatively: he is unable to act as he was supposed to according to his original state. If his original state was (a), after the villainy he cannot act as (a). Thus his function is best represented as $\bar{a}$ (non a).

The state (a) is therefore the semantic value of all that which defines the subject of the correlated sequence before the villainy: primarily the helpers of the subject of the correlated sequence as manifested either in that sequence, in subsequences of the subject of the correlated sequence or in appropriate qualifications and attributions (cf. above). The state ($\bar{a}$) (non a) is the state of a personage who is the contradictory of the subject of the correlated sequence. [The state of the villain, as opponent of the subject of the correlated sequence, seems to be ($\bar{a}$), yet this part of the model needs to be verified further before being considered as a constant.] The function $\bar{a}$ reflects how the subject of the correlated sequence "functions" when deprived from some or all of his helpers: this function is manifested in the situation of lack.

The function y is manifested by the action of the villain. It is therefore defined in the subsequence of the opponent of the correlated sequence that we termed, following Propp, the villainy, as well as in some of its subsequences (cf. above). The villain and its function can also be manifested in the topical sequence, and its subsequences, as opponent of the hero. The state (y) is manifested in the situation of lack.

Thus the semantic value of x, y, (b), (a), and $(\bar{a})$, (and also of (y) and $\bar{a}$) can be determined with the help of most of the sequences, subsequences, and qualifications of the correlated content, the topical content, and the villainy content. Yet other subsequences and qualifications cannot be considered as manifesting the semantic values of these five functions and states but rather as manifesting other semantic values. The role of these and other semantic values in the meaning effect of the narrative can be understood as providing the necessary contrasting background which allows the reader/hearer to perceive more sharply the semantic values of x, y, (a) and (b). In other words, these other semantic values are the contradictories of x, y, (a) and (b). For instance, "non-heroes" (cf. the priest and Levite in the parable of the Good Semaritan) manifest $\bar{x}$ (the function non x) and have the state $(\bar{b})$. Similarly, $\bar{y}$ would be manifested by a "non-villain". Since $\bar{y}$ is implied by x (the function of the hero) it is possible that $\bar{y}$ be the function of the subject of the correlated sequence before the villainy and after the topical sequence. However, this part of the model needs further verification before it can be termed a constant.

It is to be noted that $\bar{x}$, $\bar{y}$, $(\bar{a})$, $\bar{a}$, $\bar{b}$ are broader semantic categories than the primary categories. This can be expressed in terms of the relations of implication in the semiotic squares. Indeed, x implies $\bar{y}$ (as white implies "non black"). Yet, $\bar{y}$ because it is a broader category does not necessarily imply x (indeed "non black" can be "white" but also "blue", etc.). Because the contradictory categories are broadly defined, the sub-contrary relations--$\bar{y} \leftrightarrow \bar{x}$ and $\bar{b} \leftrightarrow \bar{a}$--are not necessarily a strict contrary relation. They might even be viewed as overlapping: e.g., green, blue, and yellow are both "non white" and "non black".

This analysis attempts to define each of the semantic categories in terms of the intra-textual relations. Certain semantic categories, especially states, are further defined in terms of extra-textual relations by the use of words or symbols like "father" which refer to the cultural codes. At this stage of the analysis, we are not taking into account the meaning, in the cultural codes, of the words and symbols used to designate the subjects of the main sequences.[9]

B. Analysis of the Parable of the Prodigal Son in Terms
of the Mythical and Elementary Structures

The purpose of this analysis is the determination of the semantic values of the eight categories x, y, (a), (b), $\bar{x}$, $\bar{y}$, ($\bar{a}$), ($\bar{b}$) and of the two subcategories (y) and $\bar{a}$. Following Lévi-Strauss' example (cf. "The Structural Study of Myth," *Structural Anthropology*, Garden City, N.Y.: Doubleday, 1967, 210ff.), we record the text in eight columns rather than in four. For Lévi-Strauss each column represents one of the four mythemes which are complex semantic units ($F_x(a)$, $F_y(b)$,...). For us, each column represents a less complex semantic unit, either a function (x, y,...) or a state ((a), (b),...). Yet these functions and states are themselves complex semantic units (rather than semantic features). Second, rather than following the order of the text as Lévi-Strauss did, we follow the order of the narrative hierarchy. This procedure has the inconvenience that it is no longer possible to read the text from left to right, yet it has the great advantage of making explicit the hierarchical relations for the determination of the functions and states.

Following carefully the model proposed above, this re-writing of the text in columns does not present major diffi-culties. The distinction between $\bar{x}$ (the contradictory of the function of the hero) and $\bar{y}$ (the contradictory of the function of the villain) is not immediately clear. We chose the con-tent of these columns keeping in mind the relations of impli-cation: x implies $\bar{y}$, and y implies $\bar{x}$. As suggested above, $\bar{y}$ seems to be the function of the subject of the correlated sequence as what is opposed to the villainy. Because $\bar{x}$ is distinct from the function of the villain, we believe that it is manifested in the topical content, thus in subsequences which are related to the topical sequence without being sub-sequences of its subject.

The states are not in the same interrelationship as the functions (because of the complex inversion in the mythical structure). Thus we cannot expect that they will correspond directly to the functions. We have identified (a), (b), ($\bar{a}$) respectively as the states of the subjects of the correlated sequence, of the topical sequence, and of the villainy (during as well as after the villainy, i.e. ($\bar{a}$) is also manifested in the topical content as long as the state of the villain is not modified by the successful action of the hero). ($\bar{b}$) is the state which is the contradictory of the state of the hero and implied by the state of the subject of the correlated sequence: this is the state of personages who manifest the function $\bar{x}$.

The display of the parable of the Prodigal Son in columns on pages 130 to 134 has been established according to the method outlined above.

Reading these columns vertically we can now attempt to formulate the semantic value of each category. The functions and states are semantic categories which we could term, paraphrasing Lévi-Strauss, "bundles of semantic features". It nevertheless remains that they are highly abstract entities, that is, merely features of the larger semantic units that Lévi-Strauss terms "mythemes" and which are manifested in "narrative figures". A given function should not be viewed as a complete and sufficient definition of a narrative figure. There is more to a personage than his actions! We are usually aware of this fact, yet we have the tendency to forget that this is also true of his state because we are so accustomed to conceive a personage as a static entity. A given state should not be viewed as a complete and sufficient definition of a narrative figure! *A narrative figure as manifestation of a mytheme is the specific combination of a function and a state.*

Function and state are themselves complex semantic units, i.e., "bundles of semantic features". We have already expressed this in terms of the narrative structure. We can be more specific by saying that the function is the interrelation of the *semantic values* of the subject, the object, the receiver; the state is the interrelation of the *semantic values* of the subject, the helper(s), the opponent(s), and also the sender.

Interpreting the various relations listed in each column we identify the "elementary mythical semantic unit" which characterizes this column. We used this long phrase as a designation for a function or a state in order to bring to the fore the fact that they are at once complex semantic units and semantic elements submitted to the constraint of the elementary structure. Consequently, we have to keep in mind that a function or a state is a "bundle of relations", i.e., it has several semantic features. In order to identify the pertinent features we can use the model for the elementary structure: the semiotic square. For instance, the pertinent features of the function x are those which set this function in contrary opposition with y, in contradictory opposition with $\bar{x}$ and in relation of implication with $\bar{y}$. Similarly, for each of the other functions and for the states.[10]

In column 1, the column of the function x, both verses 20b and 28c manifest the function "giving oneself to undeserving sons"--to sons who in one way or another cannot any longer be called son, one because he is unworthy, the other because he refuses. Verse 22 manifests the function of "giving sonship to undeserving sons". This second function, which in the narrative structure is hierarchically inferior to the first, can be viewed as a secondary form of the first function: by giving himself to his sons the father gives them the quality of "sonship".

In column 3, verse 24a expresses the state (y) as "dead and lost son". The deprived father has the state (y). In other words, the state of the deprived father is characterized by the semantic features, "having a dead and lost son" or "being without one of his sons".

(1) ·(2)

x ȳ

20b
(Father) communicating
himself to the prodigal
son (the father embraced
the young son and kissed
him)

22a
mandating of the servants
(thus, servants = metonymy
of the Father)

22b
(Father) communicating
honor and sonship to the
prodigal son (giving robe,
ring and shoes to the
prodigal son)

28c
(Father) communicating
himself to the elder son
(coming out and entreating
the elder son to come home)

31
giving a message to the
elder son

12c
(Father) sharing his be-
longings with his two
sons (he divided his be-
longings between them)

12b,c
(Father) giving share
of property according
to custom

23c, 24c
(Father) partaking food
and feast with young
son (let us eat and
make merry...and they
began to make merry)

31
(Father) communicating
himself and his
property to elder son

32
(Father) giving a feast
for the young son

(3)

y & (y)

(4)

$\bar{x}$

(y)

24a
having a dead and lost son

y

13c,d
using one's belongings
for one's self (the young
son took his journey to a
far country and there he
squandered his property
in loose living)

13b
gathering one's property

12
using his Father as helper
for his own purpose

29d
wishing to make a feast
for oneself with friends

29b-30
using the Father's belongings as the young son does
(receiving fatted calf
from the Father) and did
(spending his Father's
property for himself with
harlots)

17a
wishing to live as a
servant

18a, 20a, 21a
coming home and giving
a message to the Father
(repentance as the means
for becoming a servant,
cf. col. 8)

22a
servants acting accord-
ing to the order of the
Father

25a
working in the field of
the Father

28c
coming home (after work
in the field)

29b-30
working for the Father
as a servant

(5)	(6)
(a)	($\bar{b}$)

11b
having two sons

17b
servants being with the Father: having abundant bread

23, 24
(having a feast) with the help of servants and young son; having a young son alive and found

20b
(young son) being with the Father and having a feast

23a,b
having servants

25a
having an elder son

25a
(elder son before the villainy) being with the Father

25b
having servant; being in the house

(7)

(b)

20b
(Father) being associated
with unworthy and needy
son

22
(Father) having servants

(8)

(ā) & ā

ā

24a
(dead and lost young
son)

20b
lacking the young son

(ā)

17c
young son perishing with
hunger (in a far country)

15a
having a citizen as
helper and famine as
opponent

15b
being the servant of a
citizen of a far country

16
being without food
(even without execrable
food)

14c
being without food and
without property; being
in a far country; having
famine as opponent

19b, 21c
wishing to be a servant
of the Father, not son
(not worthy to be called
son)

(continued)

(7)

(b)

(8)

(ā) & ā

(ā) (continued)

18b, 21b
having heaven and Father
as opponents; sinning
against them

25b, 26
having as opponent the
Father giving the feast;
having a servant as
helper

28a
being angry (having
Father as opponent)

27
having a Father who
gives feast because
an estranged and un-
worthy young son comes
home in good health

28c
being the opponent of
the Father; having the
Father as opponent

29c,d
being without feast and
without kid

The other verses manifest the function y which can be expressed as "using the father's property for oneself" or in more general terms--"living selfishly".

X and y are contraries through the following features: "giving oneself graciously", i.e., having compassion, is the contrary of "living selfishly".

In column 2, "sharing one's life and property with others" accounts for what is common to the various verses and is therefore ȳ. ȳ is the contradictory of y. "Sharing one's life and property with others" is "not living selfishly". ȳ is implied in x: "Giving oneself graciously" implies "sharing one's life and property with others" (yet the second does not imply the first: e.g., one can share one's life and property in order to gain profit).

In column 4, "working for wages" or more generally "working for rewards" accounts for what is common to the various verses and is therefore x̄. x̄ is indeed the contradictory of x ("working for rewards" is the contradictory of "giving oneself graciously"), and it is implied in y ("working for rewards" is implied in "living selfishly").

In column 5, the semantic value of the state (a) is "father" defined in the narrative as "a master (having servants) who has two sons".

In column 7, the state of the hero (b) is defined as "father (master with sons) being associated with an unworthy and needy son".

(a) and (b) are contraries. The semantic features of (a) "having two sons and servants" is in contrary opposition with the semantic features of (b) "being associated with an unworthy and needy son". This opposition leads us to define (a) as "having worthy sons and servants". This semantic

value of (a) is clearly implied in the text. The state of
the father which was originally (in the initial situation
of the parable and also possibly in the cultural code, i.e.,
in the mind of the hearers and readers) "being with worthy
people, sons and servants" becomes in the topical content
of the narrative "being associated with unworthy and needy
people".

Column 6 includes the state ($\bar{b}$) of the personages "who
are with the father and have everything in abundance". The
state (a) implies ($\bar{b}$) through the semantic feature of (a)
"having servants" (i.e., "being a master") and the semantic
feature of ($\bar{b}$) "having everything in abundance". The state
($\bar{b}$) is the contradictory of (b): the semantic feature
"having everything in abundance" does not include the semantic feature "being associated with needy people".

Column 8 is the state ($\bar{a}$) of the personages "who are
without the father, have the father as opponent, and are
needy because they are without proper helpers; being unworthy (to be called son); being without feast, without
abundance, feeling needy (elder son)". The state ($\bar{a}$) is
contradictory of (a): it does not include the semantic
feature "having father", that is, "having master with worthy
son". Furthermore, the state ($\bar{a}$) is implied in (b) since
($\bar{a}$) includes the semantic features "unworthy" and "needy"
(semantic features which are also in (b)).

The function $\bar{a}$ is living without his son thus being
unable to live as "father" defined in (a) should.

We can summarize the system of elementary mythical semantic values manifested in the text in the two following semiotic squares.

giving oneself to
   undeserving sons

giving oneself
   graciously

having compassion

using the father's
   property for
   oneself

living selfishly

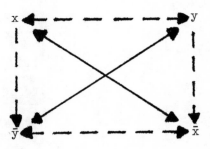

sharing one's life
   and property with
   others

working for wages

working for rewards

having worthy sons

having servants

being associated with
   worthy people

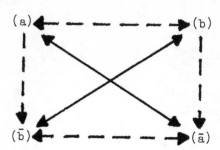

being associated with
   unworthy and needy
   (son)

being with the father
   (= not being associ-
   ated with unworthy
   people)

having everything in
   abundance

being without the
   father

having father as
   opponent

being needy

being unworthy

being without
   abundance

($F_{\bar{a}}$ being unable to
   live as "father")

At this point of the analysis we would need to study the
text in terms of the cultural codes. The preceding analysis
in terms of the narrative, mythical, and elementary structures
has pointed out a limited set of semantic features which has
been selected by these structures from the polysemic potential
of the main symbols: father, son (two terms: υἱός, τέκνον),
servants (three types of servants: μίσθιος, δοῦλος, παῖς),
far country, home, feast, robe, ring, shoes, fatted calf, kid,

etc. ... The meaning effect of the text includes also in a negative way the other semantic features that these symbols have according to the cultural codes. The fact that these features are left aside or even excluded is quite "meaning-ful". Traditional exegesis (cf., J. Jeremias, *The Parables of Jesus*) has been devoted in part to the study of these cultural codes. The results of these exegeses and philologi-cal studies can be used at this stage.[11] In the limits of this paper, which is already too long, we cannot propose the analysis in terms of the cultural codes. Among its results would be a sharper apprehension of the eight seman-tic categories.

The following stage of the analysis would demand us to take into account the "structures of the enunciation" which would include the *Sitz im Leben* in Jesus' ministry, or in the life of the early Church, according to the level chosen for the interpretation, and also the place of the parable either in Jesus' argument in his teaching, or in Luke's argument in his two volume work.

On the basis of this complete analysis we could then apprehend the mythical level of the meaning effect: that is, the implicit partial "mythical system" proposed by the parable.

On the limited ground of the analysis that we have performed, this mythical level of the meaning effect can be represented as follows, using Lévi-Strauss' formula.

Natural
  Man

(b) being associated with unworthy and needy
      people

F_y living selfishly

(y) having a lost
     and dead son

$F_{\bar{a}}$ living without
         a son

(b) associated with
     unworthy and
     needy people

F_x giving oneself
         graciously

(a) being associated with worthy people

F_x giving oneself graciously

God

If we consider this partial mythical system in terms of
the situation of the early Church and its relation with Judaism, we can tentatively interpret it as follows.

The parable addresses people who believe that there is
a strict separation *between* good people (the Chosen People)
who are rich and associated with worthy people and who in
this situation give themselves graciously (love their neighbor
(= $F_x(a)$) and evil people who are associated with unworthy
and needy people (renegade Jews who are living with the
goyim?) and in this situation live selfishly (= $F_y(b)$).

This opposition represents metaphorically an even more fundamental opposition that we could term the opposition between "God" and "natural man". The parable proclaims that this fundamental opposition is indeed overcome if one accepts as a valid mediation of the opposition between the Chosen People and the renegade Jews, people who are associated with unworthy (Gentiles) and needy (poor) yet give themselves graciously (the early Church) ($= F_x(b)$). The validity of this mediation would be established if the opposition between the early Church and the deprived Chosen People (Chosen People deprived from some of its sons) could be overcome.

It should be clear that this last interpretation is intended as an *illustration* and nothing more. Before ascertaining it we need to take carefully into account the cultural structures and the structures of the enunciation. Yet our knowledge of the two structural levels is impaired by the cultural gap which separates us from our text. The analysis in terms of the deep structures of all the Lucan corpus would allow us to overcome in part this problem: it would reveal many other elements of its mythical system.

Similarly, comparing such analysis in terms of the deep structures of all the parables with the analysis of other texts should allow us to apprehend the specific literary genre "parable" either as characteristic of the Synoptic Gospels or as characteristic of one of the Gospels (according to the level chosen for the analysis). At this point, for a rigorous and detailed comparison of the units identified by means of the analysis in terms of the narrative, mythical, and elementary structures, it will be essential to use the computer: the language "forester" and the programs that Judson F. Parker is presently creating will become a most useful and necessary tool. Furthermore, as I suggested elsewhere, there will be important hermeneutical possibilities offered by the results of such analyses.

Yet, all this demands a rigorous method of analysis. We believe we have made some progress toward establishing such a method, yet the models upon which it is built must be sharpened, refined, ascertained, verified. This paper is presented to you with the hope that you will care to criticize it. If, as a result, we must abandon substantial parts of it, you will have helped us to make important progress.

NOTES

1. Of course, there are other possibilities. Some critics have proposed that the original parable ended with verse 24, that is, that it did not include the story of the elder son. Indeed, such a text would be a complete narrative. We could eventually test this theory by performing the analysis of this hypothetical short version of the parable and comparing the results of this analysis with those of the analysis of the longer version. If we could eventually demonstrate that the two sets of semantic categories which characterize these two versions were not consistent with each other, we would have a confirmation of the validity of the theory about the shorter version of the parable. In this paper, since we have to limit ourselves to one analysis, we have chosen to analyze the longer version: the sub-narrative of the Gospel according to Luke.

2. It should be noted that the above formulation for the main narrative transformation is ambiguous. There are indeed two possible interpretations of the formula:
    (1) When the initial sequence (Cor. Seq. 1) is interrupted and consequently the receiver (R^i) of this initial sequence is deprived of the object (O^i) which the subject (S^i) of the initial sequence was supposed to transmit to him. In the reestablished initial sequence (Cor. Seq. 2) R^i can at last receive O^i. Thus the narrative transformation could be represented as

$$R^i \cap O^i \quad \rightarrow \quad R^i \cup O^i$$

This transformation is indeed present in the narrative, but this is a secondary transformation and not what we term the main narrative transformation.
    (2) The object of the main transformation is the object (O^t) that the hero (S^t) transmits to a receiver (R^t) who is also the subject (S^i) of the initial sequence. The transmission of the object (O^t) by the hero is the very topic of the narrative: this is why the sequence of the hero is appropriately termed "topical sequence". It is in fact the transmission of a helper to S^i. If we term the actants of the initial sequence Se^i (sender), O^i, R^i, S^i

(subject), H^i (helper), Op^i (opponent), and the actants of the topical sequence: Se^t, O^t, R^t, S^t, H^t, Op^t, the formula of the main transformation can be written:

$$S^i(=R^t) \cap O^t(=H^i) \quad \rightarrow \quad S^i(=R^t) \cup O^t(=H^i)$$

This is how we understand the formula.

3.   As Louis Marin pointed out during the discussion of this paper, the way in which the narrative structure is actualized is in effect determined at the level of the enunciation.   The *author chose* to tell the story in a specific way.

4.   Following the discussion and as a response to Professor Culley's criticism printed below, we should emphasize that this breaking down of the narrative into narrative sequences or narrative programs is justified by the fact that a narrative can be viewed as the intersection of several narratives (cf. above).   Each narrative sequence is potentially one of the five elements (Cor. Seq. 1, villainy, situation of lack, topical sequence, Cor. Seq. 2) of the broad narrative structure.

5.   Thus in the most common case the subject of the subsequence is one of the actants of the sequence.   It is through its subject that a subsequence is linked with the sequence.   If, furthermore, the receiver of the subsequence is also an actant of the sequence, the subsequence qualifies this other actant by attributing to him an object.   In this case there is a double link: both the subject and the receiver of the subsequence are actants of the sequence.   By contrast in the case of the "qualifications" (i.e., of the subsequences for which the sole attribution of an object to a receiver is actualized) the only link with the sequence is that the receiver of the subsequence is one of the actants of the sequence.

6.   The following analysis is deductive.   It is important to keep in mind that the models presupposed here are representation of the *constant* network of relations found to be characteristic of narratives in any culture.   For a discussion of the type of research involved in establishing and verifying these models see Jean Calloud, *Structural Analysis of Narratives*, Daniel Patte tr. (Scholars Press/ Fortress Press: Missoula and Philadelphia, 1976), chap. I and II and the translator's preface.   Each analysis is also

a verification of the model which might lead to its modification.

7. Note that this shift of program is indicated in the Greek text by the participle δέ. This particle indicates a mild contrast which we would not usually indicate in English by a particle. It is interesting to note that in each instance in our text δέ indicates a narrative shift.

8. We denote the implicit actants by recording them between parentheses. As implicit actants, we record only those actants who are manifested by other sequences. In this case the "father" is manifested as helper for this performance in sequence (3).

9. Yet, of course, by the very fact that we are using the other words according to the meaning they have in the dictionary we are making use of the cultural codes.

10. This interpretation does not present any difficulty as long as we avoid confusing functions and states. For instance, reading verse 20b we could be tempted to consider "compassion" as the state of the "father-hero", although it is a function--father (S) communicating himself (H) to an unworthy and needy son (R). In fact in this verse the state of the subject is defined by his relation to the sender: the unworthy and needy son. The state is "being with an unworthy and needy son".

11. In the case of our text we should not forget that according to the level at which we want to interpret the parable we would have to deal with either Palestinian or Hellenistic cultural codes.

12. This display has been generated with the help of the computer using the computer language "FORESTER" created by Judd F. Parker. This language has special characteristics which will allow the use of the computer to facilitate the structural analysis of text. Its vocabulary is basically the same as the one found in this paper. Note simply that S6 refers to sequence (6); QSS means qualification or subsequence; QSS-H means QSS of the helper of the preceding sequence at a specific "statement" written STMT, which can be CS1,...PS3 or, in the case of a qualification, ATTR (an attribution). We are presenting only an abbreviated form of the hierarchy.

CORRELATED CONTENT #1 : Father and sons before the villainy

```
SEQ(S27A)
   PS2=STMT
   :   QSS-S(1)=QUAL(S1)
   :       ATTR=STMT
   :   QSS-S(2)=SEQ(S4)
   :       PS2=STMT
   :       PS3=STMT
```

VILLAINY CONTENT: y.s.'s prodigal life in a far country

```
   :   QSS-H=QUAL(S28)
   :       ATTR=STMT
   :       :   QSS-R=SEQ(S6)
   :       :       DS=STMT
   :       :       PS2=STMT
   :       :       :   QSS-S=SEQ(S5)
   :       :       :       PS3=STMT
   :       :       :       :   QSS-H=SEQ(S3)
   :       :       :       :       CS1=STMT
   :       :       :       :       PS2=STMT
   :       :       :       :       :   QSS-SE=SEQ(S2)
   :       :       :       :       :       PS3=STMT
   :       :       :       :       PS3=STMT
   :       :       PS3=STMT
```

CORRELATED CONTENT #1 partially restored: the feast

```
   :   QSS-S(3)=SEQ(S27)
   :       CS1=STMT
   :       PS2=STMT
   :       :   QSS-H(1)=QUAL(S29)
   :       :       ATTR=STMT
   :       :   QSS-H(2)=SEQ(S25)
   :       :       CS1=STMT
   :       :       PS3=STMT
   :       :       :   QSS-S=SEQ(S26)
   :       :       :       CS1=STMT
   :       :       :       PS3=STMT
```

TOPICAL CONTENT #1: Father welcoming the y.s. home

```
:      :    QSS-S=SEQ(S20A)
:      :       PS2=STMT
:      :       PS3=STMT
:      :       :  QSS-S=SEQ(S20)
:      :       :     CS1=STMT
:      :       :     :  QSS-SE=SEQ(S16)
:      :       :     :     CS1=STMT
:      :       :     :     CS2=STMT
:      :       :     :     :  QSS-S=SEQ(S13)
:      :       :     :     :     DS=STMT
:      :       :     :     :     :  QSS-O=QUAL(S14)
:      :       :     :     :     :     ATTR=STMT
:      :       :     :     :     PS3=STMT
:      :       :     :     :     :  QSS-S(1)=SEQ(S15)
:      :       :     :     :     :     PS2=STMT
:      :       :     :     :     :     :  QSS-R=SEQ(S10)
:      :       :     :     :     :     :     CS1=STMT
:      :       :     :     :     :     :     :  QSS-S=SEQ(S11)
:      :       :     :     :     :     :     :     CS1=STMT
:      :       :     :     :     :     :     :     DS=STMT
:      :       :     :     :     :     :     :     PS2=STMT
:      :       :     :     :     :     :     :     PS3=STMT
:      :       :     :     :     :     :     :     :  QSS-S=SEQ(S12)
:      :       :     :     :     :     :     :     :     CS1=STMT
:      :       :     :     :     :     :     :     DS=STMT
:      :       :     :     :     :     :     :     PS1=STMT
:      :       :     :     :     :     :     :     PS2=STMT
:      :       :     :     :     :     :     QSS-S(2)=QUAL(S9)
:      :       :     :     :     :     :     ATTR=STMT
:      :       :     :     :     :     :     :  QSS-H(2)=QUAL(S8)
:      :       :     :     :     :     :     :     ATTR=STMT
:      :       :     :     :     :     :     :  QSS-S=QUAL(S7)
:      :       :     :     :     :     :     :     ATTR=STMT
:      :       :     :     :     DS=STMT
:      :       :     :     PS2=STMT
:      :       :     :     PS3=STMT
:      :       :     :     :  QSS-R=SEQ(S19)
:      :       :     :     :     CS1=STMT
:      :       :     :     :     :  QSS-R=QUAL(S18)
:      :       :     :     :     :     ATTR=STMT
:      :       :     :     :     :     :  QSS-R=SEQ(S17)
:      :       :     :     :     :     :     PS2=STMT
:      :       :     :     :     :     :     PS3=STMT
:      :       :     :     :     :  QSS-S=QUAL(S22)
:      :       :     :     :     ATTR=STMT
:      :       :     :     :     :  QSS-R=SEQ(S21)
:      :       :     :     :     :     PS2=STMT
:      :       :     :     :     :     PS3=STMT
:      :       :     :     DS=STMT
:      :       :     :     PS2=STMT
:      :       :     :     :  QSS-S=SEQ(S23)
:      :       :     :     :     PS3=STMT
:      :       :     :     :     :  QSS-R=SEQ(S24)
:      :       :     :     :     :     CS1=STMT
:      :       :     :     :     :     PS3=STMT
:      :       :     :     PS3=STMT
:      PS3=STMT
```

147

CORRELATED CONTENT #2: the e.s. coming home from the field

```
:   QSS-S(4)=QUAL(S30)
:      ATTR=STMT
```

VILLAINY #2: e.s.'s refusal to come home

```
:     :   QSS-O(1)=QUAL(S31)
:     :      ATTR=STMT
:     :   QSS-O(2)=SEQ(S32)
:     :      DS=STMT
:     :      :   QSS-H(2)=SEQ(S33)
:     :      :      CS1=STMT
:     :      :      PS3=STMT
:     :      :      :   QSS-R=QUAL(S35A)
:     :      :      :      ATTR=STMT
:     :      :      :      :   QSS-O=SEQ(S35)
:     :      :      :      :      PS2=STMT
:     :      :      :      :      :   QSS-S=QUAL(S36)
:     :      :      :      :      :      ATTR=STMT
:     :      :      :      :      :      :   QSS-O=SEQ(S34)
:     :      :      :      :      :      :      DS=STMT
:     :      :      :      :      :      :      :   QSS-S=QUAL(S37)
:     :      :      :      :      :      :      :      ATTR=STMT
:     :      :   QSS-S=QUAL(S38)
:     :      :      ATTR=STMT
```

148

TOPICAL CONTENT #2: father inviting the e.s. to come back home.
```
   :   QSS-S(5)=SEQ(S39)
   :       DS=STMT
   :       PS2=STMT
   :   :   QSS-OP=SEQ(S40)
   :   :       PS3=STMT
   :   :   :   QSS-S=SEQ(S45)
   :   :   :       CS2=STMT
   :   :   :   :   QSS-S=SEQ(S41)
   :   :   :   :       PS2=STMT
   :   :   :   :       PS3=STMT
   :   :   :   :   :   QSS-S=QUAL(S42)
   :   :   :   :   :       ATTR=STMT
   :   :   :   :   :   :   QSS-O=QUAL(S43)
   :   :   :   :   :   :       ATTR=STMT
   :   :   :   :   :   QSS-SE=SEQ(S44)
   :   :   :   :   :       CS1=STMT
   :   :   :   :   :   :   QSS-S=SEQ(S48)
   :   :   :   :   :   :       PS3=STMT
   :   :   :   :   :   :   :   QSS-R=SEQ(S46)
   :   :   :   :   :   :       DS=STMT
   :   :   :   :   :   :   :   QSS-S=SEQ(S47)
   :   :   :   :   :   :   :       PS3=STMT
   :   :   QSS-S(0)=SEQ(S39A)
   :   :       PS3=STMT
   :   :   QSS-S(2)=SEQ(S49)
   :   :       PS3=STMT
   :   :   :   QSS-R(0)=QUAL(S50)
   :   :   :       ATTR=STMT
   :   :   :   QSS-R(2)=QUAL(S51)
   :   :   :       ATTR=STMT
   :   :   :   QSS-S=SEQ(S52)
   :   :   :       CS1=STMT
   :   :   :   :   QSS-SE(0)=QUAL(S53)
   :   :   :   :       ATTR=STMT
   :   :   :   :   QSS-SE(2)=QUAL(S54)
   :   :   :   :       ATTR=STMT
   PS3=STMT
   ABORT??
```

149

RESPONSE TO DANIEL PATTE

Robert C. Culley

McGill University

I find myself in an ambivalent situation. I am intrigued
by what is going on in structural analysis, but I have some
nagging problems which keep hanging on. Patte's paper is
full, detailed, and technical and probably deserves a better
critique than I am in a position to offer. As an Old Testament scholar, I have not spent the time and effort on parable
study which a New Testament scholar would have, nor am I
especially confident about my grasp of the particular structuralist tools used by Patte to be able to respond to his
paper at the level at which it was written. As an alternative
approach, I will try to articulate some general feelings of
uneasiness, endeavoring to be specific where I can.

Patte mentions four models which he seeks to apply to
the parable of the Prodigal Son. My response will concern
itself mainly with the first, and I will add one or two
comments at the end about the others.

My first problem in trying to follow the general discussion about parable which has filled the first two volumes
of *Semeia* and continues in part in this conference is simply
this: what is a parable? I raise this question because I
wonder about the assumption that parable is by definition
primarily a form of narrative in the sense of story. In
Patte's paper, in a discussion of the relationship of the
elements in the Gospel of Luke to the Gospel as a whole, he
sees Luke as a complex narrative in which are embedded many

sub-narratives. Then he says: "A parable is a sub-narrative which by itself is a complete narrative." Now, it is this kind of assumption that I would like to have clarified further, especially because it leads to the immediate application of methods used to analyze folktales and other kinds of stories.

Far be it from me to instruct New Testament scholars in their craft. But, perhaps, if I just state my impressions here, you will see what I am getting at. My impression is that, in the Gospels, parables need not have an extensive narrative element. That is, parables often describe brief incidents or happenings which we do not experience as a full narrative or story. For example, the parable of the Pharisee and the Tax Collector is not much of a story—but is it any less a parable? Furthermore, I have seen the term "narrative parables" used in discussions in *Semeia*, a term which suggests that "narrative parables" (i.e., parables which seem to contain some extended story or anecdote) are a subcategory of some larger category which is called parable. What then is parable and what does it do? I will not hazard a clear answer to this question. One could say that parables are not really talking about what they appear to be talking about but are using what they say to point to something else. In whatever terms, this function of parable is best described—whether it be confronting people with how things are or giving them insight into reality or some aspect of it—it would seem to me that the primary or basic structure of parable would have something to do with this function and how parables achieve their purpose.

The point that I am trying to make here is that narrative would seem to be something separate from and subordinate to a primary parable structure. That is to say, using narrative elements would be one way of filling in a parable structure and achieving what a parable does. It is one way of filling the slots in parable structures. Thus, basic parable structure is not identical with story structure. If this were so, then it would be important to recognize that narrative elements, when found in parables, are subordinate to and therefore used in a way which is calculated best to achieve what parable is trying to accomplish. In other words, the ordering and shaping of narrative elements found in parables is governed primarily by the rules governing parable and only secondarily by rules governing narrative. This hardly means that one cannot find what appear to be fully developed narratives as parables or segments of parables. Most of the well-known parables are like this. But care needs to be taken in analyzing narrative elements because they are functioning within the larger frame of parable structure, and it may be that the parable structure itself selects or highlights points which must be picked up by readers or hearers and which are not selected or highlighted by the narrative structure alone. It is true that the presence of narrative elements invites narrative analysis, but my concern is to know the extent to which doing a narrative analysis for structure first, without determining what parable structure is, produces distortion.

Thus, in the parable work in general, I would find it helpful to see some work directed at what parable structure might be. The way I like to proceed is to start with the smallest, or shortest, examples of elements which could be called parable. These would represent something close to minimal units (i.e., the bare essentials needed for parable).

If groupings of smaller parable items can be brought together then I would think that common structural elements would show up so that it might be possible to identify certain basic parable types. Having done this, one could move to the more complex parables, better equipped I would say, to determine what role narrative and narrative elements play. All this is rather abstract. Let me try to illustrate. In the Old Testament, a couple of parables or parable-like elements are found in situations of conflict between a prophet and a king. The prophet tells a story involving an injustice which invites the king's response. The king's response is then turned on the king himself, when the real reference of the parable is revealed. Does parable not operate in a similar way on a number of occasions in the New Testament, such that acceptance of the parable (its truth, its validity) at the same time forces the hearer to condemn himself or at least admit the wrongness of his views? For example, the parable of the Lost Sheep, if accepted by the hearer, forces its application to the religious structure within the hearer's life, thereby condemning it. This is what I think I mean when I talk about basic parable structures. There may be a few other basic parables. I will not go on to comment on the parable of the Prodigal Son. It is a rather full and complex item. Several things are going on, and this is why I deem it preferable to deal with minimal units first before going on to more complex narrative structures. Basic parable structures, once identified in smaller parables, can then be used to sort out the hierarchy of elements in the parable. Patte's analysis is, of course, designed to do this kind of sorting, and so the question as to whether Patte's way of doing things will turn out to be the most accurate and most efficient.

But suppose that my misgivings about the nature of parable are set aside and that we move on to narrative analysis as Patte has done in the first and longest section of his paper. Another problem emerges. Patte outlines a series of stages: initial situation, villainy, situation of lack, performance of the hero, and reestablished initial situation. Now, when I look at the parable and this model, even after reading Patte's extensive analysis, the two just do not fall together neatly in my own mind. The story of the two sons does not seem to me, when I read it, to high-light features like a villainy which causes a lack which is overcome by the action of the hero mandated to this task. It is true that Patte is able to identify elements in the story which he sets beside the terms: villainy, situation of lack, and hero.

However, simply to express my general uneasiness in a few lines over a major part of Patte's paper is not a very productive kind of criticism. Perhaps I can be a bit more specific on a couple of points. The terminology may be a difficulty. Terms like villainy, lack, mandate, and hero come down from Propp's work on the folktale where obvious villains cause lacks which are overcome by obvious heroes who have received a mandate to accomplish a task. If these things go on in the parables, they are actions which appear in more subtle forms. For example, Patte must discuss, for a few sentences at least, who the hero is in the first sequence, the father or son. Would it be helpful to attempt to create a terminology which would be more generally de-scriptive so that it can cover both what happens in folktales and what happens in parables? This might alleviate the un-fortunate feeling that the terminology (and therefore a mode of analysis) which may be appropriate for the folktale is being forced on parables where it is not appropriate.

Such an exercise might prove useful as a way of testing whether or not there is in fact a correlation between the kinds of things which happen in folktales and what happens in narrative parables.

All this touches on a problem I have had from the start in trying to evaluate structuralist writings, and I will just mention it here without elaboration. The problem is this: what constitutes verification? Patte raises the question himself clearly in his paper when he speaks of his four theoretical models. He claims to be working with narratives close to the level at which scientists operate with natural phenomena. He seeks verification through experiment which means the kind of detailed, clause-by-clause analysis of a text displayed in his paper. He is quite prepared to adjust his models as they are shown to be inadequate. However, to phrase it in an exaggerated form, I have difficulty perceiving what has been verified when I see an analysis like this: the model being used or the ingenuity of the analyst. Of course, the proper way of dealing with this problem of verification and adequacy in a convincing way would be to follow the stages of Patte's analysis point by point. But there is no time here for such a thorough test of the adequacy and efficiency of the models Patte uses.

Still, perhaps, I can go a step in this direction by posing some questions about Patte's use of the actantial diagram associated with the name of Greimas. In Patte's analysis, almost every clause in the parable of the Prodigal Son is given a number and identified with various coded labels which indicate what the clause does in the narrative. Further more, for every clause, an actantial diagram is set down and filled in where appropriate with information found in the clause. It seems then that this actantial diagram functions for Patte more critically at the sentence level than at the level of larger segments of narrative, or the whole narrative. In my limited experience, I have always seen actantial analysis applied at the level of the whole narrative.

Having read through the analysis of all the clauses by using the actantial diagram, I have considerable difficulty recognizing the usefulness of the procedure. On the one hand, I wonder if those who are accustomed to using the actantial diagram for the analysis of narratives are satisfied with its applications to clauses and sentences. On the other hand, a discourse analysis based on the syntactical analysis of clauses would appear to be a more appropriate way of describing clause structure and the relationship of clauses to each other. In Patte's work, the sentences and clauses seem to be pulled apart and stuck in slots of a diagram not designed for this kind of analysis. An interesting "loop-the-loop" has been made here. One of the factors which led to the development of the actantial diagram was the grammatical description of sentences. Now, this is being swung back on sentences again. Switching back and forth between levels of language is a tricky business. It is even worrisome to take the first step and deal with the texts on the analogy of how one deals with sentences. Is it not more so when one swings back to deal with sentences using the very devices developed to handle narrative? Thus, I feel the need of further explanation and justification at this point, especially since this is very much in the area which Patte identifies as the corner-stone of his method.

Finally, one or two remarks on the second and third models mentioned by Patte. In general, analysis of this type (Patte uses Lévi-Strauss' formula and the semiotic square) may well be relevant to parable study in so far as there is a concern with balancing off of opposites and marking off their relationships. Parables use the balancing of opposites frequently, or at least the opposing of different elements, and so this may be something very basic in the structure or structures of parable. I do not feel that I can say much more about the specific application of Lévi-Strauss' formula which Patte sets out. My general attitude continues to be ambivalent here. Even if we agree that Lévi-Strauss' formula works for myth and even if it can be applied more widely to stories other than myths, one still wonders about its application to parable. If Lévi-Strauss sees the function of groupings of myths as blurring fundamental contradiction (but not resolving them), then I am not satisfied at first glance with the application to parables which gives the impression of doing the opposite: sharpening contradictions, revealing alternatives and contrasts which were not recognized as such.

RESPONSE TO DANIEL PATTE

William G. Doty

Rutgers University, Douglass College

1. Limitations of the paper.

I want to express appreciation to Professor Patte and his students for the substantial amount of work represented in this paper. He and his students are providing us with the data bank necessary to test the model for, and the coding tools of, an extremely complex approach to literary analysis of biblical narratives.

If results with respect to hermeneutical *interpretation* of the particular text seem relatively meager, we are not to regard this as a failure of the project: Patte aims at methodological sophistication for the task of *Vorarbeit*, a preliminary analytical stage of research that sets important contours and constraints for the eventual interpretation.

He seems well aware of the dangers of mistaking the model for the actuality, a restraint that is crucial in light of criticisms that Lévi-Strauss *imposes* his models arbitrarily from the standpoint of *contemporary* standards (see examples of this criticism in Ino Rossi, ed., *The Unconscious in Culture*, 1974, and Stanley Diamond, *In Search of the Primitive*, 1974).

Defending Lévi-Strauss, Rossi suggests that Lévi-Strauss' models are "formal models or sets of grammatical rules which express the *relational properties* of the system" (p. 138, my emphasis). And I find Jan Pouwer's formulations (*ibid.*, pp. 243, 244, my emphasis) especially appropriate to models for parable analysis: 1. "A model is basically an explicitly formulated *metaphor*, consisting of a number of interdependent elements." 2. "A models is *a compressed simile* which serves to compare the relationship between selected elements of a logical construct...."

Perhaps we are brought near to Kafka's "if you only followed the parables you yourselves would become parables... at any rate, we are near to what Pouwer calls "the unavoidabl circular nature of the explanatory process: a structuralist explains structures by a structure". He continues: "However by relating a structure to structures along the various levels of analysis [the structuralist] enriches a structure with empirical content." (*ibid.*, p. 250) I think this is sufficiently illustrated by the ways Patte treats *spatial relationships* in the Good Samaritan (in the article for *Soundings*; cf. the recent attempts at building an "imagic pragmatics").

We should not demand more than is promised--and I mean this to be taken with respect to the entire structuralist enterprise in which we find ourselves at the present time. Nineteenth and twentieth century hermeneutics should have taught us by now not to demand interpretive conclusions too early in the analytical and reflective processes. The phrase of François Bovon, "analytic then synthetic" (*Structural Analysis and Biblical Exegesis*, p. 15), provides a useful guideline, as does Dan Via's "analytical and totalizing" (*Kerygma and Comedy*, 1975, p. 15). And we should remember Robert Scholes remark that "The hermeneutic 'recovery' of meaning is often just the story of the critic's struggle to recover it." (*Structuralism in Literature*, 1974, p. 10)

2. The difficulty and complexity of the model.

 2.a. Variations in terminology in the three articles of Patte (in *Semeia* 2, *Soundings*, and here) have added difficulty to understanding and comprehension of the system he proposes, but were probably unavoidable. [Examples omitted here. W.G.D.] In as confusing a situation as this one, we must all be extremely careful to use *consistently* any metalinguistic terms such as utterance, statement, situation, narrative, *et al*.

 2.b. One of the most difficult parts of the structuralist enterprise for me has been getting in view comprehensive outlines of different systems. Here is the way I now understand Patte's system:

I.   CULTURAL STRUCTURES (specific languages of the text; cultural codes such as political, geographical; specific literary styles used in particular genres).

II.   STRUCTURES OF THE ENUNCIATION (pattern of the author's argument; authorial style; constraints of the historical setting and the author's total work).

III.   DEEP STRUCTURES

 A.   NARRATIVE STRUCTURES (in a hierarchical arrangement, each lower element representing a wider semantization of an element in the statement in the computer graph above):

  1.   *Sequences* (also defined as "narrative programs"; characterized by verbs of "doing"; N.B.: modal auxiliaries are characteristic of CS1 & CS2).

   -Initial Correlated Sequence
    interrupted by a Situation of Lack brought about by a Villainy as a subsequence

-Topical Sequence
>indicating the performance of the hero
by which he brings about a transformation
by means of a helper who is transmitted
to him

-Final Correlated Sequence
>re-establishment of the original conjunc-
tion between S(ubject) and Ob(ject)

>>Aborting of these sequences is
caused by
-Sub-sequences (of the six actants,
Se, Ob, R, H, Su, Op);
-Sub-narratives (in complex narra-
tives); or
-Qualifications (attributing of an
OB to an R; characterized by verbs
of "being" and "having").

2. *Syntagms.*

-Contractual
>(mandate + acceptance/refusal = CU = CS1;
communication + reception = CU = CS2)
(a potential program of action which is
actualized in the following syntagms)

-Disjunctional
>(arrival + departure/departure + return,
i.e., movements and encounters of the
actors...steps in realizing the contract)

-Performancial
>(PS1 confrontation with the lack; PS2
domination or submission; PS3 attribution)

3. *Narrative Utterances* (I find this a confusing term) composed of

4. *Functions* (mandating, communication, etc.) and

5. the *Actantial Model* with the

6. *Actants* set into a flow chart.

B. MYTHICAL STRUCTURE $F_x(a) : F_y(b) :: F_x(b) : F_{\underline{a}}(y)$

(featuring the relationship between "bundles of
semantic features" or complex semantic units, i.e.,
functions and states. The function is the interrelation of the semantic values of the Su, Ob, R;
the state is the interrelation of the semantic
values of the Su, H/s, Op/s, and Se.)

C. ELEMENTARY STRUCTURE   (The constraints of the
logical relationships that can obtain in a given
network--the logical square of oppositions, called
here "the semiotic square".)

D. INTERRELATIONSHIP OF NARRATIVE/MYTHIC/ELEMENTARY
STRUCTURES (which, since it is not discussed in
detail here, I take in the sense of Dan Via's
emphasis [*Kerygma and Comedy*, 1975, pp. 151f.]
upon "the relationship between different narrative
levels": "A relationship among levels is established by a unit's being correlated in some way
with units on one or more levels.")

As I understand this construct, Patte is bringing together literary-structuralist-analysis with Lévi-Strauss'
mythic-structuralist-analysis. I do not know of other
approaches to *literary* texts where this is so thoroughly
explored; part of the difficulty is that the anthropological
structuralists have often operated with entirely deconstructed texts without showing us how the deconstruction
took place, and without the regard for *particular literary
texts* that has marked analysis of poetic and biblical
materials in modern hermeneutics.

These systems, however, have sometimes tended "to
neglect the text because [they are] pre-occupied with writing
the text's pre- or post-history", as Robert Martin-Achard
reminds us (*Structural Analysis and Biblical Exegesis*, p.
35). Clearly one of the important stresses of structuralist

exegesis is its focus upon texts *as they exist in the biblical transmissions*, seeking "instead of decomposing the traditional version,...to read it as a whole" (Starobinski in *ibid.*, p. 58). Robert Polzin (April 1974 special issue of *Interpretation*) shows us some of what this means for the book of Job, which is often treated as if it were a mini-library of texts in itself.

Let me point out in passing that one remaining desideratum is the correlation of Lévi-Strauss' emphasis upon the diachronic layering of successive transformations of a myth with the biblical-critical studies known as tradition history. Peter Munz (*When the Golden Bough Breaks*, 1973) also calls for attention to the historical seriality of myths, and for typological sophistication in "reading" symbol series.

2.c. The problem of the encoding of the materials is a very real one. See for instance the works of P. and E. K. Maranda, and especially for an introduction to computer coding, articles in P. Maranda, ed., *Mythology*.

Again I have the sense of some real progress--as progress beyond the Propp-Dundes-Maranda-Güttegemanns proposals. The categories Patte and his colleagues utilize are more "deeply" embedded categories than those used earlier. Hence we deal with the intrinsic logics of discourse rather than with surface texts and textures, what Robert Scholes calls the "micropoetics" of the text (p. 91; see also Jonathan Culler, *Structuralist Poetics*, 1975).

2.d. Discussion of Dan Via's paper showed clearly the need for differentiating: A. analytical structure of the narrative, which should be verifiable by many independent codings, and B. mythological/religious--or in Via's terms, psychological--ways of comprehending ("projections upon") the underlying "meanings" of the text. The "meaning effect" that Patte refers to in the *Soundings* article includes *all* these, as I understand him: "produced by the interaction of a series of semiotic structures" (ms., p. 2).

3. Generalized consequences.

Since it is hardly to be expected that a 74 page analysis plus a 9 foot computer read-out can be performed for each of the forty-odd "parabolic" units of the synoptic tradition [but members of the research team inform me that this is indeed planned!], let alone for the vast store of narrations in Western literature, I assume that Patte intends this analysis as a programmatic analysis for the study of narratives, specifically parables. Having defined, as he puts it on p. 126, "each of the semantic categories in terms of the intra-textual relations", we may assume that he intends this particular analysis as a basis for subsequent analyses.

In this case, we must ask about the wider applicability of his results: do we learn here information that applies to *many* texts, and not just the Prodigal Son? My understanding is that this is precisely the aim of the section 3.A., "The Model and the Method", where Patte correlates the mythical state, the mythical function, the topical content, the situation of lack, and the broader semantic categories $(\bar{x}, \bar{y}, (\bar{a}), \bar{a}, \bar{b})$ with the provisional analysis in 2.A., "The Tentative Analysis in Terms of the Broad Characteristics of the Narrative Structure", pp. 74ff.

If the propositions here are accepted (for example, that "the sequence of the 'hero' [i.e., in the narrative structure] corresponds to $F_x(b)$ [i.e., in the mythical structure]"; and "that the 'situation of lack' corresponds to $F_{\bar{a}}(y)$ in the mythical structure and the topical content corresponds to $F_x(b)$ in the mythical structure", p. 120 and that certain semantic values can be derived from certain defined semantic values in the text, and I am disposed to accept them, then we have won our way to shortening future analyses. What remains to be done first, as Patte recognizes, is to establish that these valences are valid in a *number* of instances.

In that case, of course, we have established precisely the generic grouping by deduction that enables us to understand particular texts in relation to the text-type or the (inductive) genre, and we can evaluate the narrator on the basis of his fulfillment/non-fulfillment of the generic model. Or, to work out from Dominic Crossan's analytical schema for the Servant Parables, we could understand how a narrator builds a generic expectancy in a series of parables, only to reverse himself within that same generic expectancy to set on its head not just the received moral tradition, but the very tradition established within the initial parables in the narrator's own series.

It is precisely this latter aspect that intrigues me, and that will call forth a long period of rather tedious statistical coding of Jesuanic and pre-/post-/non-Jesuanic parables, as well as necessitating particular attention to the Cultural Structures. Malcom Clark's work on the pro-phetic disassembling of the received tradition and subse-quent re-assembling of it by the prophet as metaphor-ist (Batson, Beker, and Clark, *Commitment without Ideology*) can now be related to the disassembling/re-assembling within the narrator's particular narrations as well as within the

wider cultural structures of the sociological setting and
historico-cultural matrix. In that case, such features as
the "reversal" which several of us have studied can be
specified as a semantic-semiological performance and not
just as a superficial narrative technique.

From the specific coding and analysis we are pointed
to the larger contours after all, for, as Robert Scholes
remarks (p. 147, criticizing Todorov before turning to
Barthes, and arguing for inclusion of semantic dimensions
along with analysis of surface structures):

> Meaning is never simply folded into a work
> (implicated) so that it can then be un-
> folded (explicated) by a technician of
> language processes. Meaning is a continual
> shuttling back and forth between the lan-
> guage of the work and a network of con-
> tents which are not *in* the work but are
> essential for its realization. A good
> commentary sketches in this elaborate
> structure which forms around the work as
> we perceive its semantic connections with
> our world of meanings.

To construct such a commentary, Paul Ricoeur and others
point us not away from the vibrancy and polyvalence of the
semiotic objects, but towards them. If, in Ricoeur's
phrases, "True symbols contain all hermeneutics, those
which are directed toward the emergence of new meanings
and those which are directed toward the resurgence of archaic
fantasies." (*The Conflict of Interpretations*, 1974, p. 23)...
and: "...hermeneutics is thought recovering meaning suspended
within a system of symbols." (p. 30)...then I think he is
further correct in stating that:

A tradition exhausts itself by mythologizing
the symbol; a tradition is renewed by means
of interpretation, which reascends the slope
from exhausted time to hidden time, that is,
by soliciting from mythology the symbol and
its store of meaning. (p. 29)

DISCUSSION

PARKER: I want to speak to Bill Doty's comment that subsequences in our terminology have a wider semantic dimension. Generally, I see these subsequences and qualifications as being more specific as regards detail. I would see this as a narrowing rather than a widening. What happens, for example, when the hero performs some action in communicating a helper to the subject of the correlated sequence or situation is that he performs certain specific acts which go deeper and deeper, if you will, into more subsequences which themselves become more and more specific.

DOTY: Perhaps the matter is one of factual interpretation of the data. Now I find it very difficult to read the flow chart. I did not know what was 'under' versus what was 'above'. There is that confusion. I wish Daniel or someone in the work group would add some definitions on how to read the chart. My wider concern was keyed by what Daniel had to say about the left-over group of things--non-X, non-Y, non-A, non-B. He points out these are wider insofar as black and white become black-white in the first opposition as opposed to red, green, yellow, orange, etc.

PARKER: These are manifested perhaps in the subsequences. The other semantic features are in effect a widening in that sense. Another question for me, one that has concerned me in the seminar, is how the hierarchy functions. You [Doty] made a statement, if I heard you correctly, that the aborting of a sequence may be caused by a subsequence. Again, I would say that the way in which a subsequence aborts may be made *more explicit* by a subsequence. It may be that the subsequence aborts for lack of a helper or is the action of an opponent. If you wish to see that as causality all right; but essentially a subsequence is the way by which the superior action or higher level action is made more explicit; and the aborting of a lower level sequence might in fact be that which enables a higher level sequence to proceed.

DOTY: But there is quite a difference between syntagm and paradigm. Causal language goes with paradigm and not with syntagmatic analysis.

POLZIN: I have a couple of questions with regard to Daniel's understanding of the nature of the models being used, either Greimas' or Lévi-Strauss'. Bob Culley pointed out that he is more familiar with Greimas' model being used on a more global basis than in your very miniscule use of Greimas' model. I have the same sort of question with regard to Lévi-Strauss' understanding of his formula. We do not understand how Lévi-Strauss understands his own formula precisely because he has not used it very much. In fact he has used it only once or twice since that programmatic article.

PATTE: He says that he is using it constantly.

POLZIN: Yes, but not explicitly, implicitly. My problem is, if I remember Marandas' use of the formula, they use it in a syntagmatic way, whereas you say you are using it in a paradigmatic way. I am further confused: even though you say you are using it paradigmatically, I cannot see any difference between the way you are using Lévi-Strauss' formula and Greimas' formula. In other words, Greimas' formula is for syntagmatic use; it is sequential. In fact, is that not what you do in using Lévi-Strauss' formula? For in the end you use it to give a global picture of the parable and that is paradigmatic. Could you use it sequentially at points in the parable?

PATTE: To address your question directly, let us begin with the mythical structure and the formula. Lévi-Strauss says quite clearly that a mythical system--the semanticization of the mythical structure by the complete series of oppositions --is manifested through all the variants of the myth. This is interpreted to mean all the stories which in that culture express that mythical system. If that is the case, the formula points out the relationship between the stories. The question remains though how to relate the two sides of the equation. After many attempts, I determined that it is the second part of the formula which represents the story and the first part of the formula refers to other stories which are hinted at in the text. With the example I took, the opposition between good people and evil people, between chosen people and renegade Jews, is a story not told. The parable is related to this opposition as the second part of the formula is related to its first part.

POLZIN: Could you then apply that paradigmatic model to any of your crucial sequences--as for instance the initial sequence?

PATTE: We can use the paradigmatic formula each time we have a narrative, even if it is a subnarrative. For instance, in my work on the Gospel of Mark, I plan to study first the subnarratives and to apply the formula each time I encounter a subnarrative. By progressively analyzing the text in this way I hope to be able to formulate the general mythical system manifested. Coming back to Bob Culley's comment on the use of the actantial model in a microscopic way, I am doing it yes and no: yes, but acknowledging at the same time that there are only a few actantial models which are crucial for the analysis--the one of the topical sequence and the one representing the situation of lack. The actantial models of the other sequences are simply a way to understand how these two actantial models are further semanticized.

POLZIN: Do you use Lévi-Strauss' formula in a sequential way? He said that you can take elements of the story and move them about. Do you do that?

PATTE: In the columns I am not following the order of the text. You cannot even read the story horizontally as you can in Lévi-Strauss' displays. I am using the order of the narrative hierarchy because it is more convenient.

WITTIG: This comes back to the application of the macro-methodology to a micro-test and to what Bob Culley said. I am grateful to Bill Doty for the schematic analysis which helps me to understand what I take to be my own fundamental difficulty with this method. It is the only structural method I know of that offers me this basic difficulty. We are working here with three levels of analysis when we are only supposed to be working with one. There is the cultural level, the level of enunciation, and the deep structure level. However, when we work through these fifty-four sequences we are working at the surface structure of the enunciation, that is the level of discourse. Yet, we are using tools designed for the deepest structural level. The problem is that the surface structure of discourse can be realized in any number of ways. For example, there is no point in applying the actantial model at that level to sequence #1, for it may be expressed in another fashion. What is needed are some sharper, more refined grammatical tools for understanding the transformations that derive from the actantial model. That is the difficulty many of us feel: namely the case of semantic overkill. These are really tools to be used in generic analysis to make generic distinctions amongst a variety of texts.

ROTH: In Bill Doty's summary of Daniel Patte's paper he claims that the model he proposes does not claim to be the actuality, the reality. How then are the two related to each other? You say by summary that these models may be seen as structures of the human mind and in another context like the structure according to which crystals coalesce. Can any model which uses the logical square by necessity come to results that are not dualistic in character, a model which operated with white-black, left-right, in-out? I see this confirmed in the tentative conclusion on page 140 where you have two groups opposed to each other. Could you come to any other conclusion? Is there not a spatialization and a detemporalization? In short, does the model not function like a platonic idea?

PATTE: I prefer to express it by saying it functions as an archetype. I would like to keep it as a model, as an allegory, a metaphor, something which best describes what appears to be the case. Take for example electric power. What is it? There are different models which describe it and which indeed work; different models working in different situations. I am not claiming that this is the only possible one, only that it seems to work. I agree here that there is a difficulty in terms of the nature of this structure.

ROTH: If you make a programmatic test, what are the criteria according to which you can say it works or does not work, at least in this particular instance?

PATTE: I think the only possible criteria is that you have first of all to study texts which are already meaningful, which are present in our culture. And if it represents the meaning effect of the text, it is a deconstruction of the meaning effect of a text. We are establishing a method by using texts we understand and not as a tool to understand them. Only in a second step might we eventually use them to overcome some problems of communication created by cultural gaps.

ROTH: Does this mean you are moving close to the Bultmannian understanding in that you can only interpret texts in which you recognize the question of existence raised in a way similar to the way in which you raised it?

PATTE: I do not believe so in the sense that once these models are established we can move into texts that we do not understand and find the categories which allow us to reorganize or understand the cultural codes of another time. Take the example of Kittel; there is much written for each word. The polysemic nature of language is precisely what the structure of the human mind and other structures are overcoming by a filtering process, as I suggested, another kind of metaphor.

MARIN: Let me ask a very minute question first, and then a more important one. First of all, I have a problem with your use of the Greek text, especially the elimination of some parts of the text. Do you have some criteria pertaining to the use of the Greek version?

PATTE: No, but the analysis has been done on the Greek text.

MARIN: There is a theoretical problem involved here. The very same objection was raised against me in this connection! The second problem has to do with the structure of the enunciation in a very empirical way: namely, as the author's historical situation, the situation of the audience, the hearer, etc. I wonder if the structure of the enunciation can be approached in a more formal way. For example, on page 76 you raise the problem of enunciation in your analysis. It is especially important with parable to take into account the structure of the enunciation, for it may be a basic feature in the type of narrative we call parables. Another question has to do with the limits of the text. I think you evacuate very quickly the problem of the limits of discourse but we encounter very interesting phenomena at the limits. This leads me then to my general idea. I wonder if the time has not come to move from algebraic structural analysis to a topological structual analysis: I mean an analysis of limits, of phenomena of center, of relations between limits and center, of the strategy that the text develops in order to have a certain meaning effect. This is certainly a major problem.

PATTE: I agree.

PETERSEN: My problem relates initially to the nature of meaning effect. You suggested earlier that models reveal meaning effect and also that meaning effect determines the validity of the different models. I find the status of meaning effect in relation to text and model unclear. This lack of clarity is seen also in the distinction between generic structure and narrative structure that Bob Culley mentioned and which you seemed to confirm. The non-structural models are, as I suggested before, transcendant. Actantial models may provide criteria for showing how or on what basis one genre is to be differentiated from another but that is not necessarily identical with generic structure. This leads to the problem that by starting with narrative structure and relegating generic structure to another dimension of inquiry you may very well run into the problem that your narrative structural model may have to be drastically revised on the basis of a strictly generic structural analysis. You have also suggested that generic structure is also related to meaning effect. If, for example, generic structure following Proppian lines is part

of code langue and the semiotic key to narrative signification in a given text, then the generic structure will have
profound effects upon what you can say about the text. Will
this not result in problems with what you will want to say
about the semiotics of the text on the basis of its narrative structure?

PATTE: In response to both your question and Professor
Marin's questions, what we are dealing with is a specific
semanticization of the narrative structure, mythical
structure and so on. This semanticization comes from the
two 'upper levels'--that is the levels of enunciation and
culture which impose themselves as filters piling up upon
each other. As a result, the filtering of the other two
levels, the narrative structure is invested in a very
specific way. It is evoked and that is enough. We understand the text as a narrative. It has value 'narrativity',
to take the example of the narrative structure. I think the
generic level will appear as a very specific way to actualize
the deep structure.

PETERSEN: It is even more confusing when you add to the
generic structural question a non-structural question such
as how you introduce into the total analysis such phenomena
as metaphor, irony, or allegory which are probably not
structural. This returns us to my initial concern about
the relationship of model to meaning effect. It seems to
me that your meaning effect is limited to narrative structure and mythical structure which are on the level of langue
and not language. This is an end run around the concreteness
of the codal system in which an utterance is shaped.

PATTE: The only thing I can say, again, is that I did not intend at all to describe the whole meaning effect. There is a lot more to it.

CHAPTER III

THE SEMIOTIC ENDEAVOR: TWO RESPONSES

SEMIOTICS AND THE STRUCTURE OF THE HUMAN MIND

Walburga von Raffler Engel
Vanderbilt University

I come to this meeting from the field of Linguistics and this is my only area of expertise. I am neither a literary critic nor a Biblical scholar. I was trained as an anthropological linguist in the Bloomfieldian tradition and my current research follows in the lines of the new British Empiricism.

In recent times, Biblical scholars have become increasingly aware of the concept of *discourse analysis* which is defined in terms of *super-sentential grammar*. Linguists, on the contrary, speak of *supra-sentential grammar*. Discourse analysis frequently is not interpreted linguistically but according to literary standards. Linguistically speaking, discourse analysis implies grammatical rules that extend intra-sententially, such as pronominal and phrasal anaphora, the use of tenses, either of the type that we have in English where, for example, we have to opt for either the past or the historical present, or for the more complicated type of the Latin *consecutio temporum*. A good example is gender agreement in the Romance languages. In Italian one person may ask, *"Che cravatta ti metterai?"* "What tie are you going to wear?" The other person, in his answer, *"Quella gialla."* "The yellow one" must preserve the feminine gender of the object. Grammatical agreement is determined within the conversational discourse and cuts across interlocutors.

Languages differ greatly in their rules for intra-sentential and intra-phrasal relationships. The classical example comes from H. A. Gleason's seminal article on "Contrastive Analysis in Discourse Structure" (*Nineteenth Annual Round Table* edited by James E. Alatis. Washington, D.C.: Georgetown University Press, 1968, 39-63): *Before he left, he telephoned home*. As Gleason comments, "English allows us to tell a short narrative completely in reverse, though it takes some ingenuity to reorder more than three or four clauses without serious discomfort. Some other languages allow nothing of this kind. Even a simple inversion may be disallowed." (Gleason, p. 46)

Another language-specific feature of discourse is the proper choice of *register*, depending on the situational, contextual, and inter-personal relationship of the interlocutors. A famous example is Robert Burling's low caste Indian nurse addressing her high caste charge in a most deferential type of baby talk which to us would sound absolutely ridiculous.

In French one has to decide between the formal (*vous*) and the familiar (*tu*) form of address and once the choice is made the form selected at the onset has to be used consistently throughout. An interesting case is the non-reciprocity observed by Wallace Lambert among conservative Quebec families where the parents address their children by *tu* while the children are expected to use the deferential *vous* towards their parents and, in particular, towards their grandparents.

Languages differ, cultures differ, and the combination of a different language and a different culture compounds the complexity of cross-cultural communication. Biblical translation has the still further problem of a different period in time.

I am a Piagetian and for me 'language does not equal cognition. The child learning his first language is really learning a second language. The child, to begin with, had to learn how to conceptualize the world. This does not deny the Whorfian hypothesis, it only redimensions it. The rules of *language use* and those of *language form* vary enormously from one language to the other. If the structure of the human mind (whatever that means) were isomorphic with language, communication would break down, translation would be impossible. Equally, if the commonalities would not outweigh the differences among people's mental structures we could not translate either.

Some scholars do not distinguish between form and content. By definition, the form is the content. For me, the form of language, and certainly not its level of syntax alone, expresses meaning but does not constitute meaning. There are rules for the form and rules for the content. And even the semantic level is language-and-culture specific. Language does not equal cognition. To get out of this impasse by positing a deep structure of language which is supposedly identical to the structure of the human mind, is a solution in name only unless it can be rigorously documented. Chomsky posited such a deep structure: his syntactic component. A syntactically based interpretation of deep structure has been largely abandoned in present day linguistics because it was proved untenable by experimental research in psycholinguistics and in first-language acquisition. Within the current faction of Generative Semantics we are witnessing a return to the idea of a semantically based deep structure which was prevalent among linguists before the so-called Chomskyan Revolution.

Literary critics who are unaware of the variety of linguistic theories outside the transformational school and unfamiliar with the numerous factions within the transformational school itself, tend to operate on two conflicting levels: on the surface, sometimes, they adhere to a syntactic deep structure while covertly utilizing a semantic deep structure. They also generally do not specify their intermediate levels. Nobody seems capable of identifying the process by which the surface is mapped onto the deep structure. Most of the latter problem does not even come to the fore. There is a general tendency to switch from one level to the other rather than present a coherent analysis of the surface as distinct from the analysis of the deep structure. To keep these two levels distinct as one proceeds looking for structures is the first prerequisite the semiotician must establish. Each level has to be described in its own right.

Frequently, a vague term such as grammar is used as if it were synonymous with structure. Great care needs to be taken not to identify the grammatical structure with the narrative structure. I have seen cases where the two were made to coalesce. In such instances, the narrative *agent* is sometimes equated with the grammatical *subject*. I assume that this means the syntactic deep structure subject, equivalent to the psychological subject of pre-Chomskyan grammars. In the same vein, the narrative *recipient* is sometimes identified with the *direct object*, and the *affected* with the *indirect object*. Which language are such authors talking about? Languages vary enormously in the use of the direct and the indirect object to express very similar semantic relation-

ships. Even in English we see a book but we look at it.
Discourse context is not the same as *literary genre*.

Whichever linguistic model one chooses, this refers
to the grammatical organization of the text and is not
necessarily identical with the model for the literary
(narrative or other), mythical, cultural, or whatsoever
analysis of that same text.

Within one's linguistic model it is necessary not to
assume that the rules governing *sentence grammar* are by
definition identical to the rules of *discourse grammar*.
I am not in favor of considering the transformational-
generative rules for sentence formation as the basis for
all other structures.

If linguistic structure (of whichever model one chooses
and whatever theory one follows) were the structure of the
human mind, we would be in the near impossibility to communicate across languages, cultures, and time. Structural
analysis is a methodology, a methodology borrowed from
linguistics. This methodology for structural analysis
should not be confused with linguistic structure. Linguistic
structures are arrived at through structural analysis of
language material. It is important not to generalize the
results obtained in linguistics through structural analysis
simply because linguistics was the first area in which structural methodology was applied.

Non-linguists also tend to equate the transformational
concept of *deep structure* with the *underlying structure* of
Pragueian and Bloomfieldian structuralism. The former is a
given from which the *surface structure* is deduced while the
latter is induced from the *overt manifestation*. The difference is not only one of terminology. What I aim to point out

is the need for a clear idea of the linguistic model one chooses. Ecclecticism can be justified only as the beginning stage for the formation of a new theoretical model, not as an operational device. Chomsky asserts that every sentence must have a verb. This is a basic tenet of transformational grammar according to which each sentence in its deep structure consists of NP + VP. According to Pikean Tagmemics and to the neo-Bloomfieldian school, a surface sentence such as *Good morning* even though it does not represent the favorite type of the English sentence, still does not necessarily derive from an underlying form with a verb as it does for the transformational-generative school where the deep structure contains something like *I wish you...* For Fillmore's Case Grammar the verb is central to linguistic analysis.

Even if one believes that each sentence has a verb, at least in the deep structure, it does not follow that all verbs are verbs of action and certainly not that, analogically, all discourse has to contain an action. This would make my brief paper non-discourse because it obviously offers no action.

To finish with something more than theoretical observations, I shall report my interpretation of the parable of the Good Samaritan, as I have presented it in the 1973 Seminar on Semiology and Exegesis directed by Professor Patte.

The narrative structure falls neatly into Robert Scholes' three-fold subdivision of contract-test-judgment, but I disagree with Scholes when he says that the Superior Power is absent in the story.

The Superior Power is there, right at the beginning, in the quote by Jesus of the basic law of Judaism, to love God and to love one's fellowman and assist him in need (Deut. 23, Lev. 18, 19, 23, 34). יהוה established the contract:

ואהכת לרעך כמוך (Lev. 19:18)

If all those who pass by were not bound to obey the law, there would be no parable. The story would be pointless.

At the outset, *the law is established*. The law is love, life-sustaining (Keep my commandments that thou shalt live). The robbers have no love; their action is anti-law, life-destroying (Thou shalt not kill). A man's life is in jeopardy. *The law is broken* by the robbers who threw the man in the ditch. Two Jews of the highest social standing, a Cohen and a Levite, come by and fail the test. Then a Jew of the lowest social standing, a Samaritan comes by and passes the test. His action is one of love, life-preserving. *The law is reestablished*.

The parable has a social message. Who is ὁ ἄνθρωπος? A structuralist's interpretation would show him to be an Israelite. The central characters in the story are defined by their social class, the priest, the Levite, the Samaritan, leaving undefined only the Israelite. There is only one open spot and one more possible social category. It is also the most common one and appropriately rendered in Greek by ὁ ἄνθρωπος. The two persons of higher social standing than himself pass him by and the one person of lower social standing saves his life.

STRUCTURALIST CRITICISM OF THE PARABLES:

A BRIEF RESPONSE

David Roberson

University of California, Davis

I am not learned in structuralist lore, nor do I employ structuralist methodology in my own studies. So I come to this conference as a fascinated onlooker, anxious to learn more, but not always able to evaluate the cogency of arguments or assess the significance of conclusions.

When, after reading structuralist criticism of the Bible and after listening to the papers so far given at this conference, I try to evaluate the structuralist phenomenon in biblical studies, I am reminded of the situation of a physicist friend of mine. He has become interested in a form of algebra which allows one to handle with great efficiency problems that presuppose four dimensions. Since Einstein in his theories added to the three dimensions of space the one of time, he felt that this particular algebra might provide a simplified way of solving problems in relativity. He also found, to his delight, that application of the rules of this algebra also enabled him to deduce the fundamental equations of quantum mechanics, raising the possibility of uniting relativity and quantum mechanics in a single theory.

When he approached some of his fellow physicists with his ideas, the response he got went something like this: your ideas are all well and good, but what have you told us that we didn't already know by other methods of calculation?

What unsolved problems can you help us solve? Does your method of calculation show us that our picture of the universe is fundamentally inaccurate in some way? My friend admitted that so far, anyway, his ideas yielded no new information nor necessarily raised new problems to be dealt with. Well, then, the reply came, you have supplied us not with a new theory, but a new form of notation.

It is instructive, I think, to set over against the above the example of any successful theory, such as Einstein's special theory of relativity. At the time Einstein proposed this theory, major problems existed that Newtonian physics could not solve, like peculiarities in the orbit of Mercury or the results of the Michelson-Morley experiment, according to which the speed of light did not vary regardless of which direction it took through a hypothetical ether. Einstein's theory offered solutions to these problems, fundamentally changed our view of the nature of the universe, and pointed to new directions for research.

Returning now to the problem of structuralist biblical studies, I find myself somewhat in the position of my physicist friend's colleagues: you seem to be giving me a new notation but not new solutions. In other words, when I add up the data supplied by your methods of computation, the answers seem quite precisely the answers I already had. To be specific, this conference is on parables, particularly the parables of Jesus. Alternative ways of organizing the data of his parables have been illustrated by several of the presentations. Yet, when these papers draw conclusions about the meaning of any particular parable, like the Good Samaritan or the Prodigal Son, I am told that the parable means what I have all along thought it meant.

Whether the objection I have raised here is a valid one is hard for me to judge. It is possible, even likely, that I do not sufficiently understand the implications of what biblical structuralists are saying to me. Certainly much structuralist criticism, like that of Lévi-Strauss, has led to solutions that are not only new but also most provocative. Nevertheless, it is disconcerting, vis-à-vis biblical materials, to be encouraged to use a notational system that is difficult to comprehend and laborious to apply, and when I finish, to be apparently no farther ahead than when I started.

In conclusion I would like to emphasize that these remarks are made by a sympathetic outsider, one who wishes the structuralist enterprise well. I have tried to state what seems to me to be a very substantial shortcoming of most structuralist biblical studies to date.

CHAPTER IV

CONCERNING INTERPRETATION:
A PARABLE OF PASCAL

Louis Marin
The Johns Hopkins University

To raise the question of the very notion of parable--
whether in the Gospels or in modern narratives which appear
to deserve that appellation--is to raise in concrete terms
the question of a basic, presupposed theory of the interpretation of literary texts. One of the essential propositions
of such a theory must be an axiom regarding the plurality of
meaning. This axiom must be clearly understood. It does not
imply that there are several meanings, and that the truth of
the interpretation therefore depends on such variables as the
contingencies of the critical approach employed, the arbitrary
choice of the point of view, the analytical procedures and
methods, or the historical, cultural and ideological position
out of which the critical discourse is shaped. This axiom
states rather that meaning is plural, and that its very definition embraces the possible and the divergent. (We speak here
not only of a theoretical definition but also of concrete
practice, whether of the writer or of the receiver of the
message, each in his own particular moment in history and
place in culture.) So a truly fundamental theory of interpretation must take its rise from the elaboration of a logic of
the possible and the plural, of a logic of diversity and dis-

parity. In such a logic, meaning is not attributable to a closed system of univocal signs, but is produced (and indicates the processes of production) by the displacement of signifiers and the condensation of signifieds.

To sketch in this theory, I have chosen to analyse a piece from Pascal, *The First Discourse on the Condition of the Great*. (See appendix.) Here we can clearly see a production of meaning and can set forth the pragmatics which correspond, in the interpretative discourse with this production. The essay deals with ordinary language--with the discourse of the people as Pascal perceives it: "The people's opinions are sound, but they do not know what they say. The people are vain." They do not know how to discern the cause of the meaning effects ("*la raison des effets*", to use Pascal's terms) in their discourse. Learned men, astute men ("*les habiles*") speak like the people, but they know what they say. To be sure, their knowledge is ignorance, and in this respect they find themselves in the same ignorance as do the people. They do "come back to the same ignorance from which they set out, but it is a wise ignorance which knows itself".

At this point, we raise the questions which will occupy us from here on. It is hoped that they will lead us directly to a specific theory of interpretation: (1) What is the illusorily true content of ordinary language? (2) How does the transition from natural ignorance to knowing ignorance allow one to discover the truth of the illusion? (3) How and why is it not possible to express this truth, to construct the theory of ordinary language while unveiling its structure? How and why will this structure appear to us as a structure of referral and displacement toward a discourse--a "text"

which is always "other"? These are the characteristics
which resemble also the structure of the biblical parable--
a genre which may well constitute the model for the Pascalian discourse. For the chief characteristic of narrative in
this genre is that it offers itself immediately to interpretation, yet disallows its fixing in a univocal allegorism.

The First Discourse on the Condition of the Great may
give us an opportunity to analyse a modern parable and its
meaning effects. In my first draft (which was available to
the respondents in French) I attempted to relate the text's
parabolic structure to the cultural and ideological structures operative in such a seventeenth century French text.
The text itself is the transcription of a lecture which
Pascal delivered to the members of a Port-Royal Jansenist
circle. It reflects some of Pascal's essential ideas regarding society, but it also refers to specific rhetorical
devices which he used in order to persuade his interlocutors
and to induce them to specific existential attitudes. The
rhetorical patterns appear to me to be linked to some of his
basic conceptions about the various uses of language and
about meaning in general. These structures impose their
constraints upon the discourse. But, to quote Professor
Patte, "this should not be construed as a negative factor
since, without them, the discourse would be meaningless...
the structures select the pertinent connotations, those
which will participate in the meaning effect." And I should
add that these structures appear to be directly related to
the problems with which this colloquium is dealing: the
semiotic study of religious parables, and, more broadly, a
semiotic approach to religious discourse in general.

My purpose tonight is to analyse the deep structures (narrative and elementary structures) of the *First Discourse*, in order to show specifically how they operate in the text, and so to illuminate something of the way in which parables function. But before that, I would like to emphasize the question of the level of the enunciation, because it seems to me to be an integral part of the whole process of meaning and of its effects in the parabolic narrative.

My first observation is that the text calls us from the outset to understand that the story we are told requires an interpretation. The text explicitly tells us that our reading must not be a "mere" reading, but a commentary. The story claims to be an image of our condition. Such is the functional sense of the first sentence: "In order to come into the true knowledge of our condition, consider it in this image." Second, we are explicitly posited as the receivers of the message: we are participants in a dialogue. This is the function of the imperative mood. Moreover, the ultimate meaning of the story is given: we are told that the story we are about to read is coded and that its paradigm is "the true knowledge of our condition". But at the same time, the narrator warns us that this true knowledge is not completely exhibited by the story or by its possible commentaries, even in a metaphorical way. The "image" gives us only the way to this knowledge, simply the entry into it.

I would say, then, that the opening sentence frames the entire story in two ways. (1) It clearly defines a structure of enunciation. There is a sender (the narrator) who addresses a receiver (the reader) in a dialogue. To use the Jakobsonian communication model, the whole narrative set is framed by a conative function through which the sender gives to the receiver a message, if not of command, at least of advice. This is not advice about action, but about knowledge--or perhaps it influences the reader to conceive true knowledge as an act. (2) The opening sentence also frames the story in another sense, by giving the receiver a rough sketch of the specific code which ciphers the story. Properly speaking, it is a metadiscursive statement which plays the role of an introductory formula. This of course is not unlike the biblical formula, "He who has ears, let him hear." It means that the narrative message indeed has a narrative meaning, a referential function regarding its context. But it also means that this narrative meaning is itself, in turn, the signifier of a signified which constitutes the "actual meaning". The whole story connotes a secondary meaning, which is the signified metaphor. But since this code is not completely given, we as readers must construct it. So we are not only the story's readers, but its interpreters. Further, we are enjoined to know our condition and simultaneously to clear a way toward its final knowledge. Thus, our reading is admittedly constrained by the narrator's explicit warning that a code exists. Yet we have a certain, if limited, freedom to construct that code in accord with the sketch he has provided us. This freedom, however limited, is verified by the way we as receivers are called upon to interpret from out of "our condition"--the forms, dimensions and features of our historical, social and existential situation. So when we discover, toward the end of our reading, that the receiver of the message is the son of a duke, we have already interpreted the story from our own viewpoint. We have already begun to substitute our condition for that of the young duke. In other words, by the

time we know that the addressee of the message is a young
seventeenth century French nobleman, we have already applied
the narrative metaphor to ourselves. In so doing, we have
transformed the decoding processes set in motion by the text
itself. We have displaced them in accord with our own intellectual, moral and religious needs as twentieth century
readers. But this shift is possible only because the way
in which the story is narrated allows such a displacement
to take place. This is one of the practical effects of the
story, an effect resulting from the complex interaction between the interprative constraints signified by the text,
and the locus from which we read it--a locus both free yet
bound by the text. This specific practical effect of the
narrative I propose calling the "parabolic meaning effect".

I should like to broaden the scope of these initial
observations by outlining a more general hypothesis for the
reading of parables. More fully than one could perceive
at first glance, the parabolic narrative belongs to the
realm of metaphor. Not only is it a narrative which serves
as a metaphor for another narrative already given in the
text; it is a narrative which says something about metaphor
itself. Its referential object is communication, especially
metaphorical communication, and, to a certain extent, the
rules at work therein. Briefly, while overtly telling of a
castaway who is thrown by tempest onto an unknown island,
the parable is covertly speaking about its own communication-
process. Of course every literary text is self-referential
to the extent that the meaning of each of its parts is determined by reference to the context in which each is set,
rather than by reference to any outside object. But the
self-reference of the parabolic narrative is more specific.

It refers to the very process of communication and enunciation which produces the text as a coded message. This coded message is decoded by the addresser in such a way that the addressee is enabled to construct another code (by displacing the signifiers and condensing the signifieds) so as to understand the message addressed to him. This is the operation of which the parable speaks in its own metaphorical way.

Now we come to Pascal's parable. We observe that the story is told on two separate isotopies. The first one is properly the narrative level. The second one is a description. On the first level, we read a series of narrative sequences which unfold the story in time. On the second level, the final situation of the main character is analysed from his own point of view. This description, which actually is a part of the narrative, is also an attempt to construct the narrative's code--or to enable us to do so by providing us with the pieces.

After this first part, the decoding begins. This is the metaphorical application to the addressee, the duke's son, of the signifying parts of the story. These are the parts which illuminate the socio-political status of a nobleman in seventeenth century France; and this role has already been defined for these conceptual tools by the description of the narrative situation. But it is striking that this decoding process assumes a narrative form, albeit quite different from the first-level narrative. In my first draft I attempted to show how this form moves beyond a recounting only of the life of the young son of the Duke of Chevreuse, for it follows the characteristic biographical structure for the life of a nobleman in general. Had I the time, I would try to demonstrate that such a biographical structure is the result of the projection of the castaway's story, though the description of his final situation, upon the life of the duke. This description has the function of filtering the story through its codic net and of transforming it into a model, a paradigm, which nonetheless retains some narrative features.

A third part of the text constitutes a conclusion for the biographical scheme. Its function is the same as that filled by the description at the end of the parable. But this conclusion, which constantly refers to the story, is also a transformation wrought by the biographical model. The chief characteristic of this transformation consists of its shift from description to prescription, injunction.

The final paragraph of the text corresponds to its first sentence. By "corresponds" I mean that the dialogic injunctive frame of the story has been transformed by the whole text which we have read into a negative description of the condition of the great (noblemen). The great do not know their condition; they fail to recognize who they are, and are mystified by their own social and political status. In so saying, Pascal re-opens his discourse, not into another discourse but into a procedure that does not belong to the realm of discourse. And the whole text becomes an instrument for clearing the way toward such a procedure. The pragmatic effect of the text results from the combination of an injunction and a description. But the effect of this combination is not cumulative. Instead, it reveals a lack, an empty space which has to be filled by an existential transformation. If you prefer, the frame is so shaped as to enclose another narrative, a narrative which is not recounted or written, but which has to be lived. This empty space is that of the reader. This is why I have sug- gested that the structures of enunciation in parables are not only those constraints imposed upon the narrative from the outside--by the narrator and his concrete situation in life--but also by parts of the narrative itself. The text is so constructed as to provide us as readers with a place which only we ourselves can define, in interaction with the text. When we read a narrative, including its decoding and metaphorical application to the concrete life-situation of a past reader (here, the son of a French duke), we are still led to interpret the narrative in our own way. By displacing or completing its own decoding, we metaphorically apply the story to ourselves. While reading the text, we are led to write our own narrative by producing meaning effects which accord with the narrative as the narrator related it to us.

I shall limit my analysis to the narrative proper, and shall elucidate the syntagmatic and paradigmatic structures together. By syntagmatic structure I mean the sequence of major episodes and the sequence of actions within them. At this level, I shall consider the various modalizations of the narrative, the modal statements seeming especially im- portant to me. By paradigmatic structure, I mean the charac- teristics of the participants and, especially, of their inter- actions.

The introduction opens up and resolves the question: How can one who is/has practically nothing (almost a zero) come to be/have practically everything (almost an infinite)? It is a problem of strategy, insoluble in the terms in which it is posed. This is why the syntagmatic structure is so important, for the sequence of episodes and actions displays

some principles of this strategy--or at least it points out
the basic problem of the strategy. And as we shall soon
see, this problem involves the very strategy of the communication process, of discourse itself.

The story follows the general scheme of an action:
situation - action - resolution. It begins with a description of a two-sided situation of lack, then proceeds with
actions and ends with the resolution of the initial situation. The outcome is a rather paradoxical situation in that
the initial situation is solved, yet is not solved. The
paradox is developed by what I am calling the description
of the final solution. It opens up into the second-level
narrative which is simultaneously narrative and meta-narra-
tive. This second level comprises what is perhaps one of
the basic features of the parable as such, a narrative code
which provides for a decoding of the story. As usual, then,
it is the middle part of the story, here a short phrase,
which carries through the essential operation of transforming a situation of near nullity into one of near infinitude,
and of taking this transformation as a paradox since everything is changed, yet nothing is changed.

Two episodes characterize the initial situation. It
is described in terms which imply the construction of a
matrix or model. Only a small part of this matrix is
represented by those elements of the code which are explicitly given in the text, for this matrix receives a
specific investment by the narrator himself.

1. A man is cast away by a tempest upon an unknown
island.

2. The inhabitants of the island are striving to find
their king, who has been lost.

This is a good example of a situation of lack and distress. The first action is a movement which entails a disjunction: the man is violently removed from his originally ordered setting, his ship, and cast into an unknown place, the island. But this disjunction is accompanied by a conjunction: he is not drowned during the shipwreck; he reaches the coast of the island.

The second episode is also a movement which involves a disjunction: the king of the island is lost. So the islanders as a whole society are in a state of disjunction from their king, the center of their island universe and its leading, organizing principle. Now this real disjunction accompanies a potential conjunction: there is hope that they will possibly find their king. The two disjunctions imply a lost object--in the one case the ship, in the other the king. The shipwreck cost the man the cosmos or place of which he was a part. The king's disappearance deprived that other cosmos, the island, of its center. But the castaway recovers a place by being thrown upon the island. This place is substituted for the one he lost. The islanders, by contrast, are only hoping to find their king and ruler, their leader and father.

We may presuppose that the man decided to make his journey to perform a task. But obviously, being cast away upon the island was not this task: he is not an explorer of unknown islands. His coming into the island can be considered as a *negative mandate* and as a *negative volition* to carry out his task. This constitutes an interesting characteristic of our narrative. By contrast, the people, ruled by a king, forming a state, a kingdom, and loving their king, are positively mandated to find him. Their quest for the king can be characterized as a *positive volition* and we may presuppose that they *know* who their king is and that they have the *power* of finding him. We presuppose, therefore, the communication of power and knowledge to the personage which the narrator calls the people of the island.

To summarize this first step of our analysis, we may say that the initial situation of lack and distress is articulated by the following functions: 1) disjunction/conjunction; 2) communication (of knowledge and power); 3) mandating. But simultaneously, the situation is divided into two opposite sets: 1) a positive set which characterizes the people; 2) a negative one which characterizes the castaway. I mean that the way in which the two first actors of the story are narrated implies: 1) a situation of lack; 2) that one actor combines a certain number of narrative functions; 3) that consequently the other actor is deprived of these functions, except the first one: conjunction/disjunction; 4) that these two actors are both symmetrical and opposed in the situation of lack in which they partake.

One of the problems we face in our analysis of the story is the fact that the castaway seems to be sent from outside (from the outer world into the island, but also from without the story to within) in order to occupy the space left empty by the lost king at the center of the island, but he is also sent in order to start the narrative process, the telling of the story. It seems that the man is an object whose function is to overcome the lack of a ruling center of the island. So as an actor, the castaway occupies an ambiguous actantial position. He is a subject symmetrically opposed to the other subject, the people.

But the fact that he is not mandated to accomplish a definite task, and that he has no specific volition to carry out this task also defines him as an object transmitted by a mysterious sender to a receiver, the people.

Perhaps I can rephrase the problem in more general terms by focusing the analysis on the only functions that the man manifests as a personage of the story: disjunction/conjunction. By being cast away upon the island, the man defines the position of a limit, a limit between inside and outside the limit of a closed system, the island, the text itself. He sets up this limit and he transgresses it. He is an intruder from without. But simultaneously we read that the people are looking for their lost king. The closed world of the island has no center. Thus the closed system is no longer a system since it is deprived of its center. It lacks the privileged element that links the parts together in an organized whole. The castaway sets up a limit from without for a system which has no center. His coming into the system is the precise corollary of the king's departure from the system. This observation allows us to establish an interesting relation between the limit of a system and its center. It is as if the limit were a pseudo-center or as if there were an equivalence between them. It recalls Pascal's famous thought about the universe: "It is an infinite sphere whose center is everywhere and the circumference nowhere." According to our story we can rephrase this in this way: the island is a finite sphere of which the center is nowhere and which is given a limit, a circumference from without, from everywhere. This is the spatial translation of the contingent and aleatory coming of the intruder.

Whatever else the island may be (whether a political, cultural, cosmological system, or even a linguistic or semiotic system), we may view it as a system which signifies its own complete meaning. It is a whole with its closed horizon, its structural center around which it has organized itself, its norms of valorization, and its rules of functioning. It is the larger entity which emerges from the total interaction of its parts.

In my first draft, I make intertextual comparisons with an arbitrarily-defined corpus designated as Pascal's *Thoughts*, which provides what may be regarded as variants of our narrative. There I attempted to show that the parable which opens the *First Discourse* can simultaneously be deciphered in terms of a cosmological code and a theological-spiritual code, as well as through the socio-political code developed in the text itself. So the three semantic axes of knowledge, charity (i.e., desire), and power become simultaneously explicit in the one narrative. This codic overdetermination of the parable allows us to construct a more general model which can be variously invested by diverse kinds of discourses and manifested in various types of narratives. This matrix of signification I designate a "signifying system", and I consider the parable a narrative representation of the way it functions. It would certainly be possible to translate this signifying system into the morphological or taxonomic model of Greimas in which four terms are defined as two paired relations of contradiction and opposition. But what strikes me with Pascal's parable is that Pascal questions the very construction of that kind of model. Or, if you prefer, he questions the epistemology of sign and the philosophy of representation

upon which semiotic studies are grounded. How? By raising
the problem of the center and of the limits of a signifying
system. All the basic concepts used by Pascal belong to a
domain defined in Greimas' model as the "neither...nor"
relation (the relation of opposition between two previously
negated terms). More deeply and more generally speaking, I
should say that this "neither...nor" relation (the neutral
axis in Greimas' terms) is perhaps the basic relation at
work in the parabolic discourse.

When the center of a system is defined as missing, as
being lost, when there is no longer an ontological and
axiological central locus for the regulation of its operations, then such a system as an organized whole is changed
into a chaos; it becomes a non-system, an undifferentiated
system, or a paradoxical system without differentiations,
and without any principle producing and regulating its
differentiations. More specifically, we have a system
which is paradoxically organized and regulated by a missing
center, by an absent principle.

The intrusion of the castaway, unmotivated though it
is, posits a limit and draws a distinction by transgressing
that limit. By his coming, the castaway articulates the
difference between inside and outside. He is an aleatory
and contingent event who establishes a limit precisely by
breaking through it.

We have just noted that in the story the castaway is
sent by no one. He has no mandate, no will to perform a
task. He is a message without a sender. Or better, the
sender ("*destinateur*") is the narrator, the subject of the
enunciation. But in terms of the story, this subject is
defined as contingent. His only textual necessity is that

of the chain of signifiers constituting the story itself.
This chain links an "everywhere" (the outside of the text,
which the story represents in its narrative way) to a "nowhere" (the missing center, the hole in the middle of both
the island and of the story itself).

This story which we are being told serves on a deeper
level to narrativize the relationships between an event and
a signifying system. The lost king of course constitutes
the referential frame of the whole story, the focal point
from which the successive sequences of the story acquire
their meaning. But this focal point, or frame, is present
only as absent. It operates through the story by its very
absence. By his coming, the castaway provides the system
with a new referential context. But, to use the terminology
of communication theory, he is a "noise", an uncoded element
intruding upon the system from without. If the system were
not already disintegrating for lack of its center, he could
only be excluded from it or remain in it only as an alien
body. In this way the story tells us how a noise can become
a signifying part of a system, and even how it can come to
serve as its structural center. But it also tells us that
the new system so constituted is in fact a pseudo-system--
not exactly a false one, but only a simulation of the true
one. Its only value is pragmatic; its only truth is that
it works *as if* it were a true system. In this sense, the
story narrates itself. In an image, the story reflects its
own way of working, its own meaning process. It narrates
what a parable is and how it is to be used.

The analysis of a narrative is itself a discourse which
seeks to reproduce the generative process of the narrative
as a whole. But at the same time, the very analysis is also

represented narratively by the narrative under analysis. This means that, as exegetes or interpreters of the text, we are already in the text we interpret. In our studying of the text, in our determining of its meanings, we are written by the text. We are parts of it. We become the text, and the text in turn acquires an existential actuality.

Now we may return to the story. Our analysis has to describe the transformations coming from the initial situation, by articulating them from the viewpoint of the final situation. What are the possible final situations? 1) One alternative would be that the people find their missing king. In this solution, the castaway would remain a castaway, an element excluded from the system. 2) The people might replace their king by the castaway. With this solution, it is the king, defined as the center of the system, who is excluded. The king remains lost. We could evoke this possibility by substituting for the text we read, another text in which the castaway is endowed with all the moral and political qualities which make him acceptable to the islanders as a king. 3) The castaway could be the real king, who comes back to his kingdom after a long and mysterious absence. We might imagine two possible variants for this solution: a) the people discover that the castaway is their real king and rejoice at his return; or b) they never recognize the castaway as the missing king. They continue to wait for him and banish or even kill the castaway.

What is the solution adopted by the narrator? It is a complex one, since in the story the castaway *is* and *is not* the king. The man is *apparently* the king and *actually* he is not. This means that in a certain sense the man remains out of the system and in another way, is integrated into the system as its center. How is this possible narratively? By paradoxically joining together and identifying the *limit and the center*. The solution found by the narrator for the initial situation of lack and disintegration is the building of a traitor structure as a kind of transformational narrative device. Yet this traitor structure is given to us as the final solution. 1) To the people the castaway *seems* to be the king, but he *is not* the true king. Physically he *looks like* him; but he is a false king taken for a real one. 2) The castaway deigns to play the role of the king but he *knows* that he is not. He *willingly deceives* the people, but *knows* he is deceiving them. Reciprocally, 1) the people now have a king: they do not look for him any longer; 2) the people do not know that the king they recover is not the real one.

This is an extraordinary attempt to deconstruct the very notion of "meaning" as an "ultimate ontological presence" providing any signifying system with its transcendent guarantee of fundamental truth. The origin and the telos precede the system and construct it. We are shown the paradox: for us to live is to render the world meaningful; and in order to construct these signifying systems, we first need such a "meaning". But at the same time, we must recognize that this ultimate truth, this transcendent presence, this originating logos and ultimate telos is a *simulated* truth, presence, origin, and telos. Meaning, as a fundamental ontological and axiological notion, is a fiction. But it is a necessary fiction without which man could not exist.

How can such a deconstruction be expressed narratively?
The key to a solution lies in substituting modal statements
for descriptive or assertive ones in the narrative's topical
sequence (the central sequence, which relates how the initial
lack is overcome). This fundamental substitution needs
further explanation.

(modal
qualities
or by
to
parole)

The axis around which the narrative transformations
occur is the castaway's physical resemblance to the king.
Such a likeness may be considered a marker or an attribute
which qualifies the anti-subject as hero of the story. The
man's resemblance evokes the mythical hero's magical ability
to change himself into another being. By looking like the
king, the man is simultaneously the same and an "other".
He is two in one. He is the mediator between the two contradictory extremes of the opposition which the narrative
has to solve. The question we ask here is: who gives the
man this magical mark qualifying him as the hero of the
story? In a sense, we repeat the question which we have
already raised: who sends the man? The only possible
answer given by the story is *chance*. If we had enough time
to analyze the whole *Discourse*, we could show that this
notion of chance, or *alea*, is the fundamental notion of
the codes which cipher the story and through which Pascal
decodes it. In other words, the notion of chance, presented as the paradigm of the story, is a pseudo-rationali-
zation of the absent ultimate meaning, of the lacking
logos, of the king who was lost. The physical resemblance
which, by chance, endows the man with his qualifying mark,
is the narrative representational feature of the missing
king. But at the same time, this pseudo-logical solution
introduces an important characteristic into the story--

namely, the *modalization* of the further narrative statements
We can identify modalization as the opposition between
simulation, pretense and *appearance*, on the one hand, and
actuality, veracity and *truth*, on the other. The equation
which characterizes seventeenth century philosophical thinking and, more generally, the whole matrix of the sign and of
the signifying systems, is the equation of appearance and
being. The equation is the fact that a subject gives himself appearances, through language, in order to signify
being without any lack or excess either on the side of
language or on the side of reality. Now this equation is
being radically called into question. Here the subject is
not in a position of ultimate mastery. He is caught in a
symbolic chain. He is subjected to language independently
of--or rather prior to--its meaning.

This modalization commands the whole narrative performance of the story. To be sure, we acknowledge a succession
of descriptive and narrative statements: "The man is not
recognized as the king by all the people." "He accepted
all the homage they chose to render." But these statements
are subjected to two kinds of modal statements: willing
(or its contradictory, not willing) and knowing (or not
knowing). (See appendix.) The reversal of the syntagmatic
line of the story which results from the first opposition
between "appearing" versus "being" is the move from not
willing to willing. The man who *did not want* to be acclaimed as the king by the people *makes up his mind* and
finally resolves to give himself up to his good fortune.
In more abstract terms, while the descriptive statement
"being acclaimed as the king" remains unchanged, the negation of a potential program (a wish) is transformed into

assertion. Nevertheless, we have to acknowledge that the negation of this wish is, at the same time, the correlate of the assertion of truth or reality: "I am not the king, I am a castaway." By contrast, the assertion of this wish is correlated with the negation of reality and truth, i.e., to deception. To follow Greimas, since the descriptive statement remains unchanged, the transformation can be interpreted as a substitution of a modal statement concerning existence for a modal statement concerning will or wish. "Wanting or accepting to be recognized as the king" becomes "being recognized as the king". The wish modality allows the construction of a modal statement with two actants, the subject and the object. The wish axis which relates them to each other permits their semantic interpretation as potential objects of the performance and as objects invested with value. If the wish modality valorizes the object, the object as an actant of the modal statement is here converted into an attributive statement: the kingship is attributed to the man.

The other modality introduced into the story is "knowing": the man *knows* that he is not the king. Conversely, the people do not know it. But the castaway *actually* acts as the king: he *actually* realizes his wish. He knows the truth but he behaves according to the appearance. And the story ends with this contradiction. We may observe that the resolution of the situation maintains the initial contradiction but displaces it. At the beginning, the situation of lack was characterized by the contradiction between two negative description statements: "The islanders were striving to find their missing king;...the man was cast by the tempest upon an unknown island." Through the mediation constituted by the man's physical resemblance to the king, the contradiction is displaced into this one: the man knows he is not the king; nevertheless, having *decided* to be the king, he behaves as if he were. By contrast, the people who do not know that the man is not the king, realize illusively their wish to have a king. The resolution of the situation is characterized by the contradiction between two positive modal statements concerning knowing and willing, knowledge and wish.

What does this transformation mean? As Benveniste shows, narrative is characterized by the dissimulation of all marks of enunciation into the "*enoncé*". The story is told in such a way that it seems that the events narrate themselves. Now the fundamental categories of narrativity are "doing" and "being". "Doing" characterizes the acts, the processes, and "being" the qualities and attributes. By introducing modalizations, by defining the actors of the story by their wish, their knowledge, their power, the narrator who conceals himself as narrator, appears in his story under the cover of the actors. He simultaneously posits and negates his own narrative performance (his discourse, in Benveniste's sense) by displaying for his reader what the actors secretly wish, know, what they are capable of doing, that is, everything which does not belong to the realm of events. He constitutes, within the narrative statements, an enunciative network in which he captures and captivates his reader.

One of the basic features of our narrative is the narrative representation of such a process. The castaway who becomes the king knows he is not the king whom the islanders seek, but he acts as if he were. This is the

deceptive operation of the narration. The islanders who believe that he is their king and who behave accordingly represent the very act of reading a tale; an act characterized by
the referential delusion, by the belief that there is an
adequation between the "*récit*" and the "*histoire*". This
adequation defines the truth value of the narrative.

We may now come back to the narrative performances of
our parable and analyze it as the confrontation of two
subjects, the islander, S1, and the castaway, S2. We may
represent the syntagmatic train of the narrative as follows:
(NSt = Narrative Statement; F = Function) First:
NSt1:F:confrontation (S1 $\leftrightarrow$ S2). This narrative statement
is the combination of the modal statements defining S1 and
S2. Second: NSt2:domination (S1 $\rightarrow$ S2). It is an operation of negation by which S2 negates S1. This transformation
consists in the move from potentiality to realization or in
the substitution for the modal statement concerning will (or
wish) of the modal statement concerning reality. Domination
is substituted for the will to dominate. Third: NSt3:F:
attribution (S2 $\leftarrow$ O). A valorized object is attributed
to the dominating subject S2. This is an assertive statement according to Greimas.

But in our parable, this narrative performance is
entirely caught up in the traitor-structure, i.e., the
syntagmatic chain of the narrative statements is unfolded
on a deceptive level, and this is the ultimate word of the
story. *The narrative mode is here that of deception*, the
opposition between truth and deception being based upon a
fundamental grammatical category, "being versus appearance".
The traitor is a man who seems or appears to be who he is
not and who is what he does not seem to be. By looking like

the king, the castaway subverts being or reality, by its
representation, but he does so objectively and passively;
actually he does not want to look like the king, he does
not intend to deceive the inhabitants of the island. And
now when he suffers himself to be treated as a king, he
subjectively assumes his fate of being objectively an im-
postor. In so doing, he pretends to be what he is not,
for he actually feigns being the king. He is induced to
act according to what he does not think or believe and to
think or believe according to what he does not express by
his behavior. He is induced to be a hypocrite, that is to
say, to mystify the people by his own alienation. These
three moments of the traitor-structure correspond to the
three functions of the narrative performance: confrontation, domination, attribution. But, at the same time, the
deceptive mode of the narration displaces and subverts
them. The confrontation is not a true one since there is
no real struggle between the two subjects; on the contrary, if there is a struggle, it is a self-reflective
struggle of the castaway with himself. It is the same
with the domination. Indeed, the castaway becomes king,
but it is the people who negate themselves by asking to
be dominated by the man whom they take for their king.
The attribution is not a true one either, since the new
king considers himself as not actually possessing kingship,
as not truly ruling the kingdom.

If this analysis is correct, we can then apprehend
an interesting structure of exchange (or communication)
characterizing our parable. The starting point, or better
the center, of the traitor-structure is ontological: the
mysterious and fortuitous resemblance of the castaway to

the king who was lost. The consequences of this physical likeness articulate the story. If so, the traitor-structure is the locus where an operation of exchange can take place. What is this exchange? The king is the absolute value, the structural center of the system, its axiological norm. But he is not there, he is absent. The man is a castaway, an almost non-being, non-value; he is coming as an intruder from without, he breaks the limit of the system and sets up such a limit. But he represents the king. What the parable narrative tells us is that representation is an exchange or, more generally speaking, since representation defines the fundamental matrix of the sign, it tells us that signifying systems are places where an exchange occurs. On the one hand, being and value are absent. On the other hand, non-being and non-value are present. But the fact of representing being, value, through a sign—something which is almost equal to zero, to nothing—gives a derived presence to being, value, truth which are absent. The result is that this almost-zero is infinitely valorized by being, truth, value. But conversely, the quasi-zero receives from the infinite value, from being and truth its absence and it devalorizes them; it corrupts and subverts being and truth by its quasi-nothingness. The elucidation of such a structural exchange is not possible except through the general modalization of the narrative discussed above.

Now if in fact the operation of exchange between presence and absence, between being-value-infinite and nothingness-non-value-zero, characterizes every signifying system and the sign in general, then the text we read, the narrative we are told, is itself deconstructed by the very operation which it narratively describes as well as by the relationship between the narrator and the reader. This means that the origin and the telos of the text, of communication through signs, of meaning, are subverted and deconstructed as representational processes in order to give way to a strategy, a textual strategy we may call parable. Its effect is not a meaning effect, but its *simulation*, in which our own commentary is caught and by which both our own discourse and Pascal's own decoding are deconstructed and are obviously invalidated as the ultimate meaning of his parable. I attempted in my first draft in French to reach the same results in Pascalian terms, by showing that what Pascal calls the thought-in-the-back-of-the-mind and his conception of judgment imply a thorough reflection about the deconstructing effect of infinity and nothingness upon our mind's contents, upon theoretical knowledge and finally upon language in its ordinary use.

In concluding this paper, I shall emphasize a few points in order to show how in his own discursive practice, Pascal lets the displacement of the signifiers occur and how, through it, he lets his reader produce his own discourse. As we saw, the mimetic representation of the king by the castaway was the turning point of the parable. Then when Pascal decodes the parable, he reproduces such a representation at the level of the code, but in a reverse way: a duke's *corporeal* and spiritual qualities and those of a boatman are of different natures. They are heterogeneous and a difference is founded on their own merits. But, at the same time, there is no natural link between the social status of a duke and that of a boatman, nor between their respective merits. There is no natural link between the qualities of body and soul. The first difference defines

the normative model of the ordered conception of society.
It defines its truth. The second difference articulates
the real society according to the distance between two
social conditions and the real, however false, valoriza-
tions of these two conditions. Because a duke has the
social status of a nobleman, he is considered as having
greater merits than a boatman. Such a model suggests what
would be a possible code of the parable, but, in the
parable, it is because of the physical likeness of the
castaway to the king (an instance of the wrong assimilation
of corporeal and spiritual qualities to a social status),
that the castaway, once king, has the right attitude in
distinguishing his political behavior with the people,
from his beliefs and thoughts with himself. But in proceeding in such a way, the narrator signals the ideological
operation of representation by which the idea of reality,
its sign, is taken for the reality itself. This is a
violent operation; yet its violence is dissimulated by
the operation itself, since it is only "reproductive". If
the relationship between a social status and qualities of
body and soul is an ideological one, the parabolic narrative makes obvious the production of the ideology by showing that reality is reproduced in the form of a sign which,
substituting itself for reality, becomes reality. If
there is no pure simple decoding between the two levels
of the narrative and its interpretation, it is because
the form of visible and faithful representation, that is
that of the castaway, introduces a signifying displacement
of great efficacy with regard to the "theoretical" distinction of the actual political and social situation and

the ethical norms. In looking like the king, the castaway
is automatically king. This certainly is a representation
but it is used only in order to show how representation
functions: the signifier takes the place of the referent
and hides it; there is an usurpation of power by the
initial violence of the substitution. The signifier (the
castaway as body and face) takes the place of the referent
(the lost king). The parable means that meaning is always
lost and that we take for meaning, for *true* meaning, only
signifiers and their interplay.

This is exactly what happens in the *Discourse on the
Condition of the Great*. By carefully decoding the political and social meaning of the parable, Pascal offers to
his interlocutor a meaning. But in perceiving this meaning following the injunctions of Pascal's discourse, the
young duke dissimulates from himself the other meaning,
that plurality of meanings which the political and social
meaning conceals and manifests. And it is not possible
for the discourse itself and for him who utters it, to
utter this multiple meaning, to fix it in a meaning that
would be *the* meaning, except by the rhetorical detour of
the parabolic narrative which then becomes, by its very
decentering, the vehicle of the plurality of meaning.
Moreover, the parable expresses this impossibility. It
represents narratively that a universal or dogmatic interpretation giving the ultimate truth of the parable
would be a sign of violence and usurpation. But simultaneously, it shows that such an interpretation is always
in process: it cannot but be carried out. This is a
kind of textual fate from which it is not possible to
escape. The only way to point out a solution is to make

the narrative and its interpretation an opaque object. The reader can then become aware that this very opacity, this secret, is, if not meaning, at least the instrument of meaning which no longer belongs to the speculative or theoretical understanding but to an existential practice.

A striking paradox closes the explicative commentary of the parable image. Everything has been said; the political meaning has been explicated, the code of the fiction unveiled with precision and the theoretical model traced with exactitude in its representation function. Pascal adds: "What I tell you does not go very far. And if you stop there, you will not save yourself from being lost. But at least you will be lost like an honest man. The way which I open to you to lose yourself is doubtless the most honorable. But in truth it is always a great folly for a man to expose himself to damnation; and therefore he must not stop at this....Others than I will show you the way to this...." The perception of a meaning was a dissimulation of another meaning that the parable expressed already in saying the first, but without knowing that it expressed it. Such, briefly sketched is, what Pascal calls the astute man's movement of discernment. It requires recounting the narrative, then expressing yet another meaning encoded in the narrative primitive meaning. Then, this meaning unveiled, it requires implying that this unveiling is an obscuring, though practical, displacement in which appears the withdrawal of every meaning in an endless decoding, a withdrawal of meaning through the constant and violent imposition of *meaning*. This is what the parable was already saying through its narrative.

APPENDIX

In order to enter into a real knowledge of your condition, consider it in this image:

A man was cast by a tempest upon an unknown island, the inhabitants of which were in trouble to find their king, who was lost; and having a strong resemblance both in form and face to this king, he was taken for him, and acknowledged in this capacity by all the people. At first he knew not what course to take; but finally he resolved to give himself up to his good fortune. He received all the homage that they chose to render him, and suffered himself to be treated as king.

But as he could not forget his real condition, he was conscious, at the same time that he was receiving this homage, that he was not the king whom this people had sought, and that this kingdom did not belong to him. Thus he had a double thought: the one by which he acted as king, the other by which he recognized his true state, and that it was accident alone that had placed him in his present condition. He concealed the latter thought, and revealed the other. It was by the former that he was treated by the people, and by the latter that he treated himself.

Do not imagine that it is less an accident by which you find yourself master of the wealth you possess, then by which this man found himself king. You have no right to it of yourself and by your own nature any more than he: and not only do you find yourself the son of a duke, but also do you find yourself in the world at all, only through the infinity of chance.

Discourses on the Condition of the Great,
I, Beginning

Trans. O. W. Wight

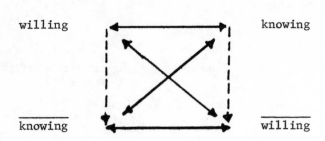

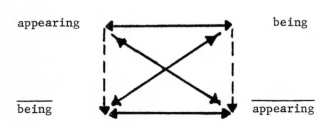

RESPONSE TO LOUIS MARIN

Larry S. Crist

Vanderbilt University

> It is, then, a strange fact that we cannot
> define these things without obscuring them
> (*Pensées*, Trotter transl.; Brunschwicg 392,
> Chevalier 383, Lafuma 109).

In "traditional" criticism, it is often held that one of
the functions (non-structuralist word here) of the parables
of Jesus is to surprise the hearer/reader, to shock him/her
loose from her/his moorings, so as to be opened to a new--
unexpected--message.

Even so it was/is for me, since my response for tonight
was prepared on Professor Marin's French paper, replaced
yesterday and today by a quite different English one. I am
rather sorry about this, since I had become rather fond of,
familiar--in the etymological sense--with that French paper
through numerous readings, efforts at decoding it. Yet,
since we are in the realm of meta-discourse, I will merely
keep on my first track, and thus furnish a sort of meta-
and parallel-discourse, taking some sort of consolation in
the thought that the two other respondents will hew more
closely to the English text.

We find ourselves here in a very familiar situation for
the medievalist that I try to be; I must add that this means
that we are thus firmly in the rabbinical tradition. Pascal
presents an *exemplum*, a parable if you will, which he then
immediately glosses. Professor Marin glosses these two now

one and we three here are glossing Professor Marin's gloss
of Pascal's *glossa cum exempla*. Then we will all gloss our
glossings. Thus meta-to-the-nth-degree-commentary/discourse.
Pascal would laugh, along with Plato and Aristotle. Furthermore, in light of the discussion by Professor Marin, Pascal
would have us realize that all this is mere verbiage. But
in the hope and trust that knowing that all is nought is
nonetheless knowing, I make bold to proceed.

Blaise Pascal died on 19 August 1662; his three *Discourses on the Condition of the Great* (five and a half pages,
small octavo, in the Chevalier/Pléiade ed.) can be dated in
the last quarter of 1660. As for his *Thoughts*, they can
reasonably be dated between 1657 and the beginning of 1659;
his sickness prevented him from finishing his classification
by subject of these mostly short notes and all the more so
from beginning to draft his *Apology for the Christian Religion*. The parable that we have before us was, then, written
after the sketches or *Thoughts* as part of a work--as opposed
to the *Thoughts*--with a clear beginning, middle, and end.

I am going to examine, first, two *Thoughts* to which
Professor Marin referred, both from the same section in the
three now-classic editions, bearing the generic title in L.
Lafuma's edition; "*Raisons des effets*": "The reason for
things" (Cohen), "The reason of effects" (Trotter). Both
of these translations are inadequate; Professor Marin's
(in his English paper) is much better: "The effects of
meaning". These two *Thoughts* can be used as sketches for
the parable written later or, recursively, as glosses there
for; the parable can be regarded as *exemplum* for the declara-
tive *Thoughts*.

The first is *Thought* 328/309/93, and is schematized in the first table (I) "The reason of effects" [The effects of meaning]. Continual alternation of *pro* and *con*. [*sic*]

> We have then shown that man is foolish, by the estimation he makes of things which are not essentials; and all these opinions are destroyed [I, line 1 //]. We have next shown that all these opinions are very sound, and that thus, since all these vanities are well founded, the people are not so foolish as is said. And so we have destroyed the opinion which destroyed that of the people [I, line 2 //].

> But we must now destroy this last proposition, and show that it remains always true that the people are foolish, though their opinions are sound, because they do not perceive the truth where it is, and, as they place it where it is not, their opinions are always very false and very unsound [I, line 3].

SCHEMA I

		A	We B
1 Man	opinions	+ → things which are not essential	←opinion − (destroys opinion 1A)
2 Man	opinions	+ → (very) well founded	←opinion + (destroys opinion 1B)
3 People	opinions (sound)	+ → non-truth − ✗↓ truth +	←opinion − (destoys opinion 3A and opinion 2B)
*4 We	opinions	+ → truth +	--------------------

If you have followed Pascal's train of reasoning as sketched out in Schema I, you will note that we are left with the existence of *truth, but the means of proceeding from the situation in lines 2, then 3, to a *(possible)4(+n), where "we" replaces "people, man" and where the destructive force of B gives way to the positive force of A, is not given (*quartum non datur*).

I add a *Thought* here, no. 327/308/83 (needing no schematization), which explains the two natural extremities of ignorance:

> The world is a grand judge of things, for it
> is in natural ignorance, which is man's true
> state. The sciences have two extremes which
> meet. The first is the pure, natural ignor-
> ance in which all men find themselves at
> birth. The other extreme is that reached by
> great intellects, who, having run through
> all that men can know, find they know nothing,
> and come back again to that same ignorance
> from which they set out; but this is a learned
> ignorance (*une ignorance savante*) which is
> conscious of itself.... [I leave off the
> rest.]

The end of natural knowledge is thus the *docta ignorantia* of a certain Western tradition. But this still leaves us in an unsatisfying state. We know that we know--*sed quid est veritas?*

This dialectic process, especially as we saw it in the first *Thought* examined, is repeated in another *Thought*, no. 337/312/90 (see Schema II): "*The reason of effects*" [The effects of meaning].--Degrees. "The people honor persons of high birth" [II, line 1 //].

"The semi-learned despise them, saying that birth is not a personal, but a chance superiority" [II, line 2 //].

"The astute [*les habiles*--Prof. Marin's translation for the misleading "learned"] honour them, not for popular [= the people's] reasons, but for secret reasons [*par la pensée de derrière*]" [II, line 3 //].

"Devout persons, who have more zeal than knowledge, despise them, in spite of that consideration which makes them honoured by the learned [the astute], because they judge them by a new light which piety gives them" [II, line 4 //].

"But perfect Christians honour them by another and higher light" [II, line 5 //].

So arrive a succession of opinions for and against, according to the light one has.

SCHEMA II

Attitude →

I	1	People	+	Men
[Nature]	2	Half-educated	−	of
	3	Astute	+	high
II	4	Devout [half-Christian?]	−	birth
[Grace]	5	Perfect Christians	+	

$3 \simeq 1(+n)$ $5 \simeq 3(+\infty)$, thus $5 \simeq [1(+n)]+\infty$

You will note that I separate these five categories into two general ones, defined by the references of the latter two as being in the at least semantic field of Grace.

The "parable" itself deals only with categories 1 and 3 as set out above. It sets forth, in its turn, two categories (Schema IIIa):

SCHEMA IIIa

		Agent	Process	Patient	
Manifest (to Do)	I	King	to Act (to Reign)	People	I Agent ≠ Patient
Hidden (to Be/Have)	II	Man	to Think (to Regard)	Oneself	II Agent ≃ Patient (+ Awareness)

SCHEMA IIIb

the Astute → the Instructor → Awareness of → the Instructed → the Astute
  (I = Pascal)   (necessary)   (You = Duke)
            coexistence
        (thus conjunction)
            I + II
        (with "content" IIIa)

The astute man is aware of the disjunction between categories I and II; the process in the first *Discourse* is shown in Schema IIIb, one of making the patient of the discourse a member of category 3 of Schema II, astute himself, as is the speaker. One must divide in order to unite: being aware of disjunction is a necessary condition for its reduction to conjunction. I note, in passing, that my category I here is transitive, thus Agent is not the same as Patient, whereas category II is reflexive, Agent being equivalent to Patient possessing awareness and thus category II is a figure of Schema IIIb.

Now since category (of Schema II) 4:5::2:3, and since Pascal omits any sort of category 2 in his parable, we might also expect no mention of category 4 further on—which is precisely the case. The parable is thus a reduction to the essential of the categories expressed in Schema II. It is a political parable, directed to a nobleman, to instruct him how to comport himself properly in his world. Astuteness is necessary for a person of high birth, since he is not of the people—that is, the people define him as nobleman in accepting his high position. But astuteness, as Professor Marin shows in the long analysis in his English paper, is merely awareness of the necessary—in all sense—falsity of one's own position as nobleman. We remain in a situation of destruction (as in line 3 of Schema I). In the final part of his gloss on the parable, in the last part of the third and last *Discourse*, Pascal leaves a way open to a solution, as shown in category 5 of Schema II—by way of the *"pensée de derrière"*, but on a much (infinitely) higher level. This *"pensée de derrière"* is connected to the sort of mental reservation as expressed in the French: "Say what you will, *mais j'ai ma petite idée derrière la tête*" = "I've got my own idea."

These are some of my own reflections on the materials brought forward by our speaker. I must now turn to his paper more closely, if not more faithfully, noting that a commentary is not the same as a presentation, and is not held--happily for me--to being an organically organized whole.

The parable of Pascal is indeed not fully--because that is, on Pascal's own terms, impossible--read out/exegeted by Pascal; he leaves it open--but with an "intended" meaning outside. His process in the parable and in the three *Discourses* is one of creation of ignorance--thus creation of a "destruction", the which is likewise one of his principle lines of attack in the *Thoughts* in general. Everyone who humbles himself...

We then move on to a double allegoresis of the parable, as *exemplum* for: 1) the human--postlapsarian, I add--condition, and; 2) the divine position: *Deus absconditus (Veti Testamenti), Deus absconditus (in carne nostra, Novi Testamenti).* Here I will simply throw forward the intriguing thought--at least to me--that Pascal does not bring up the commonplace modern theological position (at least in Catholic thought) of *Deus et Dominus Jesus absconditus in ecclesia, id est in corpore christianorum.*

These two readings coexist, even though Pascal in his own exegesis stays in the socio-political realm until the end of the *Discourses*, and there, where he moves to the supra-socio-political realm, that of the Kingdom of God, he does so only negatively. The "reality" of the existing socio-political realm being shown to be based on nothing but error and ignorance--in either order--we have no need to change or abolish it, but are called on to rise/pass above it (echoes of Dante's verb *"transumanare"*).

I can follow without question or dissent then down to the middle of the discussion of the socio-political code, where I pick up the statement that the parable as analogy for the situation of the young duke shows that, "representation is without value in reality". We must make--as is, indeed, made a bit further on--the distinction between things as they are--existential reality--and things as they should be--non-perverted, as created prelapsus--essential reality. In the former reality, in which Pascal and his addressee lived, representation is precisely what determined the way things are--if you are called king, then you reign. Professor Marin does then refer to two "heterogeneities", the one "normative or ideal", the other "de facto and real".

The discussion of the "realization" of a "false" relation, the creation of an essentially-false existential fact, to the ruler as based on some essential difference between said ruler and the ruled, is an illustration of the process of ideology; as noted by Pirandello: *"E vero, se vi pare"*-- "It's true, if it seems so to you."

The falsity of kingship--since all kings, actual or imitation, are based on non-essentially-real situations-- is realized when the distinction between categories I and II of the parable (of Schema IIIa) is lost or not even established, when we have:

King → (to) Think → King.

RESPONSE TO LOUIS MARIN

Robert Detweiler

Emory University

In situations like this conference, self-consciousness
leads to self-consciousness, so that I have been led to ask
myself how one should respond structuralistically to a structural analysis. One way, and the way I propose to take, is
to do a reading of the deep structure of Professor Marin's
analysis, which in itself is, of course, an analysis of the
deep structure of Pascal's parable. Because of time limitations, my effort has to be a kind of shorthand, and hence I
will deal with three concepts that inhabit and illuminate
the deep structure of Professor Marin's study: the three
concepts are absence, deception, and simulation. I think
that this exploration will be less a criticism of Professor
Marin's study and more a meditation on it.

Professor Marin discusses absence in terms of the
missing king, who is also the missing center of this
island's social structure, the missing center of a closed
system, whose absence threatens to disrupt and even destroy
the system. As such he is also, more theoretically, the
absent principle of organization and, more structurally,
he is the missing signifier. Yet Professor Marin argues
that the lost king remains the focal point or referential
frame of the story and that his very absence determines the
further structuring of the narrative. What is the importance
of all this? I see some possible clarifications here regard-

ing the nature of parable that are certainly implicit in Professor Marin's paper but that may not be altogether manifest. The influential and determining presence of absence (represented by the lost king) applied to the study of the nature of parable suggests above all that the parable, more so than other kinds of fiction, demands a filling-in by the reader—a filling-in that is not merely an interpretation but an existential response. Why is this so? It is so because the true parable, unlike simple metaphor or allegory or similar pedagogical literary forms, eludes mere intellectual solution. Parables can never be satisfactorily solved or resolved; they must at last be reacted to by the whole person. That is to say, the influential absence of the lost king in Pascal's parable points to a determining absence in all authentic parables, to a lack inherent in the structure of parabolic narrative that frustrates all interpretation and demands instead action—as Professor Marin states quite lucidly in the French version of his paper.

All of this is familiar to us in terms of the claim of kerygma generally that it (kerygma) cannot be treated causally or intellectually-neutrally but only decisively or judgmentally. But Professor Marin helps us to see further that the parables function as the kerygma of kerygma, as the decision-provoking "phonemes" or basic constituent units of the New Testament gospel. Now it is fascinating to me that this decision-provoking quality of parables is extended to discourse in general by Jacques Derrida. Derrida argues in *L'écriture et la différence* that modern discourse as a whole has lost the king and is marked by the presence of absence, that our thought and language are determined by

efforts to think, speak, and act around the knowledge of the
empty center. In this situation, what Professor Marin treats
casually as chance, the aleatic appearance of the castaway,
Derrida treats as "freeplay", a sophisticated version, I
think, of Lévi-Strauss' *bricolage*: the process of filling
in the empty center with configurations of whatever material
may be at hand. We can now observe a difference between a
theological and a non-theological understanding of parable
in relation to discourse. A philosopher like Derrida, who
sees himself engaged in the task of dismantling the whole
tradition of western metaphysics from the inside, attacks
the foundations of language and fills in the resultant void
with his aleatic configurations, whereas the theologian (at
least the Christian theologian) is likely to replace the
lost king, the empty center with the castaway who is Christ
--and the castaway's language, as we recall, is the language
of parable that asks for decision as well as interpretation.
The radical theologians have already set about replacing the
lost king, but they have not done it very skillfully in
terms of language, especially kerygmatic language.

Second, in Pascal's parable, Professor Marin emphasizes
the dynamics of deception involved in the castaway's new
vocation. The people think he is their lost king, and although he knows that he is not, he decides to act *as if* he
is and live publically and politically in a deceptive mode.
Applied to the structure of parable generally, this situation
of the castaway suggests that the presence in parable that
takes the place of what is absent is *always* deceptive.
Things are never what they seem. Social structures, communications, the creation of meaning exist and take place
via fictions. Picasso said that years ago regarding the

function of art, when he remarked that art is a lie that
tells the truth.   Lévi-Strauss said something like it more
recently: "To reach reality we must first repudiate experience, although we may later return to it."   Now Professor Marin is interested mainly in pointing out in this
context, I think, that both the "ordinary" and educated man
lives in deception, but the educated man knows that he is
being deceived--that the castaway is not the real king--
and learns to accommodate and utilize the deception.   Lévi-
Strauss has declared an interest in this problem: "I claim
to show not how men think in myths but how the myths operate
in men's minds without their being aware of the fact."   In
any case, a parable is a fiction, and as such it is a deception that is used both to hide and to convey a "truth".
The truth that the castaway hides is that he is not the
king; the truth that he would convey to the educated--and
none of the islanders is educated--is that their system has
been destroyed and hence they must change their lives.
Putting things that way reminds me of the conclusion of
Rilke's marvelous poem, "Torso of Apollo".   The final line,
the response to looking at the great statue--essentially
a deception and a fiction, is, abruptly: "You must change
your life."   Hence--and I wish I could develop this el-
liptically--the structure of parabolic narration always
produces a call to repentance--another, more emotionally-
loaded way of declaring that a parable eludes mere interpretation and demands decision.   Here we see an intensification
of the assertion that all good art demands that one change
one's life: the recognition of the fiction, the realization
of the deception practiced upon us, makes us attempt to
escape the deception by becoming someone else, and thus the

fiction is replicated but also fulfilled. We are asked to become the lost king, and in deciding to do so, our lives are changed. Or to put it another way: whoever becomes educated and learns that the castaway is not the lost king is bound to assume a part in the deception.

Third, Professor Marin shows that the castaway's deception is successful because of simulation. The castaway *looks* like the king and hence he is accepted *as* the king. In this operation is revealed another sense in which parable is extended metaphor: a metaphor creates a likeness out of things that are disparate but nevertheless possess hitherto undiscovered similarities. Parables build on this creation of likeness (and I remind you that the German term for parable is *Gleichnis*), but it is a likeness that exists via simulation. What is the difference between simulation and imitation? An imitation produces a representation; it is not like its object in all respects, and it produces a representation, moreover, in order to derive power from its object. A simulation reproduces the conditions of its object in order to develop an independent power. The castaway does not imitate the lost king; he *looks* like the lost king, and the power he derives from that resemblance becomes his own. It is dependent on his likeness, on his own physical features, and not on second-guessing the lost king. Thus the castaway gains a power that enables him to look forward to a kingship of his own making even though, paradoxically, it is a creation by simulation. What could keep the castaway honest in his kingdom? Certainly the possibility that the real king might return--and if you hear overtones here of Pascal's wager, you are thinking with me. The chance that the real king might return thus gives the castaway's kingship an eschatological coloring: the simulation may someday be checked against the real, and hence one had better be oneself in order to justify one's role. The implication of this is that the structure of parabolic narration is eschatological, and I mean just that. The parable not only demands completion and fulfillment through decisive action; it not only asks that one change one's life; it anticipates a radical change in world order--and in this way also it serves as a microform of kerygma. Above all, the parable is eschatological by its drive toward absorption. It exists in the expectation of the reality that will render it (the parable) superfluous. It is fragile, partial, tentative, just as language and just as ourselves. It wishes to fade through a greater illumination.

Thus, three essentially negative terms in Professor Marin's deep structure analysis--absence, deception, simulation--become positive when grasped in terms of the gospel parables, and we see that parable is structured so that it calls for decision, *metanoia*, and eschatological hope. I hope now that my response has not appeared to ignore or attempted to displace Professor Marin's study. Roland Barthes has remarked that the best interpretation of an imaginative text is another imaginative text, and I have tried very modestly to compliment and complement both Marin and Pascal by extending the language of their discourse, which in both cases is the language of parable.

RESPONSE TO LOUIS MARIN

Lou H. Silberman
Vanderbilt University

I sometimes wonder if we may not be engaged in an under-taking that makes more of the parable than meets the eye; that indeed, parables are only what they are and are nothing more; that they serve a particular purpose, which is to allow the parablist a chance to say what he wants to say. So it is only the opening of a door, a way of catching attention; in a sense a way of fooling the hearer so that the parablist may quickly get beyond the parable to what he has in mind.

There are some people who assume that everything is or must be a parable. Nothing can really be as simple as it appears. My teacher, Jacob Z. Lauterbach, told me of a man in his town in Austrian Gallicia--a sort of "enlightened one", still very pious but having fallen far enough from grace to have learned German--who had heard of the wonders of German literature and most particularly of Schiller's great tragedy *Wallensteins Tod*. So he read that masterpiece and read it over again and then read it a third time. He was convinced something was wrong. It simply could not be what it appeared to be. Who would waste time writing about a general and his death? Therefore, he applied to the understanding of the text that which he knew best, talmudic hermeneutics and thus dis-covered what *Wallensteins Tod* really meant. Unfortunately he did not disclose the secret to my teacher, so I am unable to tell you what *Wallensteins Tod* means.

When I read Professor Marin's paper and turned to
Pascal's *Discourse*, there suddenly came into my mind another
story--not a parable--by one of Pascal's contemporaries.
I said to myself, but this is exactly the same story. It is
by La Fontaine and is called, in English, *Puss in Boots*.
It begins: "There was once a miller who left no more estate
to the three sons he had but his mill, his ass, and his cat.
The division was soon made. Neither the clerk nor the lawyer
was sent for. They would soon have eaten up all the possessions. The eldest had the mill; the second, the ass; the
youngest had nothing but the cat." The story is, I know,
familiar to you. The cat--a talking cat as is proper in
such a tale--soon ingratiates himself to the King on behalf
of his master whom he refers to as the Marquis of Carrabas,
already an intimation of Pascal's castaway. One day, when
the cat knew that the King and his daughter--the most beautiful princess in the world--were to take a ride along the
river, he said to his master: "If you will follow my advice,
your fortune is made. You have nothing else to do but to go
and wash yourself in the river in that part I shall show you
and leave the rest to me." The Marquis [his simulated or dissimulated title] did what the cat advised without knowing why
or wherefore. While he was washing the King passed by. Whereupon, the cat began to cry out in a loud voice: "Help, help!
My Lord, Marquis of Carrabas is going to drown!" At the
noise, the King put his head out of the coach window and seeing it was the cat who had so often brought him such good
wild game, commanded his guards to hasten to the assistance
of his lordship, the Marquis of Carrabas. While they were
drawing the poor Marquis out of the river, the cat came up
to the coach and told the King that while his master was

bathing, there came by some rogues that went off with his clothes [--so he is now naked as the castaway--], although he had cried out, "Thieves! Thieves!" as loud as he could. The cat had, of course, himself hidden them under a great stone. The king sent for clothes suitable for one of high rank and--so the tale continues--"caressed him after a very extraordinary manner, and, as the fine clothes he had given him extremely set off his good frame--for he was well made and very handsome in his person--the King's daughter took a secret inclination to him. The Marquis of Carrabas had no sooner passed two or three respectful and somewhat tender glances, than she fell in love with him." The King invited him into his coach; the cat conquered the local ogre and bestowed his lands and possessions on his master, etc., etc., etc. The princess and the marquis were married and lived happily ever after. Pascal's parable is nothing but a tale for children.

Let me call your attention to yet another tale--a novel set in modern India by R. K. Narayan, *The Guide*. It is the story of a young fellow who had earned his living as--watch this--a guide; who had become involved in ever more complicated schemes to rise in the world; who had overstepped the bounds and found himself in prison, where, in his own words, he became "the master of the show" for his gift of gab that had both raised him up and brought him down did not fail him. He became *Vadhyar*--Teacher. On release from prison, wandering about aimlessly, he had idly taken over a place that once had been the abode of a holy man and had slowly become entangled and interwined in the life of a nearby village and the lives of the villagers. In the beginning, it had all been a sort of a well-intended joke. He had no plans to

stay but only to enjoy his momentary influence and the
material rewards gained by his verbal dexterity. In the
end, the faith of the villagers had seized and transformed
him. On the one hand, he knew himself to be only a guide
who had gone to prison and was indeed a fraud. But the
villagers knew he was a holy man, so that in the end, when
the village was endangered by drought and famine, he was
called upon to save it. He longed to stand up and shout:
"Get out, all of you, and leave me alone, I am not the man
to save you. No power on earth can save you if you are
doomed. Why do you bother me with all this fasting and
austerity?" But instead, he fasted, for rain, until at the
end: "The eastern sky was red. Many in the camp were still
sleeping. Raju could not walk, but he insisted upon pulling
himself along all the same. He panted with the effort. He
went down the steps of the river, halting for breath on each
step, and finally reached his basin of water. He stepped
into it, shut his eyes, and turned toward the mountain, his
lips muttering the prayer. Velan and another held him each
by an arm. The morning sun was out by now; a great shaft of
light illumined the surroundings. It was difficult to hold
Raju on his feet, as he had a tendency to flop down. They
held him as if he were a baby. Raju opened his eyes, looked
about, and said, 'Velan, it's raining in the hills. I can
feel it coming up under my feet, up my legs --' He sagged
down." The guide had become a guide. Or had he?

In each case we have the tale of an imposture. Only in
the first do we have a parable; or are all three parables,
two in potentiality, one in actuality? We know that it is
a parable because we are told so; we do not know that the
other two are not parables, but we do not know that they are.

Parables are then very strange things. We must pay careful
attention to them for they may be nothing more than stories
until we intend them to be more than that, but we cannot be
sure. Although anything as late as the 17th century causes
me uneasiness--I seldom venture beyond the early 5th century
--, nonetheless as we view Pascal's parable--seen now in a
dialectic relation with the "mere" stories I have brought
together with it--I find myself fascinated and excited as
I watch these words, these few lines develop. I suspect
that given the structure of Pascal's thought, given the
structure of French, of European intellectual life in the
17th century, we have come to understand, through Professor
Marin's exegesis, the manner in which this particular kind
of parable functions.

The question I have to ask of myself is, will it indeed cast light upon the kinds of parables in which I am
interested, the parables of the rabbis, the parables of the
New Testament? Or is not something else going on, something
in its own way more demanding and less demanding at the same
time? Which leads me to a crucial point that carries us back
to my teacher's acquaintance. One of the things that has
been missing in our discussion are the hearers of the parable;
the role they play. I have become more and more convinced
of the most important role or at least the no less important
role the hearers play along with the speaker. I have spent
a great deal of time studying preaching in the synagogues of
Galilee in the 5th century. Despite the many problems I still
face after 10 years of labor, one salient point has emerged.
I have discovered that there is a secret, unexpressed contract
between the preacher and the congregation. When he uses a
parable, there must be an agreement, a saying of 'yes' on his

hearers' part. He cannot force them to hear the parable; they have to be eager and ready to hear. And so it is with Pascal's parable as Professor Marin has indicated. A wide horizon of possible meanings is offered; there is that of the speaker; there are those of the audience as their own lives, their own minds, their own experiences play over his words and are illuminated by them. Out of this interaction, the action of the speaker, the reaction of the hearer confronted by the parable, a transformation occurs, as Professor Marin has pointed out in the case of the young duke. What is important, then, to recognize is that in dealing with parables we are not readers of a text but hearers of a discourse so, as we listen, we too find ourselves strangely warmed. We come to know that despite its deceptions—for in the beginning a parable deceives—a parable discloses as well. And it is this double movement that a parable is all about.

DISCUSSION

MARIN: I have just delivered a four hour seminar paper at
Cornell University on *Puss and Boots*. (Lou Silberman can
appreciate this after his comments.) The title was "A
Mythical Eucharist in a Seventeenth Century Fairy Tale".
I think you have pointed out a fundamental problem by comparing the approach of *Puss and Boots* to Pascal's parable.
We have in *Puss and Boots* in a different way what I could
call power speech; speech which transforms words into
things. For example, the cat is always lying, and at the
end of the play all of his lies become reality. The main
difference, from my point of view, is that in *Puss and
Boots* the king is not missing. That is very important,
for if you analyze carefully you will notice that the
king's presence frames all of the stories--for example there
is constant reference to the king and the king is always
present when something occurs--when the cat engages in
performative processes. First of all, I think we can relate this kind of story--that is *Puss and Boots* and Pascal's parable--to what Professor Patte calls cultural structure. And the argument of these stories recurs to the
general conception of language: representation, the relationship between language and being in seventeenth century
philosophy and metaphysics. To speak at the level of cultural constraints of the story, Pascal presents in this
survey a rather extreme case to the extent that his thought
moves within this cultural and philosophical conception;
but it is for the purpose of subverting this philosophical
framework. That is my first point.

Secondly, do you think that in our present way of dealing with problems of signs and signifying systems we have really moved out of this general framework? Some years ago I studied *Cartesian Linguistics* by Chomsky and I was interested in the way Chomsky thought of the seventeenth century grammar and logic of Pascal's France as sort of a nucleus for his own conception of language. We can find many examples here of the permanent philosophical grounds of our western conception of sign and signifying system.

So my intent was to use Pascal, who in the seventeenth century provided a subverting analysis of the conception of sign, in order to question our own structural analysis. So it was a parabolic way of posing the problem of the metaphysical or philosophical ground of our reflection. I don't think that scientific theories in the social sciences or linguistics are neutral. They are linked: they are based upon a general conception of language, man, etc. That is the way I tried to use Pascal in my paper. With respect to the relationship of the parable's role and the expressed contract between the preacher and the congregation, the parable was set to work without specifying the contract. You (Lou Silberman) are right in pointing out the difference between modern parables and the New Testament parables. That is because we have to think about the change in the audience to whom the parable is addressed. We have another type of community or society in which the only way the parabolic structure can work is through this kind of negation. The conditions of parabolic reception are changed.

Concerning the matter of "*raison des effets*" and the difficulty we have in translating it, I wonder if "*raison*", which is usually translated "reason" or "cause", does not refer to "ratio"--not in the sense of logos or cause, but as proportion. Pascal thought of *raison* not as reason, but within the realm of physics, as componential forces, a structure of manifestation of forces without any emphasis upon the metaphysical substance. It is just a way of showing the structure in which we compose effects of forces which are only knowable through their effects. From my point of view that is the real meaning of *raison* in this phrase *raison des effets*.

WHITE: I have what is perhaps a misguided question. Correct me if it is. I would like you to compare what I sense to be a fundamental binary system under which you are operating here with the binary system of Greimas and Lévi-Strauss. I see language functioning over against a meaningful absence. At the center of this system which you are working on, the missing king is the meaningful absence and the castaway is language functioning over against that absence as a system of meaning. You have a meaningful absence as one pole and a concrete symbol functioning in a polarity over against that absence, and the meaning of the whole structure comes out of that polarity. Whereas in Lévi-Strauss' and Greimas' binary systems it is between two more substantial poles--a metonymic polarity--a concrete plus its negation.

MARIN: I agree that there is a great difference. What I try to show through the text is in fact a kind of reflection about what is a signifying system in Pascal's sense. It is really an operation which intends to dissimulate the fact that there is a missing link, the very point which gives the system not only its consistency but also its meaning. The way in which the story tells us how it is missing, that there is a hole in the middle of the system, is dissimulated by a representational apparatus. Perhaps the system is a way of dissimulating the ontological existence of some elements which gives consistency to all of the terms.

I had in mind the reflection of some people like Lacan on the notion of subject. The fact is that Pascal's parables or metaphors are a way of closing or filling the holes which the chain of signifiers is endlessly attempting to reach. This is but a general reflection on the notion of subject. That is my point. It is a very difficult thing to move from the notion of model to the notion of strategy and the way that Pascal seems to me to use the notion of presenting is very similar, for example, to the use Lacan made of the Saussurian structure of the sign. It is a way of taking a definitive system and displacing it--that is the meaning of strategy--and a way of manipulating and simulating truth and being.

CHAPTER V

PARABLE, ALLEGORY, AND PARADOX

John Dominic Crossan

DePaul University, Chicago

What is laid upon us is to accomplish the
negative, the positive is already given.[1]
                    -Franz Kafka

What I claim is to live to the full the
contradiction of my time, which may well
make sarcasm the condition of truth.
        No semiology which cannot, in the last
analysis, be acknowledged as semioclasm.[2]
                    -Roland Barthes

The fact would seem to be, if in my situation one may speak of facts, not only that
I shall have to speak of things of which I
cannot speak, but also, which is even more
interesting, that I shall have to, I forget,
no matter.[3]
                    -Samuel Beckett

This paper is less interested in the semiology of any
individual parable than in the semiology of story and the
specification of parable as one of the types or modes of
story. Parable will be discussed in relationship to example
(or exemplary-story) and allegory in an attempt to fix the
meanings of these terms as precisely as possible.*

PARABLE AND PARADOX

The title of this section and much of its content is based on the work of Heinz Politzer and especially on his 1962 book, *Franz Kafka: Parable and Paradox*. He contends that parable is narrative paradox, paradox formed into story, and it is with that claim that I begin the discussion.[4]

CONTEMPORARY PARABLE

In explaining his definition of parable as *paradox formed into story* Heinz Politzer takes for model the 125th aphorism of Nietzsche's *The Joyful Wisdom* of 1882. The tradition of the Greek philosopher Diogenes following his lantern's light in search of an honest man was given to Nietzsche. But his own parable offers us a madman instead of a philosopher, seeking God not man, declaring God dead not alive, and repeating his indictment on all, including himself, as the murderers of God. "*We have killed him*--you and I." If, then, the seeker after God is himself among the murderers of God the paradox forces the final gesture of smashing his lantern to the ground. "Must not lanterns be lit in the morning?" Therefore, "He threw his lantern on the ground, and it broke and went out." We need more light now in the darkness after the murder of God, therefore, in-crease the darkness. Which Emily Dickinson had said a little earlier: "To Whom the Mornings stand for Nights, / What must the Midnights - be!"[5]

This paradigmatic example furnishes us with the core elements of parable. The first is paradox. The second is

story. And the third is their correlation as paradoxical
story. This is accomplished by effecting a structural reversal on a traditional or expected story at its deepest
levels. Politzer gives two examples, one from Camus and
the other from Kafka.

The Plague. "The only general insight Camus' plague
conveys to the reader is the realization that there are no
general insights to be gained." Politzer's summary finds
its concentrated reflection in this comment of Jarrou to
Rieux which Camus placed centrally in his novel. "A
hundred years ago plague wiped out the entire population
of a town in Persia, with one exception. And the sole
survivor was precisely the man whose job it was to wash the
dead bodies, and who carried on throughout the epidemic."
Once again from Politzer: "For Camus...the incomprehensible
remains incomprehensible, and a paradox takes the place of
any rational maxim conveyed by the narration. It is a kind
of metadidactic prose: at the core of the secret a new
mystery is hidden." I would underline that adjective,
"meta-didactic", and return to it a little later on.

The Trial. We might expect a story structured in a
nice, polite binary opposition as follows: The Law gives
sentence of death to one convicted of serious crime but
gives no death sentence to one innocent of such crime.
Kafka furnishes us with a single reversal of this expectation: the Law sentences K. to death and he never knows of
what he is accused. This paradox is concentrated once again
in a central incident "Before the Law". (I admit to finding
both central incidents in both novels much more devastating
in their brevity than the full novels which now contain them.)
A man seeks entrance to the Law but the doorkeeper continually

denies him entrance. He waits and waits and just before
his death he asks the Doorkeeper why nobody else ever
sought entrance to the Law. "No one but you could gain
admittance through this door, since this door was intended
only for you. I am now going to shut it." Once again the
paradox gives our expectation a reversal. One expects the
Doorkeeper to admit those for whom the door was intended
and to deny entrance to the unintended ones. But the
parable has the Doorkeeper (the Law) deny entrance to the
sole intended one. I underline that this is again a single
reversal because in very many of Jesus' parables we shall
find a double reversal and their artistry consists especially in the economics of this double reversal in a very
short story. Politzer summarizes the vision of Kafka in a
phrase that every theologian might well remember. "He
created symbols which through their paradoxical form expressed the inexpressible without betraying it."

BIBLICAL PARABLE

Politzer continues his analysis of the modern parable
with some comments on its ancient biblical predecessor. And
at this point I must disagree most strongly with his conclusions.

Biblical and contemporary parables agree in posing a
metaphysical challenge. What, then, is the difference?
"The modern parable differs, however, from its model in that
it no longer carries a clear-cut message but is built around
a paradox." But what if parable _is the_ clear-cut message?

There are, of course, biblical stories with a clear-cut message but there are also biblical stories which are parables in exactly the same sense proposed by Politzer for their contemporary situation, that is, parables as storied paradoxes. It is hardly fair to blame Politzer for finding clear-cut messages in the parables of Jesus since the tradition went to a lot of trouble adjusting them to have such clear-cut messages before passing them on to us.

But long before Jesus arrived there were parables in the Hebrew Bible. Ecclesiastes posed his paradoxes to the wisdom tradition and Ruth did the same for the legal tradition. Indeed, in a rather unusual conversion, Ruth started off as an example or exemplary-story (act like this and all will be well) and was later changed into a parable (What if Obed had divorced Ruth in "obedience" to Ezra-Nehemiah intransigence?). But the most magnificent parable in the Hebrew Bible is the book of Jonah which is the precursor for the parables of Jesus and the distant ancestor of the contemporary parabolic genre.

Scholarship once liked to argue how God got whales into the Mediterranean and prophets into whales and each out of the other without serious structural damage to either. The debate is almost as hilarious as the book of Jonah itself and must have surely rejoiced the iconoclastic soul of its author. Jonah is a parabolic lampoon, a parody directed at the very heart of the Bible. It converts into paradox the prophetic traditions themselves. It is, as John Miles so aptly put it, the Bible laughing at itself.[6]

Imagine, first of all, the expected and polarized activity of prophets and pagans against the biblical back-

ground. God calls the prophet to mission and obedience is
the immediate response. Amos established the pattern and
stressed its ineluctable necessity when he said to King
Amaziah of Israel, "I am no prophet, nor a prophet's son;
but I am a herdsman, and a dresser of sycamore trees, and
the Lord took me from following the flock, and the Lord
said to me, 'Go, prophesy to my people Israel'" (7:14-15).
Amos was not a professional seer but one called as it were
against his will, or at least his plans, and he had to obey.
But not so Jonah. This most unusual prophet is ordered by
God to go east to Nineveh and he flees instead west to
Tarshish ("from the presence of the Lord"). The prophet
disobeys and it takes the famous and comic transportation
by God's great fish to deposit him eventually in the right
direction (proleptic Suez Canal?). We also know what to
expect of pagans and especially of Ninevites. The three
short chapters of the book of Nahum combine high poetry
and equal hate in announcing the fall of the Assyrian
capital. "Woe to the bloody city, all full of lies and
booty - no end to the plunder" (3:1). This gleeful description of the sack of Nineveh concludes triumphantly,
"All who hear the news of you clap their hands over you.
For upon whom has not come your unceasing evil" (3:19).
Turn now to the book of Jonah. No sooner has this most
recalcitrant prophet announced the divine message in
Nineveh than this: "And the people of Nineveh believed
God; they proclaimed a fast, and put on sackcloth, from the
greatest of them to the least of them. The tidings reached
the king of Nineveh, and he arose from his throne, removed
his robe, and covered himself with sackcloth, and sat in
ashes. And he made proclamation and published throughout

Nineveh, 'By the decree of the king and his nobles: Let neither man nor beast, herd nor flock, taste anything; let them not feed, or drink water, but let man and beast be covered with sackcloth and let them cry mightily to God'" (3:5-8). From king to kine in sackcloth and ashes. Surely the most massive metanoia in all of biblical tradition.

The parable offers a paradoxical double or polar reversal. We expect prophets to obey and pagans, especially Ninevites, to disobey Yahweh, God of Israel. But the story presents us with a most disobedient prophet and with some unbelievably obedient Ninevites. I would emphasize the literary skill which effects a double paradox in this story as distinct from the single paradox of the contemporary parables seen earlier. But what Politzer found in his modern parables and denied to their biblical predecessors is most certainly present in the case of Jonah. The term *parable*, then, should be used technically and specifically, from ancient to contemporary example, for *paradoxes formed into story by effecting single or double reversals of the audience's most profound expectations*. The structure of parable is a deliberate but comic reversal of the expected story. It is not a literal reversal as if Jonah taught that all prophets were bad and all Ninevites were good. It lays bare the relativity of plot, of any plot, and because it is paradoxical it also precludes the possibility of having its own plot taken literally or absolutely. Parable is, to borrow Rilke's phrase, a "ruin that blazingly belies its name".[7]

MYTH AND PARABLE

The function of parable can be clarified by comparing it with myth. I am accepting *myth* in the technical sense given to the term in anthropology and folklore, and I accept the definition for it proposed by the French structuralist Claude Lévi-Strauss. In his 1955 article on "The Structural Study of Myth", he argued that "the purpose of myth is to provide a logical model capable of overcoming a contradiction".[8] Edmund Leach comments on this definition by saying that, "In every myth system we will find a persistent sequence of binary discriminations, as between human/super-human, mortal/immortal, male/female, legitimate/illegitimate, good/bad...followed by a 'mediation' of the paired categories thus distinguished."[9] Categories in binary opposition to each other must be given surrogate representatives whose reconciliation persuades us that the former opposition is mediated. If one cannot mediate love and war, life and death, it may still be possible to get the Goddess of Love and the God of War reconciled with one another. And if all this sounds too abstract and aseptic, Pierre Maranda has restated the theory in more interesting language. "Myth... is the expression of the dynamic disequilibrium which is the (acknowledged) powerlessness to build adequate homomorphisms between incompatible and hence disturbing facts. It is the expression of the reluctant acknowledgment that the event is mightier than the structure. But myth is also and more than anything else, the hallucinogenic chant in which man-kind harmonizes the vagaries of history—the chant hummed for generations in the minds of man and humming itself in the human mind (that innate dream to reduce continuous randomness to a final pattern) as hinted by Plato and Jung, or, better, as amplified by Chomsky and Lévi-Strauss."[10]

It is at this point that a most obvious question can be addressed to such a definition of myth. If one accepts the prevalence of binary oppositions as being fundamental to human thinking and if one accepts myth as mediation of binary contradiction, then, *what is the binary opposite of myth itself*? My own answer is that parable is precisely such a binary opposite and that it creates contradiction where before there was reconciliation and mediation. Just as Victor Turner found that *ritual* was bifurcated into rites of order and disorder, elevation and reversal, so must *story* be dichotomized as myth and parable.[11]

All of which W. B. Yeats told us even more clearly quite some time ago in his "Supernatural Songs":

> Civilisation is hooped together, brought
> Under a rule, under the semblance of peace
> By manifold illusion; but man's life is
>   thought,
> And he, despite his terror, cannot cease
> Ravening through century after century
> Ravening, raging, and uprooting that he
>   may come
> Into the desolation of reality:
> Egypt and Greece, good-bye, and good-bye,
>   Rome!

Over against the harmonious majors of myth we hear the dissonant minors of parable and are thus prepared for Yeats' ultimate challenge: "The last kiss is given to the void."[12]

JESUS AS PARABLER

It is possible to accept the preceding definition of parable, to agree that the genre's trajectory stretches from Jonah to Kafka, and yet to insist that none of this applies to Jesus since his stories are not parables but examples. They are, one might claim, storied models of conduct or storied warnings against misconduct. They would not be parables in the strict sense of storied paradox.

In the context of this paper, I do not wish to repeat arguments already in print against understanding Jesus' stories as moral examples.[13] I shall restrict myself to one classic instance studied from a literary rather than an historical viewpoint.

One preliminary point: A parable can be either metonymical or metaphorical, as in the famous distinction proposed by Roman Jakobson.[14] Metonymical parables will subvert world by reducing a vital *part* or *representative* to paradox while metaphorical parables will do so by converting a *model* or *microcosm* to paradox. Each type has advantages and disadvantages, depending on whether one wants immediate impact or permanent challenge. The story under consideration is a metonymical rather than a metaphorical parable.

I take as paradigmatic case Jesus' story of "The Good Samaritan". The phrase has become part of the language as a cipher for concerned assistance and we seldom realize that as first uttered it was, like square circle, an oxymoron.

I would ask you to forget everything or anything you know about the story's present setting or editorial interpretation within the gospel of Luke. Here is the story, the whole story, and nothing but the story:

> A man was going down from Jerusalem to
> Jericho, and he fell among robbers, who
> stripped him and beat him, and departed,
> leaving him half dead. Now by chance a
> priest was going down that road; and when
> he saw him he passed by on the other side.
> So likewise a Levite, when he came to the
> place and saw him, passed by on the other
> side. But a Samaritan, as he journeyed,
> came to where he was; and when he saw him,
> he had compassion, and went to him and
> bound up his wounds, pouring on oil and
> wine; then he set him on his own beast
> and brought him to an inn, and took care
> of him. And the next day he took out two
> denarii and gave them to the innkeeper,
> saying, 'Take care of him, and whatever
> more you spend, I will repay you when I
> come back.'

A perfectly balanced drama in four acts. In the first act the robbers do three things: strip, beat, and leave for dead. In the second and third acts the Priest and Levite do nothing. But in the fourth act the Samaritan negates the robbers by an opposite three counter-actions: medication, transportation, shelter.

How is the story to be interpreted? The tradition's answer is unanimous. Its first evangelical interpreter, Luke, takes it as an example and has Jesus conclude with, "Go and do likewise." And a contemporary philosopher, Paul Ricoeur, concurs, "The parable has turned the story into a pattern for action."[15]

I have asked you to ignore the present gospel setting of the story and I would ask you also, for a moment, to forget you know it comes from Jesus. This is admittedly artificial but it is a necessary discipline in order to see with fresh eyes a story we have never read with sufficient attention. Roland Barthes has said that "the (actual) author of a narrative should not be confused with the teller of the story; the traces of the teller are immanent to the story and therefore perfectly accessible to semiological analysis".[16] I shall be concerned with the *implicit narrator* rather than the historical author (Jesus). And just as there is an implicit narrator in any story so there can also be an *implicit hearer* or audience. As Tzvetan Todorov wrote concerning the implied audience in fantastic tales, "It must be noted that we have in mind no actual reader but the role of the reader implicit in the text (just as the narrator's function is implicit in the text)."[17] For example, who is the implied narrator and implied hearer in a story about a U.S. destroyer and a German submarine during World War II if it is entitled "The Enemy Below" or "The Enemy Above" or "The Enemies"? If, then, we ignore our knowledge that Jesus is the historical author for this story of the Samaritan, what can we learn about its implied narrator and implied audience from within the story itself?

Notice the way in which the actors are introduced into the drama: a man going down from Jerusalem to Jericho, a Priest, a Levite, a Samaritan. I would make two conclusions from this, and they are literary judgments, not absolutes. First, the story is told by a Jewish narrator to a Jewish audience. Places known to Jews (Jerusalem, Jericho) and functions equally well-known to them (Priest, Levite) are not explained or specified in any way. Therefore, they do not need to be. But the outsider, the Samaritan, is specified

exactly in his socio-religious situation. Recall the male
chauvinism that gives us Senators and Lady Senators or that
describes a woman as "an attractive grandmother" but seldom
reciprocates on "a handsome grandfather". And notice the
different implications of those two adjectives: handsome in
itself but attractive for others/males. An outsider thinks
of Jews and Samaritans. A Jew, naturally, thinks of us and
Samaritans. Second, the story is most likely told in a
Jerusalem setting. The choice of the Jerusalem-Jericho road
is made either because it is generally notorious for such
robbery ("A man was crossing Central Park late at night...")
or because it locates narrator and hearers in Jerusalem so
that one's first instinct in detailing a journey is to make
it from-there. If I have to give students a concrete example
of a journey it would usually be "from Chicago to..." This
setting in Jerusalem is also corroborated by the choice of
Temple functionaries later in the story.

A Jewish narrator tells a Jerusalem audience a story in
which Temple functionaries fail in human kindness and the
outcast Samaritan succeeds superbly in helping the wounded
Jew. You will note how it is taken completely for granted
that this man is a Jew and can be identified obliquely as "a
man going down from Jerusalem to Jericho" without any further
social or religious qualifications. What would be the reaction of such an audience to such a story? Imagine a contemporary parallel. A Roman Catholic priest preaches as
follows from a Belfast pulpit one Sunday. A "man from the
Falls Road" lies wounded; a Roman Catholic priest passes by;
an I.R.A. member passes by; a Protestant terrorist stops and
assists him. How does the congregation react? Does it hear:
Help those in need, or, even love your enemies? Any audience

so parabled knows immediately and viscerally that an example story demanding love of enemies should *put the enemy or outsider wounded by the roadside and have him helped by such as are in the audience* and not vice versa. An example puts the Samaritan in trouble and has the Jew help or puts the terrorist in the afflicted position and has the Catholic stop to help. Examples persuade but parables provoke.

The story of Jesus is not an example but a parable. It presents the audience with a paradox involving a double reversal of expectations. The forces of good (Priest, Levite) do evil; the forces of evil (Samaritan) do good. It is exactly the same structure as in Jonah where prophets disobey and Ninevites repent. And it is exactly the same structure found in Jesus' paradoxes or counter-proverbs. Who loses life, saves it; who saves, loses it. Who has, receives; who has not, gets it taken away. But just as the tradition attempted, rather unsuccessfully, to change these paradoxes back into proverbs, so it attempted, with no greater success, to divert the radical thrust of his parables by turning them back into the more normal channels so that parables became examples.

I said earlier that the tradition had been unanimous in taking "The Good Samaritan" as an example rather than as a parable. If you turn, however, from direct commentary by exegetes to indirect commentary by novelists the tradition is not quite so unanimous. Leo Tolstoy, as might be expected, reflects an example interpretation in his story, "What Men Live By". Simon the shoemaker sees something near a roadside shrine. "To his surprise it really was a man, alive or dead, sitting naked, leaning motionless against the shrine. Terror seized the shoemaker, and he thought, 'Someone has killed him,

stripped him, and left him here. If I meddle I shall surely
get into trouble.'" But he relents, covers the man with his
own coat and takes him home. He helps Simon so adeptly at
his craft that "from all the district round people came to
Simon for their boots, and he began to be well off". Finally,
the stranger reveals that he is an angel but before he departs he recalls their first meeting, "When the man saw me
he frowned and became still more terrible, and passed me by
on the other side. I despaired; but suddenly I heard him
coming back."[18]

Henry Fielding, however, offers a far different retelling of the story. Since he is much more interested in parodic
satire than in exemplaric conduct he senses far more accurately than Tolstoy the parabolic nature of the story of Jesus.
The incident is in Chapter XII (*"Containing many surprising
Adventures, which Joseph Andrews met with on the Road, scarce
credible to those who have never travelled in a Stage-Coach"*)
of his novel *Joseph Andrews*.[19]

Joseph is travelling on foot as was the man in Jesus'
story and exactly the same fate befalls him. "He was met
by two Fellows in a narrow Lane, and ordered to stand and
deliver...and both together fell to be-labouring poor Joseph
with their Sticks, till they were convinced they had put an
end to his miserable Being: They then stript him entirely
naked, threw him into a Ditch, and departed with their Booty."
It is an eighteenth century version of Jesus' summary, "fell
among robbers, who stripped him and beat him, and departed,
leaving him half dead".

The *successive* arrival of Priest, Levite, and Samaritan
is developed by Fielding into the arrival of a coach so that
there is a *simultaneous* dialogue between the negative and

positive reactions of the travelers to the man in the ditch. The coach has six main characters: Postillion, Coachman, Lady, her Footman, Old Gentleman, Young Lawyer. These engage in parodic debate over four major points (recall the Samaritan's action): to stop or not, to help or not, to transport or not, to clothe or not.

To Stop or Not? The Postillion wants to stop. The Coachman objects that "we are confounded late, and have no time to look after dead Men". The Lady wants to stop out of curiosity.

To Help or Not? The Coachman asks who will "pay a Shilling for his Carriage the four Miles: and the two gentlemen refuse to do so. But the Lawyer's reiterated warnings of their legal responsibilities make them all agree "to join with the Company in giving a Mug of Beer for his Fare".

To Clothe or Not? Lawyer and Gentleman refuse because they are cold and wish to keep their overcoats. The Coachman ("who had two great Coats spread under him") and the Lady's Footman refuse lest their coats become bloody. Finally, it is the Postillion who acts: "It is more than probable, poor *Joseph*...must have perished, unless the Postillion, (a Lad who hath been since transported for robbing a Hen-roost) had voluntarily stript off a great Coat, his only Garment, at the same time swearing a great Oath, (for which he was rebuked by the Passengers) 'that he would rather ride in his Shirt all his Life, than suffer a Fellow-Creature to lie in so miserable a Condition'."

Coachman, Lady and Footman, Lawyer and Gentleman all refuse assistance or do so for self-serving reasons. But it is the Postillion, the lowest member of the Coach hier-

archy, one whose rebuked swearing is an omen of his future
penal exile, who *stops*, who *goes* to Joseph, and alone will
clothe him with his own and only outer garment and so make
transportation to shelter possible.

It is clear that Fielding presumes one should give aid
to those in distress and that Jesus extends such aid even
to enemies. But these are the *presuppositions* rather than
the *points* of their respective stories. To say that Jesus
or Fielding created their stories to furnish models of
neighborliness is to interpret Kafka's *The Trial* as an
argument against police brutality and Camus' *The Plague* as
a model of medical assistance. I submit, in conclusion,
that Fielding has given us the only adequate commentary ever
written on Jesus' famous story.

This paper will not concern itself with how many other
parables are present among the stories of Jesus. "The Good
Samaritan" by itself locates him as a parabler on the generic
trajectory which extends from as long ago as Jonah to as recently as Kafka.

Ben Belitt has given several different definitions of
parable in discussing those of Kafka and Borges. His reference to parable "as a hermetic directive to the 'elect'"[20]
may be too much under the exclusive influence of Mark 4 and
its tradition but, elsewhere in the same article, he suggests
a far more satisfying definition of parable, one which
specifies what parables as narrative paradoxes can functionally effect. "Finally, as insights, parables serve what
might be called an epistemology of *losses*. Their value, as
knowledge, is to enhance our 'consciousness of ignorance'--
but that is the beginning of wisdom. The vocation of Socrates
began with a visit to the Oracle at Delphi and a 'parable',

and ended with a philosopher's conviction that 'I know that
I do not know'."

PARABLE AND ALLEGORY

This section is a review and a revision of what I said
concerning allegory in my book *In Parables*. The need for
rethinking that analysis arises both negatively in a growing
dissatisfaction with the distinctions there accepted, and
positively in an attempt to consider allegory under the rubric
of play. There is also a quite deliberate shift from a
romanticist to a structuralist basis of interpretation.

IDEAS OR IMAGES

In Parables argued a distinction between metaphor, in
which images led to ideas, and allegory, in which ideas
preceded and begot images. The distinction also proposed
the ascendancy of image over idea and, therefore, of metaphor over allegory. This seemed a fairly clear differentiation and one for which there was an extremely illustrious
pedigree since I could cite Goethe and Coleridge, Yeats and
Eliot in its favor.

Since that time, however, I have found it more and more
difficult to answer three questions which cumulatively seem
to destroy those distinctions as far as either coherent
theory or practical application are concerned. First, what
exactly is the difference between an image and an idea?
For instance, Borges opened "The Fearful Sphere of Pascal"

by saying that, "It may be that universal history is the history of a handful of metaphors",[21] and he closed it with the same sentence. If history is metaphors, images, are even the most abstract philosophies controlled by ideas or by images and what is the difference between them at such a depth? Second, *if* we can distinguish, how do we know whether a given author moved in creativity from idea to image or from image to idea? For example, in "The Antique Ring" Nathaniel Hawthorne has Edward Caryl tell Clara Pemberton, "You know that I can never separate the idea from the symbol in which it manifests itself."[22] Unless we could declare by critical fiat that a bad story is created from idea to image and all great ones move in the opposite direction, it would seem that a dualism based on such a distinction is of little practical value. Third, *even if* the distinction be accepted *and if* the creative dualism be acknowledged, why should we conclude that the movement from image to idea is intrinsically superior to its opposite? The usual argument is to take bad allegory and explain its failure because of idea's distortion of image and to applaud great allegory (as symbol or metaphor) because of the triumph of image. But, once again, we are back in critical fiat. There might also be other reasons and even more basic ones why some allegories are admittedly bad while others are creatively magnificent.

Robert Scholes and Robert Kellogg have made very precise criticism of this distinction between symbol/metaphor and allegory in their book on *The Nature of Narratives*.[23] The distinction is fundamentally a product of Romanticism where "this invidious distinction sees symbolism as being organic, non-intellectual, pointing to some mystical connection between the mind of the poet and that unreal world which is the shaping mind or soul behind actuality, wearing what we call the 'real' world as its vestment. In this essentially romantic view, allegory is contrasted with symbolism as being overtly intellectual and excessively didactic, reflecting the real world in a mechanical and superficial way." And whatever the value of "this invidious distinction" for *lyric poetry*, it is of little value or validity for *narrative art* which "requires an irreducible minimum of rationality which inevitably tames and limits the meaning of the vaguest of images".

In seeking to leave aside this romanticist distinction between image and idea, or symbol/metaphor and allegory, I am also very conscious of the accusation of Paul de Man in "The Rhetoric of Temporality".[24] He "tried to show that the term 'symbol' [metaphor] had in fact been substituted for that of 'allegory' in an act of ontological bad faith" within romanticist criticism.

MOTIVES FOR ALLEGORY

Why would anyone want to tell a story which can be read on different levels and with diverse meanings? Critics have indicated four major reasons or motives for allegory, or, better, four main functional effects of the mode. Allegory circumvents opposition, creates separation, establishes continuation, and reveals structuration. No doubt these four merge and intertwine with one another in any given allegorical work but their distinction is helpful both to note emphases and because they indicate a more and more profound effect of allegory as one moves from the first to the last result.

OPPOSITION. You wish to tell your story, be it to re-call the past, to support the present, or to invoke the future, but you must do so in coded fashion because of per-secution. The motive here is protection of oneself against oppression and of one's message against censorship. The story communicates to insiders but not to outsiders. This is the motive stressed in Angus Fletcher's book, *Allegory: The Theory of a Symbolic Mode*. He says, for example, "Allegory...appears to express conflict between rival authorities, as in time of political oppression we may get 'Aesop-language' to avoid censorship of dissident thought. At the heart of any allegory will be found this conflict of authorities." And again, later, "Allegory presumably thrives on political censorship."[25] This motive is well known from certain books of the Bible such as Daniel and Revelation and from the apocalyptic tradition in general. Jews persecuted by Syria or Christians oppressed by Rome announced defiantly but allegorically their security in God's ultimate and proxi-mate justice for them and against their imperial persecutors.

SEPARATION. This is the motive for allegory studied by Michael Murrin in *The Veil of Allegory*.[26] For him the primary reason for allegory is less fear of persecution than fear of profanation by misunderstanding. Allegory, he claims, wishes to make a separation within its hearers to divide those who really understand from those who hear but do not comprehend. The story creates deliberately, a separation of insiders and outsiders. For example, "The allegorical poet... expends much of his energy in protecting his truth from the multitude rather than in communicating it." Fletcher had emphasized the motive of protection against opposition as in the apocalyptic tradition of the Bible. Murrin, on the contrary, stresses the divisive judgment of the prophetic tradition. "The allegorical poet affects his audience more in the manner of a Hebrew prophet than in that of a classical orator." Both speak and cause division, only the few understand while most cannot comprehend the message. The allegorical poet deliberately creates such a minority and rejoices in its elitism but the prophet does not will it nor rejoice in its presence. He simply mourns its inevitability. I find this interpretation much more persuasive for the allegorical poet than for the Hebrew prophet and would tend to bracket completely everything concerning this latter tradition in Murrin. But allegory can certainly be used in a conviction that only a few will take one's message whole and complete while most will distort and misunderstand it. "He had, therefore, simultaneously to reveal and not to reveal his truth, and for this double purpose he cloaked his truth in the veils of allegory. The many reacted with pleasure to his symbolic tales, and the few knew how to interpret them." This may be acceptable as a motive for allegory but it is somewhat strange as a comment on Hebrew prophecy. There the audience knew all too well what the prophet was saying. The problem was not misunderstanding but disobedience and the result was martyrdom not mystery. Amos' succinct greeting, "hear this word, you cows of Bashan", was presumably quite clear to the women of Samaria and while one might consider it as veiled allegory, it is doubtful if anyone in Israel needed much translation for it.

CONTINUATION. This is a more interesting purpose which intends to strengthen the persuasive power of one's story by basing it on another one which is either better known or more secure in its structure and conclusion. It establishes the continuity of the tradition and mades novelty more acceptable as well as the past more continually viable. When, for example, human actions or historical events are told in terms of the world of nature, they take on a borrowed inevitability and an intensely persuasive teleology. If heaven is harvest, then, of course, heaven will come. Edwin Honig noted this motive in his *Dark Conceit: The Making of Allegory*.[27] The new and unproven story corroborates itself by retelling an old and accepted one, and continuation is thereby established and demonstrated. "We find the allegorical quality in a twice-told tale written in rhetorical, or figurative, language and expressing a vital belief....The twice-told aspect of the tale indicates that some venerated or proverbial antecedent (old) story has become a pattern for another (the new) story." Such an antecedent could be nature, the animal world, legend, sacred book, or whatever is judged to strengthen and corroborate the new by establishing continuity with the old.

STRUCTURATION. This fourth effect may well be the least obvious, but also the most important result of allegory. When a story can be read on many different levels, such integrated structuration can be seen as the deliberate traces of divine intentionality. These layered correspondences are there to be found by us because a divine wisdom created all of them and in finding them we are but climbing similar rungs towards their common source. Allegory reveals at every level of world a similar structuration and this is,

as it were, an indirect, and therefore much more powerful
argument from design for the existence of God. As early
as the fifth century, John Cassian taught that there were
four separate levels of meaning in the Bible since, for
example, *Jerusalem* could mean an historical city in Pales-
tine, Christ and his Church, the human soul, or Heaven.
Biblical stories could thus be read in terms of the past
of Old Testament promise and New Testament fulfillment,
the present of moral action, and the future of eschata-
logical sanctions. If you have any doubt about the power
of such a hermeneutic, you may recall that it was still
viable in the Renaissance which believed, in the words of
Meyer Abrams, that "the divine Architect has designed the
universe analogically, relating the physical, moral, and
spiritual realms by an elaborate system of correspondence".[28]

Against such a background it is clear why allegory and
morality became so closely identified. The structures of
Old and New Testament, of history and eschatology, of Christ
and Church all pressed as models upon the individual human
soul which had to do this and avoid that under pain of
alienation from all the structures of reality. It was presumably considerations such as these that led to an absolute
dismissal of the mode on the part of Henry James. "Allegory
to my sense is quite one of the lighter exercises of the
imagination. Many excellent judges, I know, have a great
stomach for it; they delight in symbols and correspondences,
in seeing a story told as if it were another and a very
different story. I frankly confess that I have as a general
thing but little enjoyment of it, and that it has never
seemed to me to be, as it were, a first-rate literary form....
It is apt to spoil two good things--a story and a moral, a

meaning and a form; and the taste for it is responsible for
a large part of the forcible-feeble writing that has been
inflicted upon the world."[29] Apart from noting once again
the identification of allegory and example ("a moral"), one
finishes that quotation with the feeling of having just read
an epitaph. Is this, then, the end? Can nothing be said in
praise of allegory?

ALLEGORY AS PLAY

If that citation from Henry James reads like epitaph,
the following must stand against it as epigraph. "We seem
to have moved from an open-ended, anthropocentric, humanistic,
naturalistic, even--to the extent that man may be thought of
as making his own universe--optimistic starting point, to one
that is closed, cosmic, eternal, supernatural (in its sober-
est sense), and pessimistic. The return to Being has returned us to Design, to microcosmic images of the macrocosm,
to the creation of Beauty within the confines of cosmic or
human necessity, to the use of the fabulous to probe beyond
the phenomenological, beyond appearances, beyond randomly
perceived events, beyond mere history. But these probes are
above all--like your Knight's sallies--challenges to the
assumptions of a dying age, exemplary adventures of the Poetic
Imagination, high-minded journeys toward the New World and
never mind that the nag's a pile of bones." The words are
from Robert Coover's superb "Dedicatoria y Prologo a don
Miguel de Cervantes Saavedra" which prefaces his "Seven
Exemplary Fictions" in *Pricksongs and Descants*.[30] It is
time, it would seem, to take another look at allegory.

I have selected a very short parable of Franz Kafka as
a case study and, once again, I am very indebted to the
analysis of Heinz Politzer. In order not to prejudice the
discussion by a summary, I quote the story in full.

> It was very early in the morning, the streets
> clean and deserted, I was on my way to the
> railroad station. As I compared the tower
> clock with my watch I realized it was al-
> ready much later than I had thought. I had
> to hurry, the shock of this discovery made
> me feel uncertain of the way, I was not
> very well acquainted with the town as yet,
> fortunately there was a policeman nearby, I
> ran to him and breathlessly asked him the
> way. He smiled and said: 'From me you want
> to learn the way?' 'Yes,' I said, 'since I
> cannot find it myself.' 'Give it up, give
> it up,' said he, and turned away with a
> sweep, like someone who wants to be alone
> with his laughter.[31]

Imagine, as adapted from Politzer, some different interpretations or variant readings of this story. They are representative rather than restrictive. There could be more and even
these tend to mingle with one another.

In an *autobiographical* reading the policeman is Kafka's
father and this can be backed up quite convincingly with
quotations from his 1919 *Letter to His Father*. A *psychological* reading sees the story as an image of acute neurasthenia
in which the patient's search cannot find either the right
time or the right place and ends in frozen immobility. (I
spare you phallic clocktowers, etc.) A *sociological* reading
might discuss the claustrophobic trap of the ghetto in which
a Jewish community was immersed in a Slav city like Prague.
An *historical* reading would emphasize the ineffectual police

See Politzer; p. 14 especially: Heinmann admits that all these interpretations are finally inadequate to explain the story. The only alternative is ... to take the story as an allegory of

273

power of the Hapsburg monarchy which had been overthrown some-
time before the story was written. A *metaphysical* reading
might see in the policeman's refusal to arbitrate direction
the waning power of philosophy to answer the questions posed
to it. And a *religious* reading could find in the policeman's
silence a vision of the death of God. With analytic imagination and interpretive sensitivity any or all of those readings
could be argued most persuasively. And so no doubt could
many more we cannot even envisage at present.

What conclusions can be drawn from the above discussion?
First, the story defies singularity or univocity in its interpretation. Second, the story demands plurality and multiplicity in its reading. Third, and most important, the story
itself is a metaphor for those first two points taken together. What does the story mean? Where is the correct interpretation? The only answer, and this comes from the story
itself, is: "Give up" that question, "Give up" that search.
The policeman in the story is the story about the policeman.
Allegory allegorizes allegory. The story always has the last
laugh.

Notice, however, that it is not a question of multiple
interpretations on the same level as in the various possible
solutions to a murder mystery. It is a question of multiple
levels of interpretation on each and all of which the story
makes excellent sense, levels which range from personal to
social, from psychological to sociological, and from philosophical to theological.

I think that this gives us a helpful insight into
allegory in its most intrinsic and challenging dimensions.
An allegory is a story whose plurality of interpretive levels
indicates that the original is itself a metaphor for that

Why is it a metaphor for plurality

Or is it not an attempt to defeat interpretation.

multiplicity. The multiple levels of reading do not derive
from authorial indecision, linguistic incompetence, or
critical misapprehension. These various levels developed
by analysis are but the obedient reflection of the multiplicity imaged in and by the story itself.

This can be illustrated from a more contemporary allegory, the beautiful and beguiling novel *The Last Unicorn* by
Peter S. Beagle. And I believe in unicorns when novels can
open like this: "The unicorn lived in a lilac wood, and she
lived all alone. She was very old, though she did not know
it, and she was no longer the careless color of sea foam,
but rather the color of snow falling on a moonlit night.
But her eyes were still clear and unwearied, and she still
moved like a shadow on the sea."[32] The major protagonists
are the White Unicorn and the Red Bull and the story concerns
the Unicorn's quest to free her fellows from the power of the
Bull. I leave it totally to your imagination to interpret
the story on all the varied levels suggested earlier for
Kafka's parable. But the ultimate victory of the White Unicorn consists in being joined with a myriad of her kind from
out the sea where the Bull had trapped them in the whitecaps.
And it is the Red Bull who departs there all alone. The
magic of multiplicity is against the tyrany of univocity
and therefore demanded in the interpretation. This is also
the morality of the story. There is none of the usual reinforcement of standard virtue or punishment for standard vice
which has made allegory almost synonymous with example and
about as desirable as well.

This, then, is what allegory is all about at its best
and deepest level. Allegory is plot at play. It makes us
aware that one single story containing one single plot can

be read on every level we can imagine, from the most person-
ally private to the most cosmically transcendant. It reveals
the relativity of plot not only within the novel itself but
across all the realms of world and of reality. Why be surprised, it asks us, to discover that the way we structure an
autobiography may be exactly how we structure an epoch or
that private life and public theology may have a similar
isomorphic structuration. But here now is a most important
parting of the ways. At another time and in another place
this would have been explained, as I noted earlier, in terms
of divine design and divine purpose. In this time and in
this place I find another conclusion more compellingly imperative. It is the structuring processes of the human imagination which are at work in *all* these levels of interpretative possibility. It is the same imagination, the same
playful human imagination, which is at work in fiction, in
history, and in philosophy, and what wonder then if it can
produce a single plot which can be read on all these variant
levels.

Allegory is the laughter of plot, the triumphant
laughter of the human imagination at play with plot and in
plot. As Mikhail Bakhtin put it, "Laughter purifies from
dogmatism, from the intolerant and the petrified; it liber-
ates from fanaticism and pedantry, from fear and intimidation,
from didacticism, naivete and illusion, *from the single meaning, the single level* [italics mine], from sentimentality."[33]

There are many devices to reveal the necessity and the
relativity of plot in works of fiction and one recalls the
quite extravagant praise lavished by Victor Shklovsky[34] on
Sterne's *Tristram Shandy* for precisely this aspect of its
artistic creativity. Allegory, however, goes much deeper

than this because it reveals to our startled eyes the ubiquity
and universality of plot across all the creativity of the
playful human imagination, from autobiography to theology and
from psychology to philosophy. "Because men have seen no
unicorns for a while does not mean they have all vanished."

PARABLES AND ALLEGORIES

In classical allegory it made little difference whether
one dealt with two clear levels in the story or admitted the
possibility of multiple meanings. Medieval exegesis, for
example, could give the Bible readings almost as diverse and
as interesting as Politzer recorded for Kafka's discussed
earlier. But meanings however multiple or readings however
diverse were all held in structured harmony as layers of
divine causality and one could climb by analogy to their
common source in God. This made allegory and example so in-
tertwined that moral or exemplaric allegory is almost tau-
tologous. What God did was the most precise and imperative
model for human action and conduct and all those layers of
medieval exegesis were fraught with both ethical admonition
and moral persuasion.

A contemporary theory of allegory and a modern reading
of ancient allegory has no such security and no such serenity.
Multiplicity now bespeaks the inevitability of imaginative
structurations and hence their isomorphic relationships and
if one invokes transcendance in such a situation it must be
found not by a climb in light but rather by a leap in darkness, not as the Topmost Rung but as Altogether Off Our
Ladder. This means that allegory in a contemporary reading

will no longer be securely bonded to example but will appear
much more wedded to parable. Its multiplicity will no longer
be that of reiterated example but that of insoluble paradox.
Allegory, to borrow from Roland Barthes in another context,
is not an apricot with a stone set in its centre and we in
search of that stone, but an onion whose manifold layers
constitute its totality and whose multiplicity is its message.[35] We have been taught, of course, to prefer apricots
to onions.

When allegory is understood in this contemporary sense
it is quite possible to discuss Jesus as both a parabler and
an allegorist. No matter at what level his stories are read,
the paradox is still there. And this is axiomatic. An allegorical parable retains the paradox at the heart of every
reading. When the paradox disappears in any reading we have
slipped into an allegorical example.

In all this discussion I presume a fundamental distinction between what Jesus' language said and what the present
interpretive frames of the tradition's transmission record
for us. Jesus' stories were parables, narrative paradoxes,
and if they are read allegorically that original paradox
should still be there on any and every level of reading.

CONCLUSION

Paradox is to parable as proverb is to example. And the
generic trajectory of parable, as narrative paradox, as paradox formed into story, extends, for instance, from Jonah
through Jesus to Kafka.

Allegorical examples induce good conduct and preclude bad conduct by placing such actions in isomorphic structuration with all the various levels of externally established reality.

Allegorical parables present us with paradox on every level of interpretation or application. I interpret the presence of such narrative paradox as the admission that story is *both* ubiquitous and artificial. Allegorical parable is the conscience of plot, the revelation of plot's created isomorphism, and the epiphany of plot's absolute necessity not as *this* or *that* but as *some* structuring of the human imagination at play.

In this sense, then, "The Stone Fisherman" by Bertolt Brecht can be taken as a parable of parables:

> The big fisherman has appeared again. He sits in his rotted boat and fishes from the time when the first lamps flare up early in the morning until the last one is put out in the evening.
>
> The villagers sit on the gravel of the embankment and watch him, Grinning. He fishes for herring but he pulls up nothing but Stones.
>
> They all laugh. The men slap their sides, the women hold on to their bellies, the children leap high into the air with laughter.
>
> When the big fisherman raises his torn net high and finds the stones in it, he does not hide them but reaches far out with his strong brown arms, seizes the stone, holds it high and shows it to the unlucky ones.[36]

NOTES

*This paper is excerpted from sections of a book recently completed for Harper & Row. The title is *Raid on the Articulate*, and it is subtitled *Comic Eschatology in Jesus and Borges*.

1. F. Kafka, *The Great Wall of China*. New York: Schocken, 1960, p. 284.

2. R. Barthes, *Mythologies*. New York: Hill & Wang, 1972. The quotations terminate the introductions to the 1957 and 1970 French editions.

3. S. Beckett, *The Unnameable*. New York: Grove Press, 1958, p. 4.

4. H. Politzer, "Franz Kafka and Albert Camus: Parables for Our Time," *Chicago Review* 14/1 (Spring, 1960) 47-67; *Franz Kafka: Parable and Paradox*. Ithaca, N.Y.: Cornell University Press, 1962. Rev. & expanded, 1966, pp. 84-85.

5. E. Dickinson, *The Poems of Emily Dickinson*. Ed. T. H. Johnson. 3 vols; The Belknap Press of Harvard University Press, 1955. Vol. 2, p. 771 (#1095).

6. J. Miles, "Laughing at the Bible: Jonah as Parody," *The Jewish Quarterly Review* 65 (1975) 168-81.

7. R. M. Rilke, *Poems 1906 to 1926*. Trans. J. B. Leishman. New York: New Directions, 1975, p. 239.

8. C. Lévi-Strauss, "The Structural Study of Myth," *Structural Anthropology*. Garden City, N.Y.: Doubleday, 1967, p. 226.

9. E. Leach, *Genesis as Myth and Other Essays*. Cape Editions, 39; London: Cape, 1969, p. 11.

10. P. Maranda (ed.), *Mythology*. Baltimore, Md.: Penguin, 1972, p. 213.

11. V. Turner, *The Ritual Process*. Chicago: Aldine, 1969, pp. 109-13, 128, 169, 176-78, 185, 191.

12. W. B. Yeats, *The Collected Poems of W. B. Yeats*. Def. ed. New York: Macmillan, 1956, p. 287.

13. J. D. Crossan, *In Parables. The Challenge of the Historical Jesus*. New York: Harper & Row, 1973. See also, since this book, "Structuralist Analysis and the Parables of Jesus," *Semeia* 1 (1974) 192-221; "The Good Samaritan: Towards a Generic Definition of Parable," *Semeia* 2 (1974) 82-112, 121-28; and, *The Dark Interval. Towards a Theology of Story*. Chicago: Argus Communications, 1975 [June].

14. R. Jakobson & M. Halle, *Fundamentals of Language*. Janua Linguarum, NR 1. 'S-Gravenhage: Mouton, 1956, pp. 52-82.

15. P. Ricoeur, "The Socius and the Neighbor," *History and Truth*. Evanston, Ill.: Northwestern University Press, 1965, pp. 98-109.

16. R. Barthes, "Introduction à l'analyse structurale des récits," *Communications* 8 (1966) 1-27 (see 19).

17. Todorov, *The Fantastic*. Cleveland: Case Western Reserve University Press, 1973, p. 31.

18. L. Tolstoy, "What Men Live By," *Twenty-Three Tales*. New York: Oxford University Press, 1971, pp. 55-82.

19. H. Fielding, *Joseph Andrews*. Ed. M. C. Battestin. Middletown, Conn.: Wesleyan University Press, 1967, pp. 51-57.

20. B. Belitt, "The Enigmatic Predicament: Some Parables of Kafka and Borges," *TriQuarterly* 25 (1972) = *Prose for Borges*, pp. 268-93 (see 270, 272, 273).

21. J. L. Borges, *Other Inquisitions 1937-1952*. New York: Simon & Schuster, 1965, pp. 6-9 = *Labyrinths*. New York: New Directions, 1964, pp. 189-92.

22. N. Hawthorne, *Hawthorne's Short Stories*. New York: Knopf, 1964, pp. 399-410 (see 410).

23. R. Scholes & R. Kellogg, *The Nature of Narrative*. New York: Oxford University Press, 1966, pp. 106-7.

24. Paul de Man, "The Rhetoric of Temporality," *Interpretation: Theory and Practice*. Ed. C. S. Singleton. Baltimore, Md.: Johns Hopkins Press, 1969, p. 194.

25. A. Fletcher, *Allegory: The Theory of a Symbolic Mode*. Ithaca, N.Y.: Cornell University Press, 1964, pp. 22 & 238.

26. M. Murrin, *The Veil of Allegory*. Chicago: University of Chicago Press, 1969, pp. 9, 22-23, 168.

27. E. Honig, *Dark Conceit: The Making of Allegory*. Cambridge, Mass.: Walker-de Berry, 1960, p. 12.

28. M. Abrams, as cited in Paul de Man [see p. 266 above], p. 179.

29. H. James, as cited in E. Honig [see p. 269 above], p. 52.

30. R. Coover, *Pricksongs and Descants*. New York: New American Library, 1969, p. 78.

31. H. Politzer [see p. 268 above], pp. 1-22.

32. P. S. Beagle, *The Last Unicorn*. New York: Ballantine, 1969, pp. 1 & 6.

33. M. Bakhtin, *Rabelais and His World*. Cambridge, Mass.: MIT Press, 1968, p. 123.

34. V. Shklovsky, *Russian Formalist Criticism: Four Essays*. Eds. L. J. Lemon & M. J. Reis. Lincoln, Neb.: University of Nebraska Press, 1965 [1921], pp. 27-57.

35. R. Barthes, "Style and Its Image," *Literary Style: A Symposium*. Ed. S. Chatman. New York: Oxford University Press, 1971, pp. 1-15 (see 10).

36. B. Brecht, *Selected Poems*. Trans. H. R. Hays. New York: Grove Press, 1947, p. 145.

RESPONSE TO JOHN DOMINIC CROSSAN

John R. Donahue
Vanderbilt University

In commenting on Professor Crossan's interesting and evocative paper, I make the initial caution that I approach semiology and structuralist exegesis somewhat with the fascination of a little boy peeking through the knothole of a construction site. I am intrigued by the materials and the bustle of activity, but am not sure what the completed structure will look like. My own approach to the parables has been from the viewpoint of redaction criticism and general literary criticism, and, it is only in the reading I have done in recent weeks, that I have begun to appreciate the depth of learning and complexity of issues raised by the work done on the parables, as evident in the *Semeia* volumes. If, in my comments, I betray a naïve understanding of aspects of structuralism, I beg the indulgence of the more expert critics.

Professor Crossan's paper raises some points of clarification. If I understand him correctly he is saying that the ultimate structure of that form of symbolic speech which we call both parable and allegory is found in paradox. He writes that parables are paradoxes formed into stories which effect single or double reversals of the audience's expectations. He then states that the difference between allegory as example and allegorical parable is that in the latter case, paradox is "at the heart of every reading" (p. 275). Crossan's understanding of paradox needs further refinement,

and the relation between paradox and irony should be touched
upon. Since the term paradox is used in such a wide sense
to describe the quality of "religious" language as well as
diverse mythic structures, I fear there is danger that the
term is so broad and comprehensive that it may not be very
helpful in a discussion of the particularity of the structure of parable or allegory in contrast to any other kind of
symbolic or figurative language. A second area of clarification centers on Crossan's distinction between allegory as
example and allegory as parable. It is not clear whether
this distinction is synonymous with the distinction between
allegorical interpretation and the creation of independent
allegories. The use of Fielding seems to deny such a distinction, while the use of Kafka seems to presuppose the
distinction.

Apart from these questions of clarification, I would
like to direct the major portion of my remarks to what I
will call Crossan's "turn toward allegory". I admire his
creativity in challenging the now overworked distinction
between parable and allegory where parable culminates in
one point of comparison to the expense of the details of
the parable, and where allegory is seen as a series of
random comments on these details which originate in the presuppositions of the allegorist rather than in confrontation
with the thrust of the original text. I would like to suggest that the turn toward allegory is a necessary development from Professor Crossan's engagement in structuralist
exegesis and that this necessity arises from three sources:
(1) the nature of *parabolē* as this is found in the New
Testament, (2) the nature of allegory in imaginative lit-

erature, and (3) the nature of structuralist exegesis itself. Finally I would like to make a few comments on his treatment of the parable of the Good Samaritan.

1. The Nature of *Parabolē*

During the period after Jülicher and through the time when scholars such as Dodd, Jeremias and Linnemann posited an absolute distinction between parable and allegory, scholars such as Paul Fiebig, Matthew Black and Raymond Brown cautioned that the modern understanding of parable may not be faithful to the Greek *parabolē*, nor to its Hebrew counterpart, *māšāl*.[1] While it has been recognized that in the Old Testament *māšāl* is used for such widely differing material as proverbs, riddles, taunt songs, allegories and a long historical psalm (Ps. 78) recounting the saving history of Israel, and, in the Intertestamental literature, for long allegories in which hidden revelation is communicated to the elect, there is reluctance to admit that *parabolē* in the New Testament is as multifaceted as its Old Testament counterpart. In light of Crossan's turn toward allegory, and his discovery of a similar structure in both parable and allegory, must we not question whether further work on the structure of the parables can be limited to the narrative parables of the New Testament. In effect I am asking whether there is any structure which underlies not only the recognized parables of Jesus, but also much of the other discourse material which has been variously classified as apothegms, wisdom sayings, apocalyptic pronouncements, and which, in their own way, are as imaginative as the narrative parables and equally the heirs of the Old Testament *māšāl*. Another way of posing the question would be to ask whether there is any structural unity which allowed the ancient writers to describe such diverse material as *māšāl* or *parabolē*.

2. The Nature of Allegory

In his paper Professor Crossan analyzes allegories from a period later than the New Testament and finds that paradox unfolds into allegory, equally as into parable. He thus gives due credit to allegory as an artistic product of the human imagination. He writes that "an allegory is a story whose plurality of interpretative levels indicates that the original itself is a metaphor for that multiplicity" (pp. 273-274). In taking such a position Crossan not only legitimates allegory, but suggests that allegorical interpretation may be a valid interpretation of a parabolic original. Concretely, if we are to return to the New Testament we might have to question the manner in which allegorical interpretations within the New Testament itself have been handled. For example, the interpretation of the Parable of the Sower in Mk. 4:13-20 has usually been discussed only in negative terms as a misinterpretation of the parable of 4:1-9. Its positive value is seen only as an entree to the theology of the early church. Thus far little attempt has been made to suggest ways in which the allegory may be a valid trajectory from the original parable. If the original is a metaphor for the multiplicity of the allegory, questions should be raised as to how the motives which Professor Crossan sees at work in the formation of allegory (opposition, separation, continuation and structuration) are operative in the allegorical interpretation of the sower. In other words, what is the unity between the parable and its interpretation?

3. The Nature of Structuralist Exegesis

Thirdly I would like to suggest that the turn to allegory may well be the natural outgrowth of the desire of
structuralist exegesis or at least some branches of it to
seek the deep structure which underlies a given text. Dan
O. Via has written of structuralist exegesis that "structure
is applied from outside and is not derived from the book;
the book belongs to the structure without containing it",
and he states that Lévi-Strauss's ultimate goal "is to discover the very structure of the human mind".[2] In applying
this method to the parables the particularity of a given
text is quickly left behind in search of a structure which
unites different texts, whatever their final form or original function. It is my contention that it is this same sort
of quest, although in different guise, which lies behind
allegorical exegesis. In order to illustrate my point I
will take an example from this exegesis as it flourished
in the high medieval period. In distinguishing between the
sensus litteralis (the *literal* as well as the *literary*
sense)[3] and the *sensus allegoricus* or *mysticus*, the medieval
exegetes affirmed that behind the historical sense of scrip-
ture was a signification which permeated different levels of
human existence. The explanation which Dante gives in his
letter to Congrande della Scala best illustrates this point.
In describing his work, Dante says that it is not *simplex
sensus*, but *polysemum*, that is, of different levels of meaning.[4] Dante states that there is a sense *qui habetur per
literam* and another *qui habetur per significata per literam*,
that is a meaning which is found through those things which
are signified or pointed to by the literary sense. He then
goes on to illustrate the different senses by commenting on

the first verse of Ps. 114, "In the exodus of Israel from
Egypt, the house of Jacob from a barbarian people, Judaea
was made his sanctification; Israel, his power."[5]   On the
historical or literal level the psalm refers to the historical Exodus; on the allegorical to *nostra redemptio per
Christum*. The moral sense connotes the *conversio animae*
from grief and misery to the state of graciousness and the
anagogical sense is the *exitus* or departure of the soul from
the slavery of corruption to the liberation of glory.   The
constant in all these levels for Dante is the polarity of
bondage--liberation which exists for him on different levels
of existence and which all arise from the polysemous possibilities inherent in the first words of the psalm, *In exitu*,
the departure from one state to another.   Therefore the
medieval allegorist senses that behind the signification of
a given text is a series of deep significations which in
turn may be related to a whole complex of other significations which are found not only in other texts but also in
art and ritual. The point of contact I see between the
allegorical method as practiced in past centuries and the
quest for deep structure in contemporary structuralist
exegesis is precisely in the fact that when a text is
divorced from the particularity of its literary and historical context it becomes a code leading to deeper levels of
meaning which may, in effect, be as culturally bound and as
subjectively eclectic as the universe of theological discourse which characterized patristic and medieval exegesis.

4. Remarks on the Good Samaritan

It may be questioned whether Professor Crossan's exegesis of the parable as well as much of the recent exegeses

is true to the present literary configuration or context of
the parable. A presupposition of my remarks is that we no
longer have direct access to the parable as it was originally
uttered. Whatever form criticism says about reconstructing
the original words of the parable, we still have the parable
only as text, not as the form of oral communication in which
it first took life. My contention is that the parable as
text cannot be considered apart from text in context and the
primary context is the context the Evangelist gives it. The
context in the teaching of Jesus is always the result of
problematic reconstruction.

As the parable stands in the Lukan context it is part of
a unit which embraces the lawyer's question (10:25-28), the
parable itself (10:29-37) and the story of Martha and Mary
(10:38-42). The fact that these comprise a unit is supported
by the observations that in the surrounding verses (10:21-24
and 11:1-4), Jesus is pictured in a state of private and
public prayer, and the juxtaposition of the Good Samaritan
with Martha and Mary betrays the common Lukan compositional
device of joining together a story about a man with a story
about a woman. In his introduction to the parable Luke alters
his Markan source (Mk. 10:17-22) by reducing the two-fold
command to love God and neighbor to one great commandment.
It is my contention that the parable of the Good Samaritan
and the story of Martha and Mary constitute for Luke a two-
part illustration of the fulfillment of the commandment and
each does this by way of paradox. The Samaritan is an example
of one who is active in loving compassion for the neighbor,
and the paradox is that the one who does this is the hated
Samaritan. The story of Martha and Mary also functions as

parable and paradox. An initial paradox is conveyed by the picture of Mary "sitting at the feet of the Lord", which is a technical term for discipleship so we have the paradox of a woman as disciple. There is also surprise in Jesus' praise of Mary's inactivity, especially in a context so close to the Good Samaritan. Luke is saying, in effect, that the command to love is fulfilled by the double movement of going out to neighbor as well as a silent sitting before the Lord. This rhythm of non-activity, waiting and going out or movement is a pattern which characterizes major parts of Luke-Acts.

Therefore it seems that any attempt to arrive at the meaning of the Good Samaritan should not only take into consideration the structure and meaning of the parable as text, but also the possible structures and meanings that it receives in its present context. Parables which had a context originally in the ministry of Jesus and which now have a context in the work of a given Evangelist cannot be studied as if they were independent tales or a bit of folklore. Not only text but context must be the object of any exegesis be it structuralist or redaction, critical or historical.

NOTES

1. A. Jülicher, *Die Gleichnisse Jesus*, 2 vols.,
Tübingen: Mohr, 1888, 1899; C. H. Dodd, *The Parables of
the Kingdom*, rev. ed., New York: Scribners, 1963 [1st ed.
1935]; J. Jeremias, *The Parables of Jesus*, rev. ed., New
York: Scribners, 1963 [1st ed. 1947]; Eta Linnemann, *Jesus
of the Parables*, New York: Harper and Row, 1966 [1st ed.
1961]; P. Fiebig, *Altjüdische Gleichnisse und die Gleichnisse Jesu*, Tübingen: Mohr, 1904; M. Black, "The Parables
as Allegory," *BJRL*, 42 (1960), 273-287; R. Brown, "Parable
and Allegory Reconsidered," *NT*, 5 (1962), 36-45.

2. *Kerygma and Comedy*, Philadelphia: Fortress Press,
1975, pp. 7, 10.

3. Too often commentators translate *sensus litteralis*
as simply literal without realizing that this *sensus* also
embraces figurative language. For example, St. Thomas says
that the *sensus parabolicus* is contained in the *litteralis*,
Summa Theologica, I, art. 10, ad 3.

4. The quotes are taken from the Latin text of the
letter as found in *Tutte de Opere di Dante Alighieri*, ed.
E. Moore, Oxford: University Press, 1894, p. 415. The
translations are mine.

5. This is a literal translation from the Latin
Vulgate. The play on words which allows Dante to develop
the four senses of the text is lost when a proper translation
of the Hebrew original is used as in the R.S.V.

RESPONSE TO JOHN DOMINIC CROSSAN

John R. Jones

Vanderbilt University

In the vexed questions of generic distinctions the two
main criteria, developed through the religious and literary
analyses of texts, have been those of form and of function.
So myth, for instance, can be formally identified, as by
Gunkel in *Die Sagen der Genesis*, as "stories of the gods"
(*Göttergeschichten*)--a designation retained by Eliade[1] and
Frye.[2] On the functional side, myth is sacred narrative
which endorses man's significant activities, providing a
warrant for those deeds requisite to social order. So myth
serves the sociological function of preserving ancient mores,
re-affirming cultural values. This function, formulated by
Malinowski[3] in 1925 and refined by Eliade,[4] is in fact already recognized by Aristotle in his discussion of the
cathartic purpose of the Greek drama. In the classic message of tragedy that the will of the gods must rule is heard
the austere voice of Apollo: a higher rationality, a higher
order than man's is at work in the reversals and puzzles of
history. Man's role is that of Sophocles' Oedipus, who must
accede to that higher order, must discover and expiate past
wrongs, and restore the ancient virtues. Weal can only replace woe when social and moral order return.

But there is another way of providing for such order.
As Bascom has observed concerning "the basic paradox of folklore",

> while it plays a vital role in transmitting
> and maintaining the institutions of a cul-
> ture and in forcing the individual to con-
> form to them, at the same time it provides
> socially approved outlets for the repressions
> which these same institutions impose upon
> him.[5]

Here catharsis means release.[6] In Euripides' *Bacchae*, the
Thebans' sufferings are not now due to contraventions which
must be righted, but to Pentheus' unbending rule. Their
mantic revels foreshadow the ultimate release of the whole
land, with Pentheus' banishment. So myth's function of
preserving social order must first be acknowledged to progress along two routes: from disorder to re-established
order, and from oppressive order to freedom and release.
If there is Apollo, there is also Dionysus.

This already suggests that within myth itself there is
room for the narrative counterparts to Turner's rites of
order and of disorder. To be sure, the second myth-pattern
exists ultimately for the sake of the order again. So in
fact do the rituals of reversal.[7] Our point here is simply
that the functional definition of myth (as a kind of folklore that re-affirms social order and religious values) may
itself present a sort of "disordering" mien. To the matter
of whole or broken models we must return later.

But the central question is the one of correlation
between these functional criteria of genre and the approach
of Lévi-Strauss. His criteria, derived not from literary
analysis but from linguistics and anthropology, are aimed
at defining myth as expressive of deep structures common to
man as man. The result is a treatment of myth on quite

another level of abstraction. Rather than the syntagmatic, diachronic aspect of myth as a recounting of deeds done in the primordial *Urzeit* (and thus warranting certain deeds/events in the present), we are confronted now with a static, paradigmatic "picture" of an unconscious structuring function of the human mind. "Myth as charter" becomes "myth as model".[8]

Such a model of course is not intended to elucidate questions of literary generic distinctions. Its focus on what is common to all forms of human communication enables Lévi-Strauss to seek it not only in such narrative forms as myths and folktales,[9] but also through systems of kinship and table-manners. The difficulty arises, then, just when we do accept "the prevalence of binary oppositions as being fundamental to human thinking".[10] How may so fundamental a conception point to "binary oppositions" between literary genres? For if this model is to be taken as Lévi-Strauss does, it places us on a more elementary plane or grid, quite below the generic distinctions.

Part of the difficulty, of course, is in Lévi-Strauss' own use of the word "myth". By interposing myth between the Saussurean levels of language as *parole* and as *langue*, he can represent it as combining the properties of both. On the one hand, myth is narration. "To be known, myth has to be told; it is a part of human speech."[11] As the spoken recounting of a story's sequences, it belongs to the non-reversible time of *parole*. On this level the question of genre has some bearing, for every human communication will be actualized in some generic mode. But this is not the level on which Lévi-Strauss focuses, precisely in his recognition of genre's culturally-specific nature. His quest for what is common to the operation of all human minds leads him to the reversible time of myth as *langue*. Here myth comprises the "specific pattern" of the timeless relationships underlying the narrative performance. Whatever Lévi-Strauss may mean by myth as a third level distinct from both these two, he is able to describe it only in its participation in them. And this bridging notion has doubtless contributed to the slipperiness of the term. This is in fact a matter of levels--levels which are fully intelligible only when each is viewed in relation to the other, but also only when each is preserved distinct from the other. And it is on this second, paradigmatic level that mythical thought reveals itself as mediating between polar oppositions. But to speak of myth here is no longer to speak of it as one of the sub-categories of "story", but to speak of one mental phenomenon --a phenomenon Lévi-Strauss in fact applies across generic distinctions and across cultures.

To come at the question from the cultural side, it is again a matter of the extent to which narrative and mythical levels are collapsed together--that is, the extent to which the religious and cultural setting is seen to impinge on the operation of the mythical structure itself. It is true that the mythical model is to be traced only when filled with a specific (narrative) content, just as the grammatical structure of a language is first discernible only through its syntagmatic performance. And that logical model is perforce filled in terms wholly meaningful only to its own native socio-religious setting. But the universal nature of the unconscious operation (as Lévi-Strauss would have it) requires that this deep-structural level be held separate from that of myth's narrative expression. As soon as we speak of the level of the narrative expression we must speak of culture. For the expression must take place in terms of one or another genre, to be intelligible to the culture it addresses. And a genre is a culturally-conditioned phenomenon.[12] The model itself, by contrast, claims to bear no reference, positive or negative, to culture. "A myth may well contradict the ethnographic reality to which it is supposed to refer, and the distortion nevertheless forms part of its structure."[13] It may be filled so as to reinforce or to undermine, but its operation is independent of that.

Such a reading of Lévi-Strauss' intent should still respect his refusal to drive a wedge between form and content. I do not mean to imply for him that "unconscious" necessarily means "unacculturated". For the filling of the deep-structural model in terms meaningful to any particular culture is itself an unconscious process, as well. And again, the form is to be traced only through its repeated and variant content, which will always address the culture which so invests it. But the humanist impulse, the universalizing anthropological thrust, and structuralism's debt to what Pouillon calls "*l'attitude totalisante*"[14] have combined in Lévi-Strauss to propose a model that transcends the interaction between literary genres and cultural patterns. Whatever may be the case for generic distinctions in terms of reinforcement or dissolution of cultural norms, that case does not rest upon the presence or absence of the deep-structural operation of mediating between binary oppositions. Two traditions have produced two sets of criteria for dealing with two levels.

If we should accept Lévi-Strauss' claims to universality for his model, the pattern should appear consistently in all forms of communication. A "polar reversal of the audience's profound expectations"[15] should not exclude it, nor should "reconciliation and mediation" be identified with reaffirmation of those expectations, if "mediation" here means the deep-structural operation of mediation between binary oppositions.

Such mediation is demanded by the construction of Lévi-Strauss' canonic formula, $F_x(a) : F_y(b) :: F_x(b) : F_{\bar{a}}(y)$, which follows the pattern of discontinuous analogy: "A is to B as C is to D." In this instance, the relationship between expressions A and B is one of binary opposition. Two functions and two states are combined in mutually exclusive poles. This opposition is mediated by the second pair, whose relationship is still one of opposition, but a closer opposition. The relation between expressions C and D may be called a metaphor for that between A and B. The mediating principle lies in the way in which they each borrow one term from each of the expressions in the first pair. Thus the analogy is not strictly discontinuous, after all. This is visible easily enough in expression C, whose components are x from A, and (b) from B. Expression D in fact does the same thing, employing (permutations of) the other two remaining components, (a) and y. In this way the two expressions C and D each participate in something of each of the first two poles. Such double participation moves C and D closer together than are A and B, and permits them to mediate that more fundamental opposition.

$$F_y(b)$$

$$F_{\underline{a}}(y)$$

$$F_x(b)$$

$$F_x(a)$$

We have called the relationship between expressions
C and D a metaphor for that between A and B. But there is
a certain contiguity in the C - D relationship, in the sense
that they represent the division of expressions A and B along
another axis:

$$F_y \leftrightarrow (b)$$
$$F_x \leftrightarrow (a)$$

Terms y and b, which were paired, now stand as counterparts,
as do x and (non-)a. In other words, what were contiguous
terms are now opposite each other.

This brings us to the special dynamic of the interaction
between C and D. If they are to provide a valid metaphor for
the relationship between A and B, they must likewise stand in
some sort of opposition to each other. Their contiguity does
not provide this. In fact if expression D were composed of
the two remaining terms, as an expected $F_y(a)$, then expressions C and D would simply consist of the same functions as
A and B, with exchanged states. Such an arrangement would
make of the entire formula a tautology, for it would be to
say that the only pertinent opposition is that between the

functions; the states are interchangeable. To hold the
second pair separate from the first, then, it is necessary
to open up a new opposition between them. This is achieved
through two alterations to the terms of expression D: the
reversal of the function and state values of terms "a" and
"y", and the nullification of term "a".[16] The first of
these two changes pits each function against its contrary
in state form. Such a twist provides for a different interaction between C and D from that between A and B.

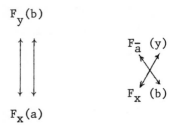

A and B in themselves represent an insoluble standoff;
function x is pitted against function y, state (a) against
state (b). Between C and D, however, this is no longer the
case. Here, the deadlock is broken: the functions, the more
dynamic aspect of each expression, are brought to bear upon
opposed states. Functions are characteristics which work
change; they effect the transformations from state to state
which comprise narrativity.[17] This is where the second
change becomes important, for it stacks the deck in favor
of C over D by effectively neutralizing D's function, so that
it is no threat to C's state. In narrative terms this means
that the hero, C, is able to overcome the situation of lack,
D, without himself being overcome by it.

So the Samaritan, for instance, can counter the
traveler's wounded and robbed state with his action of
healing and giving.[18] The effect is to initiate the
transformation of the traveler's state back to that of
being healed/enriched. As for the traveler, in the situation of lack his wanted orderly functioning is interrupted.
Not only is he unable to continue his journey toward Jericho; he is unable to order: to maintain his ordered universe by physically withdrawing from the Samaritan, or to
exert the Jewish demand that the Samaritan should become
part of his ordered universe. He has been rendered help-
less. This in fact is what brings the Samaritan and the
wounded man together. For it is precisely in his role as
a "chaos" figure that the Samaritan is able to reach the
man. If the Samaritan were himself set in the ordered universe of the traveler's definition, he like the priest and
Levite would remain separate, impervious to the man's
plight. But as it is, he is free to act. The traveler,
for his part, has not moved all the way to function b; he
has not become a "chaos-working" or "disordering" figure.
He is simply no longer functioning in his orderly capacity.
Since b is a sub-category of its implication, non-a, the
hero's state characterizes him as a part of the larger
category represented by the victim's nullified function.
This metonymic relationship allows the conjunction of the
two so they can interact. Because the Samaritan's state
is that of the "chaos" element, he is in contiguity with
the traveler's function, $\bar{a}$: "not acting in an orderly and
ordered manner". And out of this contiguity emerges the
rectification of the villainy. In sum, by virtue of the
state/function reversal, the Samaritan can act upon the

traveler to transform his state. Because of the second modification, the nullification of a, the traveler is not able
to change the Samaritan's state. And in their contiguity,
the two stand closer together than do the two extreme positive and negative poles, the religious and the brigand, and
so mediate between them.

The model permits us, then, to speak of both "mediation"
and of "reversal". But on this level these terms have to do
with semiotic relationships, not narrative performance or
cultural affirmation/dissolution. The mediation is the
product of the way in which C and D each borrow one term
from each of the expressions A and B. The reversal is the
double permutation which reverses the nature of the relationship between C and D--a reversal which both holds them
separate from the first pair and which renders their relationship unstable, capable of further resolution.

As for the relation to culture, there may in fact be a
reversal of the audience's most profound expectations, as
well. And this pattern we may then choose to label "parable".
Such communication may call into question the traditional
values by confronting them with an inimical alternative
model. Or it may just distort the elements of the accepted
one enough to disturb and probe. It may indeed simply break
the traditional model open and laugh at it. But all of this
is independent of whether or not we have a complete semiotic
model on the mythical level. That is another matter, only
partly related to the question of the ethical model.

A complete deep-structural model requires mediation.
And even parable can--usually will--have a complete model.
Parable does not simply disassemble the mythical model, to

in some negative way break apart the pieces and move them farther from each other. The Samaritan is good precisely in that he combines in himself elements from each pole, thus mediating rather than heightening that polarity. Parable's power lies in the mediation's appearance in new and surprising ways, or from unexpected quarters.

It is true that even this semiotic model may appear in broken or incomplete form. But this has to do with the completeness of the story rather than directly with the question of the ethical model. Such in fact is the case with the Kafka parable. In narrative terms, the situation of lack (lack of knowledge of the way) remains unfilled for want of a willing hero (informer). So the story stays hung up at the point of the topical sequence. This gives it the ambiguity which is such a strong element of its strangely disturbing power. But this narrative incompleteness is not a necessary feature of parable. In ethical terms, there has been a single reversal; the policeman rejects his conventionally "good" role. We are at the point of the traveler when he has been passed up by priest and Levite. To affect a double reversal, the "I" in the Kafka story should get his directions from a mugger, and so successfully complete his program. Far from re-affirming cultural expectations, such a development would further confound them, even while providing a mediating hero. The completeness of the mythical model is a function simply of the completeness of the narrative model. Narrative incompleteness may indeed be a likely feature of parable, to heighten its unsettling appeal. To that extent, there may in actuality appear some correlation between the wholeness/brokenness of the mythical model and the myth/parable distinction. But that correlation is not an inherent one. In fact our work at Vanderbilt with most of the synoptic parables has not found such incompleteness (e.g. lack of hero) to be a regular feature of their mythical models. Should such prove to be a consistent characteristic of modern parables by Borges and Kafka, we would face anew the question of their relationship to the synoptists' παραβολαί.

There are ways in which structural analysis gives promise of illuminating the sociological functions served by myth and ritual, folklore and drama. Functionalist studies of religious and cultural phenomena are often accused of imposing on the material the researcher's own presuppositions as to what features are filling these functions and so deserve his focus. Perhaps such structural devices as narrative hierarchies could provide a more objective basis for isolating these features, by allowing the pertinent oppositions and categories to emerge more clearly from the material itself. And even the deeper analyses by Lévi-Strauss on the level of the mythical structures can contribute to fuller understanding of the respective functional roles served by various genres, as in his explication of dialectical relationships between myth and ritual.[19] So there is hope that the two approaches can increasingly complement each other. But when we ask of Lévi-Strauss the directions in our quest for generic determinations, it is he who turns away with his laughter.

NOTES

1. "The persons of the myth are not human beings; they are gods or culture heroes." *The Sacred and the Profane* (N.Y.: Harcourt, Brace and World, 1959), p. 95.

2. *Anatomy of Criticism* (Princeton University Press, 1957), p. 33.

3. "Myth...is a warrant, a charter, and often even a practical guide to the activities with which it is connected." *Magic, Science and Religion* (Garden City: Doubleday, 1948), p. 108.

4. "The supreme function of myth is to 'fix' the paradigmatic models for all rites and all significant human activities." *Sacred and Profane*, p. 98.

5. W. R. Bascom, "Four Functions of Folklore" in A. Dundes, ed.: *The Study of Folklore* (Englewood Cliffs, N.J.: Prentice-Hall, 1965), p. 298.

6. David Miller develops this idea of two cathartic patterns in his "Orestes: Myth and Dream as Catharsis", in J. Campbell ed.: *Myths, Dreams and Religion* (N.Y.: Dutton and Co., 1970), pp. 26-47.

7. The "salient characteristics" of rituals of status reversal include "the stressing, not the overthrowing of the principle of hierarchy..., undoubtedly purified--even, paradoxically, by the breach of many Hindu pollution rules --through reversal, a process whereby it *remains* the structural vertebra of village life." *The Ritual Process* (Chicago: Aldine, 1969), p. 188.

8. A. Dundes, p. xiii in V. Propp: *Morphology of the Folktale* (Austin: University of Texas Press, 1968), second edition.

9. This is due, of course, to Lévi-Strauss' anthropological interest in all cultural phenomena and their interrelationships, both among themselves and with the culture producing them. The depth and universality of the innate

structuring function of the human mind does not preclude
Lévi-Strauss' determining the mythical model's *content*
in any particular culture from all available artifacts;
rather, it requires him to do so. But this quest must be
pursued on an equally "deep-structural" level through all
materials—a necessity which effectively transcends their
generic distinctions.

> It must not be considered surprising if
> this work, which is avowedly devoted to
> mythology, draws unhesitatingly on
> material provided by folk tales, legends,
> and pseudo-historical traditions and
> frequently refers to ceremonies and
> rites. I cannot accept overhasty pro-
> nouncements about what is mythology and
> what is not; but rather I claim the
> right to make use of any manifestation
> of the mental or social activities of
> the communities under consideration
> which seems likely to allow me, as the
> analysis proceeds, to complete or ex-
> plain the myth...

The Raw and the Cooked (N.Y.: Harper & Row, 1969), J. and D.
Weightman, trans., p. 4.

10. Crossan's paper, p. 255.

11. *Structural Anthropology* (Garden City: Anchor Books,
1967), p. 205.

12. Norman Petersen makes the convincing case for genres
as shared cultural media in his "On the Notion of Genre" in
Semeia I, pp. 134-181.

13. *The Raw and the Cooked*, p. 45.

14. Jean Pouillon, "Présentation: un essai de définition"
in *Les Temps Modernes*, #246 (Nov., 1966), pp. 769-790.

15. Crossan's paper, p. 253.

16. This is represented as $a^{(-1)}$ by Lévi-Strauss. Our
many attempts at Vanderbilt to apply the formula have convinced us that what is actually represented here is simply

the non-performance of function a. We have come to the
practice therefore of writing it as ā, and calling it
"non-a". Cf. the similar understanding by the Marandas
in their *Structural Models in Folklore and Transformational
Essays* (The Hague: Mouton, 1971).

17. I am of course speaking here not of "functions"
in the canonic sense first catalogued by Propp, but of the
mythical semantic features characterized by the performances
of various actors. The state/function distinctions are determined from the narrative hierarchy according to the norms
given by Daniel Patte in his paper on the Prodigal Son.

18. I am of course illustrating my understanding of the
formula with the semantic features established by Daniel
Patte in his structural interpretation of the parable in
Soundings 58/2 (Summer, 1975), 221-242, though the responsibility for this treatment of his analysis is my own.

19. "Structure and Dialectics" chap. XII of *Structural
Anthropology*, pp. 229-238.

DISCUSSION

PETERSEN: First of all, let us come back to your earlier point where you said that you are destructuring paradoxes and modalities. What exactly do you mean?

CROSSAN: Well, what holds it together for me is the term I pulled into the context of this paper without any warning-- "play". I think that here is exactly the place where you find that phenomenon deconstructing most clearly visible within our human experience. You have a constant going-stopping that is part of the whole process. I am inclined to think that the destructuring which I am talking about is not exactly the same as your destructuring if you mean by that term simply setting up a structure then reassessing it.

PETERSEN: Paradox is playing on already existing structure and someone who knows that structure is using that structure to reshape it....

CROSSAN: ...to play on it.

PETERSEN: ...to play on it. But that is not inconsistent with John Jones' statement.

CROSSAN: First of all, the person understands that he is playing. Secondly, there is no alternative to playing. This is a very important point. He does not say that he is *merely* playing, merely presuming that there is an alternative. He is not playing the structure, nor changing it. The structure really is there in reality somewhere. As Crespy says, it is out there; it is there in the beginning. Now we can tamper with it, we can seek it, we can go after it more or less whole. Or do we make it up as we go? I think that is the crucial issue for me. Are you destructuring in an attempt to get at the structure which is totally independent of your own mind? Or are you destructuring to become aware that the structure that was there in the first place was a phenomenon of the human mind?

PATTE: I am wondering if there is not confusion here between system and structure. What is contested or challenged by paradox is the system and not the structure.

CROSSAN: But my instincts tell me that you don't know where structure stops and the system begins, and that is what unnerves you about it. Maybe it (paradox) just changes the structure, but maybe it also unnerves a system and subverts the whole systematization process.

PATTE: To put it another way, is the paradox not viewed as meaningful? What we are trying to grasp is precisely what allows meaning to emerge.

CROSSAN: Let me give you an example. As I imagine a hearer of the Good Samaritan, when he hears the parable, something like this is going on. "I have heard a story in which I have to admit that there is at least one bad priest and Levite in the world and there is one good samaritan." I can also imagine a spectator saying: "Is this person telling me that

all Samaritans are good and that priests and Levites are bad?
Are they saying you cannot tell bad from evil any longer?
Are we to say that there is no logic in the universe?"

WITTIG: In an article by J. Kristeva in the *Times Literary
Supplement*, October 1973, she makes precisely the same point
in a much more abstract way about the necessity of violations
of norm in order for the norm to have significance and meaning. She was tracing a problem in the development of structuralism, saying that from Saussure through Lévi-Strauss the
emphasis has been on the structure of langue and the prevalence of that code over all individualistic activities and
individualistic understanding. While Kristeva wants now to
turn back to the Prague structural distinction which was de-
rivative from the norm which she got from the Russian formal-
ists, to turn back again to the notion you were coming to
that there has to be a violation in order for the structure
itself to be seen. It must be destructured by the individual
use of language or use of code in order for the code to have
meaning. I see that as another bolster for your argument,
though from a different direction.

PETERSEN: There is a certain diffusion of paradox if you
take the Russian formalist notion of deformalization vis-à-
vis plot, deviation from a norm or defamiliarizing a norm,
and the Prague structuralist's notion of foregrounding in
poetry where there is an alternation of normal language.
One could argue that paradox is fundamental to both prose
and poetry which then leaves the question of where and how
one classifies parable within that broader field.

CROSSAN: If you take, for example, story and plot, using those terms, what you actually do is tell the whole idea of story. There are only plots.

PETERSEN: You are challenging not the story but the idea of the story itself.

CROSSAN: Well, yes, in other words it is an empty thing; it is the sum total of all the plots. It is a useful distinction to make to say well there is the story, that is the raw material or the causal connections, and the plot or the way you put it together. That's nice, except there is no such "story". Even that first thing is probably our own western way of giving you what we call an unplotted plot. I think we are still trying to get to the norm for normal and deviant language. Who is setting up these games? Who says that the language of poetry is the deviant language? Maybe poetry is the normal use of language and the other should be considered deviant. To challenge the very presupposition that we know what the norm is scares the very life out of a lot of people. Now can you play without that center? Where I see this issue very clearly is in Borges' *Labyrinths*. Most of the people I have read who talk of Borges' *Labyrinths* have trouble with it because they end up saying that the labyrinth doesn't seem to be a bad thing for Borges and they are vastly surprised with this conclusion. They can't handle it because in western consciousness the labyrinth is bad. You are trying to get into that center to catch whatever is there and to get out alive. First, Borges doesn't think the labyrinth has a center; secondly, he doesn't want to get out of it because he doesn't think he can; thirdly, he thinks he is making up the labyrinth as he goes. So he is having fun. Why on earth would he want to get out of the labyrinth? It is like a chess match; he doesn't want to get off the board because he is having a ball there. He is building the labyrinth and it really doesn't frighten him. The big difference, it seems to me, is whether you have a goal with no center without being scared.

REYNOLDS: If I may introduce a point John Donahue mentioned a while ago, for me it crosses the whole discussion of the last three days. It is the notion of integration. John mentioned that the parables as they have been analyzed here have been lifted out of their context. I see the primary norms of structuralism in relation to this whole notion of integration. If Benveniste is correct, meaning is a function of integration, content as distinguished from form; meaning is a product of integration. A word doesn't have meaning until it is integrated into another higher unit and that unit again gets its meaning or its content from its integration into still higher units. In any case, if you have a document like the Gospel which has been entirely put together by an author or compiler, the presupposition must be in structuralist terms that the whole book has a greater meaning than the sum of the meaning of its parts. That residue of meaning is a function of integration of those parts of the total. Now how can one take a parable out of that total work and operate on it as a structuralist ignoring entirely the notion of integration? If I am interested in *Sitz im Leben Jesu* and I take the parable out of context, and say I am going to sheer off the redactional elements, or if I have a unit which I try to replace into its original context which is lost, I will make up a context to give it meaning. I will try to integrate it into an original *Sitz im Leben Jesu* context. But I am inventing the context. We've got to stop cutting them up and atomizing them. That seems to me to be sinning against the primary notion of structuralism, that is, to be lifting out parables or miracle stories or any other unit in the Gospel. It has to be understood in the context of the whole. This goes for Professor Patte's work as well. He goes to tremendous rounds to structure the unit itself and there is such an enormous amount of work in his approach to parables that he can't deal with the whole Gospel.

ROBERTSON: It seems to me that often in our thinking we operate according to a model which has a center. It is a reality and has a context which will finally end the circle. We take the Good Samaritan and we want to put it into a context that is not the one it has in Luke. That context is imagined. But if you put it in the context in which it is found in Luke, then you have something solid. We don't necessarily know what the context in Luke means. Jesus says a parable and the context in Luke interprets it. Then we interpret the context in Luke but we also possibly misinterpret that. It is not the context that gives a solid basis from which we operate, for we are also imagining the context in Luke.

CROSSAN: But the term "context" is not univocal. You have chosen one context; it is a perfectly valid context--it is absolutely valid, but it is not mine.

WITTIG: The question is to build a matrix of contexts in which you can check out your constructions.

REYNOLDS: That is the point I'm making. I am not questioning the fact that we have different contexts. What I am saying is that we must take the structure of the context seriously.

CROSSAN: The context I am taking seriously at the moment is the context of the genre parable. You have used the term "genre". That is the context.

PETERSEN: To answer your [Reynolds'] question, I agree with you about dealing with the whole text, which has not been done but I think that we have to admit even with hypothetical texts that we are doing this on the basis of a source critical methodology, whether it is philological or form critical. I think *that* is the only justification. This is the point I was making about Via Thursday night. There are source critical grounds whereupon you deal with a certain segment of that narrative as a text. My criticism was that he was making formal distinctions within a text to create yet another text, therefore separating verses 2-5 from 6-8. But I think we are dealing with hypothetical texts constructed on source critical grounds I think that would answer your question.

VIA: My point has already been made but I would like to remake it again briefly. I think that you are right: a context is necessary. But I think that it is legitimate to create a context. By dealing with the various kinds of diagrams I have to use, I show that there are semantic and formal connections between narratives which may be very distinct from each other as far as their cultural context is concerned. This is what I have done in that book, or have tried to do. Todorov, for example, says that *Tristram Shandy* and *Notes from the Underground*, Part I, can be shown to comprise a genre. Well this genre would be a context which would give a broader perspective from which we could look at each use of the component parts. This was the kind of context I was trying to work within in conscious distinction from either the context of the Gospels or the context of history. Certainly, the other thing needs to be done. One of the continuing problems in structuralist thought is how one is going to relate this synchronic approach to diachronic ones.

CROSSAN: We don't really have to go to the diachronic at all. Lévi-Strauss screams about this complete lack of context in his criticism of Propp's *Morphology of the Folktale*. He says what Propp is lacking is not the history of the tale but precisely the context in which it appeared. He says the specific differentiation between Russian formalism and structural analysis is the emphasis upon the context. And he says the problem with dealing with texts is that you don't have the contexts whereas the anthropologist has the culinary customs, the dress codes, indeed many different kinds of codes with which he can compare the various structures he is investigating.

WITTIG: And yet the context that you are talking about there is not the one that Reynolds is demanding because Lévi-Strauss is asking for the performative context in which the text functions in the culture.

MARIN: I would offer a brief comment about what Reynolds said concerning Benveniste and the use of the term "integration". I think we have to clarify very precisely what Benveniste means by "integration" at the level of sentence components. This refers to the integration process in a narrow sense. At the level of the discourse you have perhaps another integrative process but it is of a very different sort. Benveniste in his last articles insists on two different linguistics: one concerned with components on the level of the sentence, and another one which deals with discourse. I think that can illuminate some of the difficulties.

REYNOLDS: Yes, I thought we were working here in the last few days on the notion that there is a true homology between the level of linguistics and the level of discourse analysis. I was assuming that what could be affirmed about the sentence on the question of integration was equally valid on the level of discourse. I presumed that Benveniste would not take that position on discourse.

ROTH: This takes us into an equation that the paradox is related to the parable as the proverb is to the example which I find very illuminating. Now I think I can point to two different texts in the Old and New Testaments that seem to suggest paradox as a very basic patterning principle on whatever level. One is the position of two proverbs that would add up to a paradox. It was mentioned before. "Answer a fool according to his foolishness lest he think himself wise. Do not answer a fool according to his foolishness lest you become like him." This is set within normal proverbs and suddenly, like a block, it hits you. Paradoxic principle

structuring here? Another example is I Cor. 7:29-31 where
Paul discusses a theological aside. The time is short;
therefore those who have wives be as those who do not have
and thus he goes through a whole category like this: the
ὡς-μή paradoxical principle. What you unearth if you wish
in the paradox as paradox-become-story seems to be a deep
structure in at least these other two biblical traditions
as well. I'm wondering whether it has something to do with
the protest against absolutizing and against idolization
that I hear in quite a few Old Testament traditions. I'm
offering it as an observation.

DOTY: I will be brief. I am very interested also in the
context, but less in historic context which I understand
you [Reynolds] to be asking for--historical, sequential context. It seems to me that Crossan is moving away from a
pure type or sort of framework where parable is this and
allegory is that--which seems to me to do violence to the
mishalim tradition in which all of these might be encompassed. So I wonder if you aren't taking us now toward a
generic spectrum which I at least find very interesting.
Parable, allegory, and perhaps myth are included in a total
sort of generic picture in ways which we have not seen before. It doesn't bother me at all for instance to think of
Jesus telling allegories. I think the sower is a fine allegory. The question then becomes, is it a good allegory, and
is the allegorization good within that spectrum. For me you
have begun to give some of the narrative dynamics which will
enable us to place things within that spectrum rather than
by putting on lables describing this as parable I, this as
allegory II, and so on.

CROSSAN: They must pass a lithmus test. See if the allegory allegorizes allegory. If it does, I suspect it will be
superb.

DONAHUE: What I was trying to say in my remarks was that
I thought last night when Professor Marin was doing a parable
of Pascal that he showed precisely that it could not be taken
independently of diverse contexts. It would be interesting to
me to see what would have happened to that parable had it been
given to the Vanderbilt Parable Seminar with no indication
from where it had come. That is my plaint. This is what is
happening to the Gospel parable. I talked in my brief exegesis, whether it is right or wrong, about the Good Samaritan,
and its rhetorical context in the Gospel of Luke. Now there
are three or four other contexts we can talk about. But I
am just making a plea that the context has to be taken seriously.

DOTY: I just want to say one thing in connection with Marin's
example last night. It seems we could have taken the parable
without any context at all, and found it very interesting.
That might then have helped us to understand what the actual
historical context was.

REYNOLDS: I was not referring to the historical context
but to the literary one, and I just wanted to heighten the
point I was making by referring to Crist's handout. He had
three different collections of Pascal's *pensées*. The *pensées*
as they are—what do they mean? What does any one mean if
you haven't a context for it. Now different people have
collected them and have given the *pensées* different contexts

by putting them beside different *pensées*. They have different semantic colorings in each of those three versions. That is what I am talking about. What does the parable mean where it is in the Gospel?

CROSSAN: I would like to say that that is not what I was interested in. I say that not denying the validity of your point, and not denying Susan Wittig's point that it will be much more interesting when you get all of these into a matrix so you can see how you go up and down the elevators. I am just trying to look at one area. The other point I would make is that I am convinced--talking about Jesus now from the historical-critical point of view--that what he hung on that Galilean wall was a mirror. Now if he wanted to hang a portrait which is what we all like, he could have hung a portrait. If he hangs a mirror, that means when he looks in- to it he sees himself, and so would anyone else. Now I pre- sume that when somebody hangs a mirror on the wall, they want to hang a mirror: it is not a mistake.

CHAPTER VI

MEANING AND MODES OF SIGNIFICATION:
TOWARD A SEMIOTIC OF THE PARABLE

Susan Wittig

University of Texas, Austin

The structural study of the parable, like that of literary narrative, has advanced some distance beyond that first
self-confident stage when we thought we thoroughly understood
the principles of structural analysis: the accurate identification of the invariant components of the text, however
those may have been defined; the rearrangement of those units
in a meaning-producing paradigm which clearly demonstrated
their structural and functional relationships; and the classification of the basic patterns of similarity and difference
ordering each opposing paradigm. However, the programmatic
statements of philosophy and method that seemed to offer a
way into the real meaning of the text, that seemed to promise
accurate and objective measure of meaning built according to
the principles of structural linguistics and structural anthropology appear much more tentative and problematic in the recent perspectives of transformational-generative grammar, of
socio-linguistics, and of esthetics. The assumption of the
early structuralists that syntactic structure is the primary
ordering form in the sign-system of the text[1] has been
challenged by a growing conviction that semantic structures
are intimately connected with deep syntactical structures,
and that the analysis of any text will not be complete with-

out a clear understanding of its semantic dimension.[2] Further, we have learned from socio-linguistics that the performative context of the speech event, the rhetorical nature of the interchange between the sender and the receiver of the message, bound within the traditions and conventions imposed by their culture upon their communication--may be of more critical importance than the perceived structure of the text, and that its meaning may be a product of the dominant structures of the larger discourse in which it is embedded, rather than the product of its own immediate structure.[3] Further, recent work in the phenomenology of reading has suggested that it is not the structure of the text we must know if we are to understand its significance; rather, it is the structure of the reader's interaction with the text and the process of his attempts to make it meaningful that we should know.[4] And finally, the differences between pragmatic discourse--designed to shape men's beliefs or mold men's actions--and esthetic discourse--the product of creative play with the medium itself, with the dynamic, ambiguous aspects of language and with the processes of structuration and destructuration--have become clearer recently.[5] Briefly, then, a full comprehension of the significant structures that produce and govern the literary text and are at the same time reflected in it will necessarily be multi-dimensional: it will include an understanding of both the syntactic and semantic structures of the text itself; its performative, contextual, and cultural frames; and its pragmatic and esthetic purposes.

I have just described the components of what we might call a *semiotic* of the parable--an eclectic but systematic and theoretically coherent understanding of the signifying

properties of the verbal text that goes beyond any single
critical strategy to an encompassing perception of the text
as a significant whole and as a significant part of a series
of wholes in a broader and broader contextual frame.[6] No
single critical method is capable of such an all-inclusive
conception, which involves not only the text itself, but the
process of its creation, its performance, and its purpose
and effect. The semiotic model, however, a model based on
the sign theory of Charles Sanders Peirce, Charles Morris,
and F. De Saussure, has begun to seem capable of providing
the theoretical framework within which such an exploration
might be carried out.[7] I would like in this essay to provide a few tentative suggestions about what a semiotic of
the parable might look like, how it might be constituted,
and how the study of structure and meaning with which we
are immediately concerned is related to it.

Semiotics is the study of the sign--an object, a gesture, a sound--and systems of signs within the context of
their production, performance, and reception. The diadic
relations of the components of the communications act--the
sender and receiver, the sign and its referent--can be most
clearly presented in what is commonly called the "information theory triangle", a triadic representation which suggests that the sign provides an actual physical connection
between sender and receiver[8] and that a conceptual connection
exists between the referent and all other components of the
communication:

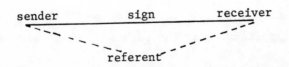

sender   sign   receiver

referent

According to Charles Morris, a complete semiotic study of a
system of signs--a verbal text, say--would focus on the sign
in its several dimensions: in its relation of *implication*
to other signs in the message, along the *syntactic axis*; in
its relations of *expression* and *impression* to the sender of
the sign and its receiver, along the *pragmatic*--or rhetorical
--axis; and in its relation of *denotation* or *designation* to
its referent, along the *semantic* axis.[9]

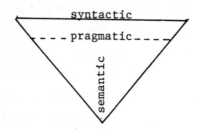

It can be easily seen, however, that each of these aspects of
the communications acts involves the other in complex, un-
measurable ways, and that the whole process of signification
is the total interaction of all three dimensions: the syntactic, the pragmatic, the semantic. For the purposes of analysi
of course, we can attempt to isolate each dimension--and that
is what literary criticism (and Biblical criticism, too) has
done for many years, forgetting or ignoring the fact that an
analysis must be followed by a synthesis, that what is taken
apart must be put back together again, and that an analysis in
part can yield insights only about that part, and not about th
whole.

    I would like now to review the basic constituents of the
semiotic model, and to discuss the possibilities of their
analytic application to the parables, which are deliberately

polysemic at several levels. Let me clarify the term "polysemic" by defining the parable first from a semantic perspective.[10] From this point of view a parable is a first-order
system[11] consisting of a linguistic sign vehicle (S_ℓ) and
the *denotatum* to which it refers (D_{en}) which has or could
have physical existence in the extra-linguistic world (e.g.
"The householder went out early in the morning to hire workers
for his vineyard."). This linguistic relationship can be
represented thus:[12]

To this point, the process I have described is the usual
process of denotation, and there is nothing unique about it.
In the parabolic system, however, the denoted object/event
does not retain its status as a mere denotatum; it is in turn
transformed into a second-order system in which the physical
form of the denotatum becomes a material sign vehicle (S_m)
designating an *unstated designatum* (D_{es}), a conceptual
referent which exists only in a world of moral and physio-
logical abstraction, which cannot be directly perceived in
the extra-linguistic world, and which must be supplied by the
perceiver of the sign.[13] (e.g. "The spirit of God at the
beginning of time began to seek out righteous men."[14])

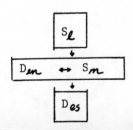

The process of signification here[15] is complicated by the fact that the whole system is a duplex semiotic in which the relationship between the first-order sign (the linguistic system) and its unstated conceptual designatum is *mediated by* a second-order, extra-linguistic denotatum (a material system), the physical, formal properties of which have been transformed into a sign and endowed with significance--although the exact nature of the designatum is not stated, and it is left to the perceiver to construct it.[16] The designatum, then, is not directly connected with the original linguistic sign; it is linked to it only through the mediation of an extra-linguistic sign.

The structure of this duplex semiotic gains its energy and effectiveness from the nature of the semantic relationships which link its components. The first order linguistic sign vehicle is linked *conventionally* and *arbitrarily* to its denotatum, as are nearly all linguistic signs; the second-order material sign vehicle, however, is linked *iconically* to its object in the same way that the structure of a diagram formally exemplifies and exhibits the structure of its object.[17]

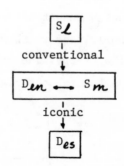

The conjunction of the conventional and iconic relationships in the parabolic system generates within the semantic structure much more energy than is generated by the conventional relationships of designation or denotation; at the same time, the fact that the final designatum is not stated gives to the system a dynamic, unstable *indeterminacy* which invites, even compels the perceiver to complete the unexpressed conceptualization.

Precisely because of this semantic incompleteness, the parabolic text may acquire a large number of different designata--all equally valid--but the nature of the relations between the parabolic sign, the denotatum, and the designatum, together with the nature of the rhetorical relations between sender and receiver, impose some important limitations on interpretation. First, and most obviously, because the sign vehicle of the designatum is similar to the denotatum (their relationship is iconic), the ideal dimensions or the thing or event which structures it.[18] For instance, the short parabolic statement we have been using as an example--"a householder went out early in the morning to hire workers for his vineyard"--could hardly be interpreted to mean that righteous men pray every morning; the two structures are not sufficiently congruent. Secondly, the designatum that the perceiver attaches to the material sign vehicle belongs within his mind to a rule-governed meaning system where it is generated by and structured according to certain conventions and beliefs with which it must conform; as this diagram indicates, it is likely that the designatum (which is created by the perceiver out of his own beliefs and experiences) owes its structure as much to the structure of the meaning system in the mind of the perceiver as it does to the structure of the denotatum itself.

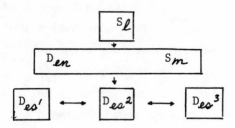

It is possible, for instance, to attribute to our short
parabolic text the interpretation "the spirit of evil went
out at the beginning of time to seek wicked men"--in fact,
if the parable were taken out of its context, it could be
read in this way. However, the powerfully stable theological
system within which this sign is generated disallows this
particular interpretation of the parable and dictates the
parameters within which the designatum may be constructed.
On the other hand, a well-organized analytic system of designata may well *generate* a certain kind of signification, even
though the structure of the material sign does not immediately
suggest it.   Let me illustrate by reminding you of the late-
medieval concept of four-fold allegorical signification, outlined so clearly in Dante's letter to Can Grande:

> ...the meaning of this work is not simple,
> but rather it is polysemous. So that this
> method of exposition may be clearer, one may
> consider it in the lines: "When Israel went
> out of Egypt, the house of Jacob from people
> of strange language, Judah was his sanctuary
> and Israel his dominion." If we look only
> at the letter, this signifies that the chil-
> dren of Israel went out of Egypt in the time
> of Moses; if we look at the allegory, it
> signifies our redemption through Christ; if
> we look at the moral sense, it signifies the

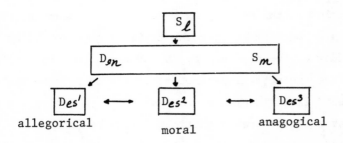

> turning of the soul from the sorrow and
> misery of sin to a state of grace; if we
> look at the anagogical sense, it signifies
> the passage of the blessed soul from the
> slavery of this corruption to the freedom
> of eternal glory.[19]

The "literal" meaning is what we have been calling here the
denotatum; the other three meanings--the allegorical, moral,
and anagogical--are all designata, all derived from the denotatum by conventional, systematic rules, and arranged in a
hierarchically ordered system of conceptual relationships:

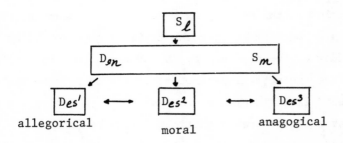

The analytic system to which this kind of complicated exegesis
belongs calls for three different but related designata; per-
ceivers acquainted with the regular conventions of four-fold
signification (as well as with the conventions of the theological system, with which the designata must also be congruent)
looked for designata to fill the empty slots in the taxonomy.
And of course the designata, once looked for, were found.[20]

Thirdly, the shape and structure of the designatum is
governed not only by the structure of the first-order and
second-order signs, but by the syntactic context in which
these signs occur:

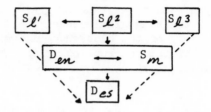

It is apparent that no single S/D relationship can be
achieved independently, outside of the syntactic relationships that govern the appearance of a particular sign at a
given point in the developing system. The process of signification is part of an on-going activity experienced by both
the sender of the sign and by its receiver, and is constraine
within the syntactical parameters of the whole sign system.[21]

These last statements concerning the rule-governed conventions which control signification can be fully explored
only when we recognize the fact that we have arrived at the
intersection of the semantic, rhetoric, and syntactic dimensions, and that we can go no further without considering how
these semantic and syntactic structures are related to the
psychological dimensions of the communications act. Let me
begin by examining the implications of the statement that the
sender of the parabolic sign presumably has in mind a meaning
system in terms of which the denotatum should be decoded--
and probably also has in mind a designatum. If the receiver
of the sign does not also possess that meaning-system, he
cannot discover the designatum intended by the sender, although he may understand very well the nature of the denotatum. Or if he possesses another, different meaning system,
with its own rule-governed structure, and if the sender does

not make explicit what designatum he intends to be derived
from the sign, the receiver will arrive at a designatum--
an interpretation of the parable--different from that which
the sender intended, although it may be fully consonant with
the dimensions of the denotatum and with his own conceptual
system. Or, finally, under the exigencies of his own particular place and time, the receiver may invert or otherwise distort what he knows to be the intended designata, in order to
fit his own meaning-system. For instance, in *The Parables
and Similes of the Rabbis*, Rabbi Feldman quotes Zech. 2:10:
"For I have spread you abroad as the four winds of heaven,
saith the Lord." Feldman comments:

> The Rabbis, in expounding this simile, de-
> clare: 'Even as the world cannot exist
> without winds, so mankind cannot exist with-
> out Israel.' Here the original meaning of
> most distant dispersion and difficult re-
> union is entirely reversed in the process
> of elaboration; a new and favourable turn is
> given to this apparently untoward prophecy
> against Israel.[22]

From the sender's point of view, the multiple designata
arrived at by these receivers are wrong because they are not
in agreement with his own. What makes possible several interpretations of the same text, of course, is its quality of
"indeterminacy", the lack of direct, immediate connection in
the text between the second-order sign and its designatum--
the dependence on the *iconic* relationship and the perception
of certain similarities of form and content. When the sender
gives no indication as to precisely what and how the sign
means, the receiver is forced to achieve whatever significance
suits his own immediate needs and purposes.

This brings me to comment on the "one-point approach" to the interpretation of the parable, a related problem of meaning which has semantic importance and can be defined in semantic terms. The basic principles of the argument can be briefly stated and as briefly dealt with. If the whole parable is viewed as a single, indivisible sign, then it is seen to have a single configurative meaning--it is seen to have one designatum, one *tertium comparatonis*:

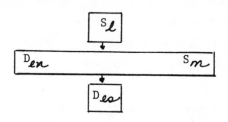

If, however, the parable is viewed as a syntactical system of related but separable signs which may have meaning independently of (although consonant with) the meaning of the whole system, the designatum system is seen to have several points of congruence with the denotatum system:

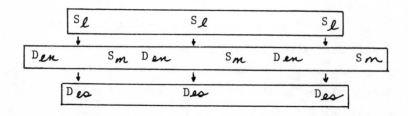

Again, unless the sender of the parabolic sign has given some indications of his intention, either directly, in the text of the parable itself, or in the context of the parable, it may be very difficult to decide whether it is appropriate to focus

on the whole text or on individual components of it. From a
semantic point of view, the question has no real answer; the
answer lies in the accepted meaning-system of the time, and
in the currently popular fashion of interpretation. In the
absence of any instruction from the sender, there seems little
theoretical problem with finding as many points of comparison
as may be found: in Tertullian's reading of The Prodigal Son,
for instance, his interpretation of the robe bestowed on the
returning prodigal as the sonship which Adam lost in the Fall
and Exile, and his understanding of the ring as the sign and
seal of baptism and the feast as the Lord's Supper,[23] none of
these violate the conventions of the theological system in
which they were born, and each seems sufficiently congruent
to its second-order system to be acceptable. It is only in
Jülicher's one-point analytical system (a configuration as
rigorously restrictive as the four-point analytic system of
Dante) that they would be disallowed.

The structure of the semantic dimension of the parabolic system--the relationship between the signs, what it denotes,
and what it designates--provides many theoretical and conceptual complexities, and there is room for research in this
area which would consider the semantic similarity between
the parables of Jesus and other parabolic systems. However,
there is one extremely interesting complexity that I would
like to comment on briefly before we go on: I would like to
direct attention to a parable which is semantically self-
referential, for it has, as one of its possible designata,
the act of parable-making itself. The Sower (Mark 4:3-8,
Matt. 13:3-8, Luke 8:5-8) can be read as Jesus' description
of himself as a speaker who cannot ensure that his audience
will hear and understand what he says and who can expect that

only a few of his listeners will be receptive; those few, however, will repay his efforts by the fullness of their understanding and acceptance--some thirty fold, some sixty fold, some an hundred fold. In semantic terms, and in this interpretation, the parable is its own conceptual referent-- it is explicitly a parable about parable-making--and those who recognize this meaning may well be the "good ground" of which the parable speaks. Other parables are similarly self-referential, but in a way which involves dimensions of the parable text other than the semantic fact of its own linguistic existence. I will return again to the question of self-reference in a moment, but first, I would like to look more closely at the rhetorical act that structures the creation and the reception of the parables, along the rhetorical dimension--and to briefly review the semiotic implications of some of the important work that has been done in this area.

Because of their status as embedded texts, the parables present an interesting, nearly unique problem in rhetorical analysis--the analysis of the relationship between sender and receiver and of the ways in which that relationship structures the message and its perception. In their first communication situation, in their first context, the parables belong to a concrete historical place and time: they are originally spoken by Jesus, to his disciples and to a crowd of listeners, and (it is argued) it is this historical con- text which imparts to them their form and meaning and is most crucial to their proper understanding.[24] Further, C. H. Dodd has suggested that recovering the historical moment in which Christ lived and spoke is critical, not just because this gives the parables greater authenticity, greater validity,

but because the parables provide brief glimpses into the
divine significance of human events--because, in what he
calls their "intense particularity as comments upon an historical situation", the parables declare the "eternal order
...present in the actual situation".[25] For Dodd, then, the
recovery of the original rhetorical context is crucial because its understanding will lead to a reconstitution in our
own lives of that intersection of the eternal in time.

Second, the parables are embedded in late first-century
narratives of Jesus' ministry, by writers who saw his teach-
ings in the light of the needs and desires of a growing heter-
ogenous church community embattled against both Jews, Gnostics, and Romans,[26] and reinterpreted the parables of Christ
to suit their own immediate and pressing purposes. Their
reinterpretation is both explicitly and implicitly perceiv-
able: explicit, because these editors and redactors have
added commentary and explanation to the parabolic texts which
gives them specific point and particularity for the early
Church; and implicit, because they have reshaped the narrative of the parables to fit their own meaning-system and because they have carefully embedded them into the larger narrative of the ministry in such a way as to control contextually
their significance to the perceiver.[27]

Finally, the parables belong to a powerful exegetical
tradition that has for centuries accumulated every possible
interpretation of the texts and attached these designata to
the signs themselves, giving them equal doctrinal authority.
Essentially, then, readers of every century come to the perception of the parables through the multiple perceptions of
earlier readers; their own expectations and understanding
are controlled to a greater or lesser extent by the under-

standing of other audiences. The fact of these imbricated communicative contexts is no doubt crucial to an historically accurate and sophisticated diachronic understanding of what the parables have meant to a variety of audiences, and it is certainly necessary to help us avoid the conflation of one audience, one rhetorical purpose, with another audience and another rhetorical purpose.

But I would like to argue that it is not *what* the parables have meant to these various audiences that is important, but *how* the parables have meaning to one reader or another and how two or more dissimilar meanings and interpretations of the same text can be at once valid. To do this, I would like to broaden our discussion of the rhetorical dimension of the parable text to include an understanding of what goes on in the reader's mind as he confronts the text, what Wolfgang Iser has called the "phenomenology" of the reading act.[28]

In *The Implied Reader*, Iser suggests that the literary event does not occur on the page, but in the convergence of the text and the reader that calls the work into phenomenological existence. Following Roman Ingarden,[29] Iser characterizes the reading activity as a "kaleidoscope of perspectives, preintentions, and recollections" in the reader's mind--expectations of what he is to see and recollections of what he has earlier seen--which make meaning out of the potential semantic structures of the text, potential because they can be actualized only by the reader's perception of them. Iser is particularly interested in those texts which display *hiatus*--the lack of syntactic or semantic connections--and "indeterminacy"--the omission of detail--and which invite the reader to establish his own connections between the lines of the text, so to speak, and to create his own significant detail, when the text does

not offer it. Indeterminate texts, he says, are "often so
fragmentary that one's attention is almost exclusively
occupied with the search for connections between fragments".[30]
In these texts, he suggests, it is not the creator's intention to frustrate or confuse us

> so much as to make us aware of the nature
> of our own capability for providing links;
> in such cases, the text refers back directly
> to our own preconceptions—which are re-
> vealed by the act of interpretation that is
> a basic element of the reading process.[31]

Iser's statement has several rather important implications.
If he is right, then we might suggest that the structure of
the parable is significant because it is the product of a
meaning-making interaction between the mind and imagination
of the author and the historical and traditional materials
out of which he fashioned his text. But if Iser is right,
we might also suggest that the structure of the parable is
not the place to look for a clue to its significance, for
that exists in the mind and imagination of the perceiver,
and is only partly affected by the structures which the
author has invested with meaning. The "real meaning" of
the parable, then, does not lie in the structure of the
text, but in the *structuring* of the text—not in the created
product but in the process of creation and perception. The
purpose of the parables, from this point of view, is not to
create one particular meaning, but to create the conditions
under which the creation of meaning can be defined and
examined by each individual perceiver, who can come to a
clearer understanding of his own expectations and precon-
ceptions—his own meaning-system. In semiotic terms, such

texts are self-reflexive in a metacommunicative dimension,
calling to our attention not their syntactic or semantic
structures, but the variety of ways in which those structures are actualized in our minds, are made to yield their
potential meanings. When we read a text characterized by
the quality of indeterminacy, as the parables are, we are
reading ourselves as well as the text, and are being forced
to an awareness of the creation of meaning in our own minds,
as well as to an awareness of the meaning itself.

And that, I submit, is one of the meanings and purposes
of the parables, in all of the rhetorical contexts that we
can define: for the audience in the physical presence of
Jesus; for the early church community to whom the Evangelists
wrote; for the readers and hearers of the parables in all
centuries. The parabolic sign, as we have seen, is highly
indeterminate at the semantic level: the ultimate designatum
is not explicitly stated, and it is left to the perceiver to
create it, using clues from the sign-context and from the
context of its own meaning-system.

I am arguing, then, that efforts to find the "real
meaning" of the parables in the historical context of a
single rhetorical act at a single moment in time reward us
with just that knowledge and no more. I am further arguing
that the parables are not authenticated by either their
original or their secondary rhetorical context, although it
may be important to us for many reasons to discover what
that context might be. Rather, the parables, unlike the
"historical" narrative in which they are embedded, present
the reader or hearer with a difficult problem in cognition
and signification, requiring his total attention--and more,
his attention *to* his attention. As Iser observes:

> Herein lies the dialectical structure of
> reading. The need to decipher gives us the
> chance to formulate our own deciphering
> capacity--i.e. we bring to the fore an
> element of our being of which we are not
> directly conscious. The production of the
> meaning of literary texts does not merely
> entail the discovery of the unformulated,
> which can then be taken over by the active
> imagination of the reader. It also entails
> the possibility that we may formulate our-
> selves and so discover what had previously
> seemed to elude our consciousness.[32]

From this point of view, the imposition of an interpretation--
any interpretation--by one reader on another reader is a peril-
ous act, for to offer a "reading" of a parable to an audience
is to circumvent this crucial aspect of the parabolic text,
and to invite the audience to participate in a ready-made
signification, instead of creating their own, and creating in
themselves an examination of the act of signification.

I would like now to turn to a brief review and critique
of structural studies of the parable, in light of the comments
and observations I have made on the nature of the semiotic
relations that govern the ways in which the parable acquires
significance. First, I would like to remind us that the
structural study of the parable, like all structural studies,
focuses on the structure of the denotatum, the first-order
referent of the linguistic sign, in an effort to understand
how that denotatum is constructed and how its construction
is related to various other aspects of the communication context. However, structural analysis (at least as it is being
practiced in the 1970's) does not conform itself to what is
apparent in the surface structure of the denotatum. All
structural studies, whether they are built on a Proppian

model of syntagmatic analysis, a Levi-Straussian model of paradigmatic analysis, or a Greimasian model of "semantic" analysis, deal with the actualization (or "semantization") of a latent pattern, a structure which is said to be a more accurate clue to meaning than the actual narrative.[33] The Proppian model enables us to describe the structures which directly underlie the "surface features" of a group of narratives and to define those narratives in terms of their generic resemblances to other similar tales. On the other hand, the Levi-Straussian model enables us to describe the paradigmatic structures of a corpus of narratives--patterns not constrained by the temporal ordering of the tale--and to see the relationship between those structures and the logical structures within which the culture creates and discovers significance. And the Greimasian actantial model enables us to see the deep structural patterns of the narrative both in Proppian functional terms and in Levi-Straussian paradigmatic terms. Structural study, then, has proven to be a useful descriptive tool in the analysis of literary form, in the retracing of an obscure compositional history, or in the establishment of generic affiliations.

However, when studying structural analysis attempts to move beyond a description of the text of the parable or a description of related texts to a study of meaning, it confronts serious difficulties. As we have seen, the denotatum and the unspecified, unstated designatum are not identical, although they appear to be iconically related: that is, the structure of the narrative of the parable is not exactly equal to the structure of the meaning the reader attaches to it. Further, that meaning is governed by factors other than the structure of the narrative designatum, as we have suggested:

the "meaning" of the parable is a product as well of the
"meaning system", the organized, stable gestalt of beliefs
and values held by the perceiver; it is a product as well
of the analytical system by which that perceiver has decided
to interpret the parables (a "one point" analytical system
like that of Jülicher, for instance, or Dante's four-point
analytical system); it is also a product of the contextual
system of narrative signs within which the parable is embedded. Most importantly, as Iser has indicated, the meaning of a text does not lie wholly in the text itself, either
at its surface or at its deep-structural level; it lies in
the coming-together of text and reader in the phenomenological convergence of mind and story that is unique to each
reading, each experience of the parable. That meaning is in
part governed by the structures of the text, but only in
part. And as far as the parables are concerned, the structure probably has less controlling effect than in any other
narrative form, precisely because of their indeterminate
nature, the fact that their semantic structure is characterized by an incompleteness, a semantic disjunction between
the manifested denotatum and the unrealized, unmanifest
designatum. Because the structure of the denotatum is only
one contributing factor in the production of meaning, and
because the significance of a parable in the mind of a reader
at any given time is the product of so many forces, it seems
that it would be appropriate at this point to caution against
treating the structure of a single parable as though it were
capable of divulging to us any special significance that we
do not already know. We may indeed discover some different
interpretations of the parable, perhaps derived from the
structure of the interpretive model itself--and at this point

we ought to remind ourselves of the autotelic danger of seeing our own meaning-making scheme reflected in the objects we
examine.[34]

These cautions may lead us to conclude that the structural study of the parable, while it is a genuinely fruitful
activity, is usefully directed to a study of genre, or to an
examination of the parable as a particular narrative type, or
to a study of the surface features of the parable as esthetic
features. I would not argue, of course, against the further
structural study of Biblical narrative in general, and more
particularly of the Synoptic Gospels; I would caution, however, against attributing to the structure of the denotatum
of the parabolic sign any more powerful influence over signification than it is properly due, and against claiming that
structural studies can help us to achieve the real, the only
"meaning" of the parable. The meaning of the parable—the
meaning of any text—does not lie wholly in the structure of
the narrative; it lies in the reader's own act of structuration, in his efforts to achieve significance, to understand
both the parable and his own system of values and beliefs
which is called to his attention by the parable. Indeed, if
the parable has any single, dependable meaning, it is that
the human mind creates significance, and can understand itself completely only when it can comprehend itself in the
act of making meaning.

NOTES

1. Vladimir Propp's syntagmatic study of fairy-tale structure (*Morphology of the Folktale*, Austin, 1970), is an early example of the formalist-structuralist emphasis on the surface structure of narrative. Published in 1928 in Russia, it has served as the starting point for many other structural analyses. Tzvetan Todorov (*La Grammaire du Decameron*, The Hague, 1969), and Eugene Dorfman (*The Narreme in Medieval Epic and Romance*, Toronto, 1970) demonstrate methodological variations of the same syntagmatic interest.

2. See John Lyons, *Introduction to Theoretical Linguistics* (London, 1971), pp. 268-269. Lyons says,

> ...one of the principle motives for the revision of the (grammatical) system has been to integrate syntax with phonology and semantics....Most linguists who accept the validity of the distinction between deep grammatical structure and surface grammatical structure...assume that there is some particularly intimate connexion between deep syntax and semantics.

3. For an example of this kind of structural analysis, see Erving Goffman, *Frame Analysis* (New York, 1974).

4. See Roman Ingarden, *The Cognition of the Literary Work of Art* (Evanston, 1973) and Wolfgang Iser, *The Implied Reader* (Baltimore, 1974).

5. Julia Kristeva is probably the most articulate spokesperson for the belief that language is a creative violation, rather than a normative act. She is concerned with "rites of rebellion" and with the "fracture" of the language code that occurs in each speech act. See "The System and the Speaking Self," *Times Literary Supplement*, Oct. 12, 1973, 1249-1250.

6. In *Language in Relation to a Unified Theory of the Structure of Human Behavior* (The Hague, 1967), Kenneth Pike

uses the example of a football game to describe a series of
overlapping hierarchies of activity which can be analyzed in
terms of waves and segments, each of which may have its own
independent structure and may share structural components
with overlapping segments. (See pp. 98-121.) Most of our
critical activity in explicating a text is directed to a
fairly confined portion of textual material. However, it
must always be remembered that we are looking at a part of
a whole, and that its surrounding contexts may create a
different field of meaning than that created by the smaller
portion.

7. See Charles Sanders Peirce, *Selected Writings* (ed.
J. Buchlev, New York, 1940) and Charles Morris, *Signs,
Language, and Behavior* (New York, 1946). For the work of
de Saussure, see *Course in General Linguistics* (ed. Bally
and Schehaye, New York, 1959).

8. The distinction between "physical" and "conceptual"
is not of much interest to us here, but generally, a semiotic
must be constructed in such a way that it is applicable to
signs in all media. It is clear that the physical nature of
the medium itself controls to a great extent the nature of
the signs that may be constructed with it. The acoustic
properties of the channel of oral communication, for instance,
make possible some communications not easily conveyed in the
graphic medium of print-patterns of intonational stress, say.
An excellent example of the application of this concept is
the Morton-McGregor theory that the length of Luke and Acts
is determined by the size of the codex on which it was
written. See *The Structure of Luke and Acts* (New York, 1964).

9. For a full description of these three processes see
Charles Morris, "Foundation of the Theory of Signs," in
Foundations of the Unity of Science, ed. Otto Neurath,
Rudolf Carnap, Charles W. Morris (Chicago, 1961) I, 79-137.
In this essay, I have used the neutral term "rhetorical" for
the term "pragmatic", which has what seems to me to be un-
fortunate philosophical overtones.

10. Jülicher's distinction between parable and allegory
depends on the perceiver's interpretation of the sign and on
his understanding of the sender intention (*Die Gleichnisreden
Jesu*, Tübingen, 1899, I, pp. 91ff.). The semantic definition
I am attempting here is more rigorously formal, although fully
carried out it also includes the pragmatic dimension. The

distinction between simile and parable according to the number of verbs (suggested by Bultmann, *Geschichte der Synoptischen Tradition*, 1931, pp. 179-222) gives us a formal description of the first-order sign system, but does not help us to understand how that sign-system (whether it is a figurative saying, a similitude, or a parable proper) is intended to mean or is perceived as having meaning.

11. For a very brief distinction between first and second-order sign systems, see Roland Barthes, *Elements of Semiology* (trans. Lavers and Smith, Boston, 1970), pp. 90-91. For a fuller, but frequently cryptic report on Russian studies in "second-order modeling systems", see O. G. Revzina's summary of "The Fourth Summer School on Secondary Modeling Systems," (Tartu, 17-24 August, 1970), *Semiotica*, VI, 3 (1972), 222-243.

12. The system of the American semioticians/and semanticists--Morris, Peirce, and Stephen Ullmann (*The Principles of Semantics*, Glascow, 1951; and *Semantics, An Introduction to the Science of Meaning*, Blackwell, 1962) seems better suited to the purposes of defining and analyzing the parabolic sign than the Saussurian-Hjelmslevian system often used for semiotic analysis. The failure of Saussure and Hjelmslev to include the non-linguistic referent as a part of the signifying construct, as Ogden and Richards have pointed out (*The Meaning of Meaning*, London, 1936, chapter 1) makes its use in this context rather difficult--precisely because the mode of signification transforms the non-linguistic referent into a sign. Further, the Saussurian separation of signifier and signified is rejected by some American linguists (Pike, p. 63), and from that point of view, Hjelmslev's four-part distinction of *two* planes of expression and content is even more difficult to work with. (However, for an example of its application, see Dan Patte's "An Analysis of Narrative Structure and the Good Samaritan," *Semeia*, 2, 1974, 1-26.) Note 15 provides a diagram of the Hjelmslevian-Saussurian system, described by Barthes in *Elements of Semiology*, pp. 89-91.

13. Morris ("Foundations," p. 83) discusses the problem of signs which refer to things and signs which refer to abstractions:

> A sign must have a designatum (that which
> the sign refers to); yet obviously every
> sign does not, in fact, refer to an actual
> existent object....Where what is referred
> to actually exists as referred to the ob-
> ject of reference is a *denotatum*. A *desig-*
> *natum* is not a thing, but a...class of ob-
> jects.

14. The interpretation here is that of Irenaeus, *Against*
Heresies, Book IV, Chap. xxxvi, 7.

15. In Hjelmslevian terms, this mode of signification
would be represented thus:

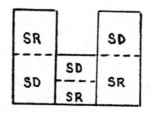

Barthes' diagram of what Hjelmslev calls a "connotative
semiotic" is oversimplified, I think (see *Elements*, p. 90).
About his own double system, Hjelmslev cautions:

> ...the distinctions we have given here of
> connotative semiotics and metasemiotics are
> only provisional "real" definitions, to
> which we cannot ascribe even operative value.

(*Prolegomena to a Theory of Language*, trans. Whitfield,
Madison, 1961, p. 114). Unfortunately, however, much structuralist work, particularly in France and Italy, relies on
just this distinction, which Hjelmslev himself finds impossible to apply.

16. In Luke's version of The Sower, this fact leads the
disciples to ask Jesus to interpret the parable for them--to
provide a stated designatum (Luke 8:9). Geraint Jones comments, "There was no indication in the parable that the Seed
represented the Word" (*The Art and Truth of the Parables*,

London, 1964, p. 101). The Evangelists, writing to a later audience, often found it necessary to provide a designatum for their readers.

17. For a complete definition of these terms, see Arthur Burks, "Icon, Index, and Symbol," in *Philosophy and Phenomenological Research*, IX, 4 (1949), 673-689.

18. For a summary application of this notion to the parables, expressed in concrete terms, see Dan Via, *The Parables: Their Literary and Existential Dimension* (Philadelphia, 1974), pp. 4-6. For a more detailed discussion see Eta Linnemann, *Die Gleichnisse Jesu*, p. 16, and Wilhelm Michaelis, *Die Gleichnisse Jesu* (Hamburg, 1956), p. 15.

19. Trans., Nancy Howe, in *Essays on Dante*, ed. Mark Musa, Bloomington, 1964, p. 37. Since Dante deliberately and carefully constructed his allegory according to this four-point model, the reader who does not know the possible modes of signification will miss much of the meaning of the narrative. It is hardly necessary to add, I think, that not all parabolic systems are so constructed, not even those parables and allegories composed in Dante's day.

20. Good examples of the generative power of this system may be found in what is now called the "Robertson school" of medieval criticism which reads almost every late medieval text as though it were parabolic system constructed according to the rules of four-fold signification.

21. On the process of syntactical cognition, Roman Ingarden writes:

> ...sentences, too, are only to a certain degree independent of other semantic units in the text and receive their full meaning, with their proper nuances, only as parts of a multiplicity of sentences. The meaning of the sentence completes itself and adapts itself to the meaning of the sentences preceding it, but not only to those preceding it. The meaning of sentences which are yet to come can also share in determining the meaning of the sentence we have just read, can supplement or modify it.

(*The Cognition of the Literary Work of Art*, p. 34).

22. Cambridge, 1924, p. 10.

23. *On Modesty*, Chap. 9.

24. Even as early as Siefried Goebel's work, *Die Parabeln Jesu* (Gotha, 1879), it was asserted that the contextual problem was paramount in any interpretation of the parables: "We must first of all ask what Jesus meant to say to those to whom he delivered it," Goebel wrote (p. 26).

25. *The Parables of the Kingdom* (New York, 1961), p. 167.

26. As an example of this view, see *Luke and the Gnostics*, by Charles H. Talbert (Nashville, 1966).

27. Form criticism and redaction criticism exemplify that critical method which intersects the syntactic and the rhetorical dimensions: it sees the Gospels as a rhetorical sign, traditional materials generically ordered, reshaped by the requirements of the later senders and receivers. From a rather different point of view, Dan Via comments:

> ...although from the standpoint of the situations in which Jesus told the parables the parables themselves were the focus, now that they have been included in a more comprehensive literary structure, that new structure has become the focus and the parables are subsidiary. To make the parables subsidiary to the larger story of Jesus and to the kerygmatic interpretation of that story was certainly the intention of the evangelists, and to the extent that their intention can be carried out the parables become vehicles for the expression of the whole kerygmatic meaning of the Gospels.

(*The Parables*, pp. 178-179).

28. See Iser, *The Implied Reader*, chapter 11 ("The Reading Process: A Phenomenological Approach").

29. Ingarden, *Cognition*. See particularly pp. 50-63.

30. Iser, p. 280.

31. Iser, p. 280.

32. Iser, p. 294.

33. Two accessible, short examples of Lévi-Strauss' structural analysis are "The Structural Study of Myth," in DeGeorge and DeGeorge, *The Structuralists from Marx to Lévi-Strauss* (Garden City, 1972) and "The Story of Adiwal," in Leach, *The Structural Study of Myth and Totemism* (London, 1969). For Greimas, see "Elements pour une théorie de l'interprétation du récit mythique," *Communications*, 8 (1966) and *Sémantique structurale* (Paris, 1966).

34. In *The Raw and the Cooked* (volume 1 of *Mythologique*, p. 5) Lévi-Strauss says,

> ...the unity of the myth is never more than tendential and projective and cannot reflect a state or a particular moment of the myth. It is a phenomenon of the imagination, resulting from the attempt at interpretation; and its function is to endow the myth with synthetic form and to prevent its integration into a confusion of opposites.

RESPONSE TO SUSAN WITTIG

John F. Plummer
Vanderbilt University

The linguistic model for structuralist and semiotic investigation presupposes a balanced interest in syntax, performative context (pragmatics), and semantics, and in this sense especially we are indebted to Professor Wittig's urging that we take care in our investigations of parables to include more than an intensive study of textual structures. Those structures of the text can be meaningful, after all, only in the context of the reader's dealing with them and of the semantic dimensions of the parable.

The paper itself provides us with: 1) a semantic definition of the parable, that is, an investigation of "how parable means", and 2) an argument for the importance of the reader in the parable activity, a new emphasis on the "right wing" of the pragmatic axis. A preliminary remark might be that this emphasis on the reader might in itself somewhat unbalance our attention to the pragmatic or rhetorical axis, in its tendency to ignore the "left wing", the fabulator of the parable. Writers are, of course, notoriously unhelpful about their meanings, and it would be unusual to find one who speaks in parables to be an exception to this rule. But to take things in their proper order, let me turn to the semantic definition of the parable which has been offered.

The definition of the parable as "...a duplex semiotic in which the relationship between the first-order sign (the linguistic system) and its unstated conceptual designatum is mediated by a second-order, extra-linguistic denotatum (a material system)..." in which the second-order material sign vehicle "...is linked iconically to its unstated designatum..." falls something short of expressing the semantic quiddity of the parable. The definition falls short of its task, I would say, in that it does not isolate the parable from many other literary forms.

I think that both elements of the definition: 1) the multipleness of the levels of signification and 2) the iconic nature of their relationships, are valid, but that both elements also characterize most if not all literary texts. The duplex nature of the parable's semiotic, first of all, seems to apply to, for example, the drama: one sees the actor who plays Richard II appear to be run through with a blade and fall to the floor, apparently dead. One's interpretation of the meaning of the play is not based directly upon what one sees (the prostrate actor), but rather upon the image of a dead king. There are then at least three elements in this multiplex semiotic event: a fallen actor, the image of a fallen king, and what that image or idea might itself be interpreted to mean. One's interpretation of Dickens' *Great Expectations* is likewise not merely an interpretation of the linguistic system. One reads: "Ours was the marsh country, down by the river, within, as the river wound, twenty miles of the sea." To understand the story as a competent reader is more than to de-code the sentence in terms of English grammar; it is to examine the "material sign vehicle", the extra-linguistic denotatum which one sees in one's mind's eye, for the meanings which it might possibly suggest beyond its mere postulation by the sentence. Literature is itself a second-order sign system built upon the natural language, or to put it another way, literature is itself, as Barthes has claimed, a language.

To say that the relationship between the second-order material sign vehicle and its unstated designatum is iconic is to refine the definition further, but still not enough. The relationship between the imagery and the meaning of all literature is iconic, and an iconic quality is, according to Charles Morris,[1] the essential characteristic of the esthetic sign. When I see *King Lear* I may feel that it is in part "about" a breakdown in communication and trust between the members of a family, and I can extend that idea somewhat to argue that it is about a similar breakdown in the structure of a kingdom, and even beyond that, a breakdown in order in general. But the play is not about incest. And it is not about the values of horsemanship as an aristocratic pursuit. Nor is it about the danger to one's health involved in taking drugs. I know it is not about these things because the nature of the relationship between imagery and action of the play and the potential meanings of the play is iconic. The elements of my interpretation of the play, that designatum which was unstated and I have supplied, and the relationships between those elements, must "fit" somehow the elements of the play in their inter-relations.

If we take a metaphysical poem like George Herbert's "Redemption", we can see that it fits the offered definition of a parable quite neatly:

> Having been tennant long to a rich lord,
> Not thriving, I resolved to be bold,
> And make a suit unto him, to afford
> A new small-rented lease, and cancel the old.

In heaven at his manor I him sought;
They told me there that he was lately gone
About some land, which he had dearly bought
Long since on earth, to take possession.
I straight returned, and knowing his
        great birth,
Sought him accordingly in great resorts;
In cities, theaters, gardens, parks,
        and courts;
At length I heard a ragged noise and mirth
Of thieves and murderers; there I him
        espied,
Who straight, *Your suit is granted*, said,
        and died.

Clearly there is an extra-linguistic denotatum here which stands in an iconic relationship to a "meaning" of the poem, its conceptual designatum. That designatum is not stated--it is left for the reader to supply that the lord in the poem is Christ, that the Lord's taking possession of some land on earth is the incarnation and passion, and that the new "small-rented lease" is the new dispensation, etc.

It might be objected that this example is not fair, because Herbert's poem is in fact a parable. We do sense, in any case, that it is intensely parable-like, although we might nevertheless classify it as a conceit. A conceit is an extended metaphor--in the case of the Herbert poem the extension is carried so far as to form a narrative. Let us take as an example another, shorter, metaphor: "When thou sigh'st, thou sigh'st not wind, / But sigh'st my soul away: / When thou weep'st, unkindly kind, / My life's blood doth decay." This is one of Donne's Songs. The imagery here is deliberately troublesome, paradoxical, "impossible" in a commonsense understanding of it. It invites us to puzzle it out, of course, to interpret it as part of an ingenious argument that the poet and his love are spiritually joined, that the woman's grieving at the poet's departure is actually destructive of his well being. One could squeeze this meaning into a paraphrase like "He says he loves her and that she shouldn't cry", and those of us who have taught Donne in the classroom are familiar with this technique, but we instinctively rebel against this as an over-simplification which dodges the challenge of the poem. Our reading ought to "fit" the material sign vehicle (that strange image of the woman's tears being the man's blood) as delicately and thoroughly as possible.

This definition of how a parable means lets in, in other words, too many things we do not want to call parables: *King Lear*, *Great Expectations*, lyric poems, metaphors. Why don't we want to call these things parables? We do feel that the difference has something to do with a meaning which must be supplied and the rules which seem to govern what kind of meaning will do. It is not that there is only one meaning for a parable, an idea which would imply that even a poor choice of words in one's interpretation of a parable would lead to disqualification, but one does somehow sense that: if the meaning of a poem can be described metaphorically as fitting into an indefinite but circumscribed space, then the meaning of a parable has to fit this circumscribed space better, more fully, even to the very edges.

It seems to me that the nature of constraints which determine the iconicism between denotatum and designatum in the parable are more intense than for other kinds of texts. I say "more intense" in order to dodge the question of whether these constraints are more numerous, or qualitatively different from those operating for other kinds of literary discourse, or both. My sense of things is that

Professor Wittig's semantic analysis of parables is on the
right track, but that it needs to be further developed along
the lines she has mapped out. To say that the semiotic of
the parable is iconic is to suggest that it is demanding.
In fact, it is more demanding, more imperious in its admonition to the reader than other forms. That remark allows me
to reiterate my desire to see an intensified study of this
iconicity and to turn my attention to the reader of the
parable.

Professor Wittig says of parable and readers that "When
we read a text characterized by the quality of indeterminacy,
as the parables are, we are reading ourselves as well as the
text, and are being forced to an awareness of the creation of
meaning in our own minds, as well as to an awareness of the
meaning itself." The problem here again is that parables are
not only *not* uniquely indeterminant (it is not claimed that
they are) but that *all* literature is to a greater or lesser
degree indeterminant. The literary sign is polysemic. I do
not want to haggle over terms, but we are involved in an
attempt at definition. I fully agree that the parable is
more indeterminant than *some* literary texts, but that is a
question of degree and not kind. A new emphasis on the
reader is one by-product of the structuralist criticism of
all literature (though it is by no means unique to structuralism). Jonathon Culler's *Structuralist Poetics* makes the
point very nicely: "The linguistic model provides a slight
reorientation which makes apparent what is needed [for the
study of literature]. Study of the linguistic system becomes theoretically coherent when we cease thinking that our
goal is to specify the properties of objects in a corpus and
concentrate instead on the task of formulating the internal-

ized competence which enables objects to have the properties they do for those who have mastered the system. To discover and characterize structures one must analyze the system which assigns structural descriptions to the objects in question, and thus a literary taxonomy should be grounded on a theory of reading."[2]

Obviously, to study how a given text means, or how literature in general means, we must study how we go about assigning and perceiving meaning. This does not thrust the author or the text out of our field of vision, or at least it should not, and this activity is not restricted to parables alone. I would disagree, in fact, that the parable is preeminently the kind of text for the pursuit of such a task, and to get to cases, I heartily disagree with Professor Wittig that "as far as the parables are concerned the structure probably has *less* controlling effect than in any other narrative form, precisely because of their indeterminate nature...." This is to argue against the very iconic nature of the parable's semantic structure which was urged earlier, that is, the idea that the meaning of the parable must *fit* the diagram of the material sign vehicle. This fit cannot be checked by the reader without a scrupulous regard for the structure of the text. Professor Wittig's own interpretation of the Parable of the Sower is based upon a perception of the ways in which the terms of the text (like the "good ground") relate to one another, in short, upon a consideration for the structure of the parable.

The paper is much more convincing when it urges us to keep semantics, syntactics, and the entire pragmatic axis in mind than it is here in its sudden tilt towards the reader. It is not enough to argue that the indeterminacy of the parable thrusts the reader into prominence. This seems to confuse prominence with vulnerability. Christ's admonition "He who has ears to hear, let him hear", puts the "hearer" on the spot; it implies in the strongest terms that something in particular is being said which must be heeded. This kind of onus is lacking in such equally indeterminate texts as Ezra Pound's "In a Station of the Metro": "The apparition of these faces in the crowd; / Petals on a wet, black bough." It seems fruitless to me to puzzle over which text allows the reader more room to maneuver (though one cannot imagine Pound saying "He who has ears, let him hear") or in which case the various levels of textual structure are more prominent. One must, as one does, utilize the entire semiotic of the parable in reading it.

To recapitulate, the paper sets out to warn, quite rightly, against premature and excessively sanguine predictions that a structural study of parables will provide the key to their entire treasure, and to draw attention to the roles of the semantic and rhetorical components of the parables' semiotic. My final impression is that the semantic investigation pulls short of its goal, leaving us with a definition of the parable which leaks, and that the exploration of the reader's role in parables (though fascinating in itself) is overstated and fails to integrate itself with, is even contradictory of, the semantic investigation.

NOTES

1. *Writings on the General Theory of Signs; Signification and Significance*, "Esthetics and the Theory of Signs," *Journal of Unified Science*, 8 (1939), 131-50.

2. (Ithica: Cornell University Press, 1975), p. 120.

RESPONSE TO SUSAN WITTIG

Gary A. Phillips

Vanderbilt University

Professor Wittig's suggestions concerning the semiotic of the parable are important for a number of reasons. First, and most obviously, she demonstrates by her argument the necessity for and possibility of eclectic model building. By appeal to literary criticism, linguistics, biblical criticism and philosophy she provides an example herself of the route any semiotic analysis of the parables must go if it is to claim even a tentative completeness. In short, she practices what she preaches. Secondly, she can proceed in this interdisciplinary way primarily because of her view of the complex, manifold nature of the structures and constraints which are part and parcel of the phenomenon of the parable's "meaning effect", a view which is shared and articulated in diverse ways in other fields such as sociolinguistics, phenomenology and, we add very significantly, in philosophy of language. The multidimensionality of the structuring components of the parable demand a model and methodology which can account for not only their individual make-up but also and most importantly, their interrelationship. It is precisely in this interrelationship and convergence of constraints that the composite meaning-effect is produced.

Professor Wittig's initial complaint against the early "structuralists" is strategic; for, if taken seriously, it blows apart any simple understanding of the syntactic-semantic, form-content relationship and attributes to the

parabolic meaning a much more complex nature. There are any
number of such models around that fail to make this important
distinction. For example, Chomsky has been criticized and
rightly so for his propounding of a syntactic model of language acquisition and use that relegates the semantic and
non-verbal components of the communicative process to a
secondary place. The semantic arises out of the syntactic,
it is secondary to the syntactic. Likewise, following Professor Wittig's suggestion, contemporary structuralist interpretation of the parable runs the risk of being criticized
for failing to appreciate the complexity of the semantic
domain. Indeed, her criticism is directed to both the structural model and the basic ontological presuppositions under-
girding that model. So, for example, we might ask do the
structural models employed in the arguments and articles of
Semeia I and II make the analogous mistake of focusing upon
the form or deep structure of the parable to the exclusion
of concern for the performative aspect of the parable in its
use and the historical context that would permit the communication to go on between sender and receiver, writer and
reader, speaker and hearer? The implications of Professor
Wittig's position seem clear: the only adequate analysis of
the parable must be a holistic one that seeks to explain the
form and function as interpenetrating, moreover that we must
go "outside of the text itself" in order to see the full
semantic picture. This leaves us with a major question:
Does Professor Wittig's criticism call into question the
structural analysis offered by D. Patte in *What is Structural Exegesis?*, especially his working model in so far as
it accounts for this broadly defined semantic picture? Is

this model unsatisfactory for explaining the extra-textual
dimensionality of the parable's meaning-effect?

It would seem clear that Patte and we who use (and abuse)
his model affirm an understanding of the meaning-effect of
the parable that is dynamic. The parabolic meaning is not
a thing but a process: "A discourse does not have a meaning
(an entity); a discourse is meaningful" (Patte, "Good Samaritan", pp. 1-2). In fact, the meaning-effect is a construct
which is produced by the interpenetration and interreaction
of a number of semiotic structures, structures defined as
the constraints of the systems, both textual and extra-textual,
which altogether produce the parable's meaning. The explanation of this process is one of explaining a phenomenon that
is already meaning-full: namely, the communication of parabolic meaning. In this limited sense the approach of our
structural analysis is phenomenological.

While it is true that Patte's method begins with a
bracketing of the investigation and focuses upon the deep
mythical, narrative and logical structures which lie at the
root of parable communication, it is not the case that we
hold that attention paid *only* to the deep constraints is
either sufficient in and of itself or holds a greater priority
over any other aspect of the total structure for disclosing
the complete meaning-effect. All of the constraints are
integral; the question is where is one to begin in the
analysis. This initial deconstruction which Professor Wittig
claims is but one-half of the goal of parabolic analysis is
complemented by a reconstruction that is accomplished when
the constraints on three strategic levels are dealt with:
the levels of cultural, enunciative and deep structures.
The analysis is only partially complete until these levels

of structure are finally integrated and the interrelationship
of the semiotic systems both textual and extra-textual which
give rise to the meaning-effect of the parable are discerned.

It is important to note that our method indeed allows
for a functional component in the structural unfolding. Precisely on the level of the enunciation the basic complaint of
Professor Wittig, we believe, can be met provided an adequate
model can be devised which will explain the pertinent features
of the performative dimension of the parable's meaning. We
agree that unless the parable is addressed in terms of the
way in which it is heard and spoken, then the deep structure
analysis will be lacking a necessary complement, a feature
of the meaning-effect of the parable that a phenomenological
attitude toward the parable readily discloses--namely that
the parable is dynamic discourse, language in use, an utterance that performs. Hence, on the level of the enunciation
we must propose a way of explaining the parable's inter-
personal, culturally expressive, performative functions.
The fact that this has not been done ought not mean that
the basic model is deficient, but only that we have not progressed to that stage in our step by step deconstruction and
reconstruction of the text.

How would we conceive of some of the constraints on the
level of the enunciation? At this juncture an appeal to the
philosophy of language is helpful. By making use of the
work of functional language philosophers and their view of
language we may have the makings for a systematic model that
can explain the phenomenon of parable use. For this we refer
to J. L. Austin, J. Searle and L. Wittgenstein.[1] What is it
about parable language that is characteristic of the *way* in
which it is comprehended and is therefore central to its

meaning-effect? Parable language may be characterized in
terms of three linguistic functions: it is referential,
that is arises out of a given historical context and so
anchors the communication by way of pointing to states of
affairs; it is attitudinal, that is it expresses an orientation toward the world that gives contour and significance
to the referents that is comprehensive in scope; it is performative in that it prompts and bolsters, teases and otherwise engages the reader/hearer in commitment to the comprehensive orientation put forward by the attitudinal force of
the language. Parabolic language functions by pointing to
an event, person, place or state of affairs. It involves
making assertions about the nature of the world. In this
regard, referentially functioning language has a public
significance whose meaning is finally qualified by the
perspective in which the referents have a status and the
degree to which the parable's speaker/hearer is committed
to that orientation, an orientation that is made visible
when the deep mythical structure is disclosed. Attitudinal
or onlook functioning language, to borrow a phrase from D.
Evans, presents interpretation and conceptualization of the
data pointed to by the referentially functioning language.
These two functions are integrally related; for the referents are constituted by the perspective which gives them
significance while the referents give content to the perspective. Finally, parabolic language has a performative
function: that is, the parable is more than just literal
statements of fact or expressive of an orientation. The
speaker/hearer of the parable accomplishes something when
discourse with performative force is employed. He becomes
self-involved with the language; he commits himself to the

onlook and affirms this stance vis-a-vis other possible onlooks. Such language functions to bring about states of
affairs by creation or modification of the present in and
through the event of the language use.

Using these categories of referential, onlook and performative functions, let us examine the nature of what I
understand to be parable more closely in terms of the definition given by Dodd. Expressed in terms of Dodd's definition
we can in fact locate these three specific functions of
parabolic language which together in part give the parable
its distinctiveness. Recalling Dodd's formulation, (1) "At
its simplest, the parable is a metaphor or simile drawn from
nature or common life": that is, the language of the parable
has reference to and is funded from the hearer's ordinary,
everyday experiences; the parable functions to refer to and
to identify various things in the world. (2) "Parable is a
metaphor...arresting the hearer by its vividness and strangeness": that is, the referential functioning language in a
certain way brings a new onlook to the attention of the
hearer so that the referents presented are viewed now in a
different light. That is its attitudinal or onlook function.
(3) Finally, "Parable...(leaves) the mind in sufficient
doubt about its precise application to tease it into active
thought": that is, parabolic language functions with a
force upon the hearer, inducing, teasing, inviting the hearer
to look on the referents in a special way. This is the
text's performative function which acts upon the hearer and
leads him to action through participation in the proffered
onlook.

Parables are drawn from real life; they are rooted in
things as they are, having "immediate realistic authenticity".

The everyday images and references of the parable are not merely incidental to its meaning; therefore, a parable's realism must not be considered a device by means of which the intellectual point is made. This referential component is constitutive of the parable's total meaning-effect. Put in other words, the use of parabolic language asserts that such and such is the case when the *whole* parable is articulated. It is the nature of parabolic language that it has an odd logic about it. That means in determining the meaning of the referential language the context becomes crucial: the referential language can never be isolated from the speaker/hearer's context and way of seeing things.[3] This is precisely one of the concerns voiced by Professor Wittig-- to ground the semantic in the historical context and the way of understanding or interpreting. What is the odd logic or structure? It is related to the logical uniqueness of the parabolic onlook itself which stands over against the ordinary way of looking on things that characterizes our everyday existence. In every respect the parable is based upon the everyday and the ordinary; the parable functions by referring to the everyday world.

But in terms of comprehending the parable we do not always immediately know the meaning of the parable's referents. As we enter the world of the parable we bracket these references for a time only to return to them later. As Funk says we look *through* the language at first and not directly *at* it. To put it in Professor Wittig's words, the parabolic language becomes a denotatum for a designatum whose meaning is not clear until the total parable is read or heard. The reference is ambiguous. Once the attitudinal function of the language is discerned then we can understand how the

referents are intended to be used and hence their meaning.
Thus, the parabolic process involves a new, imaginative
grasp of the ordinary referents by way of presenting a
new or superordinary way of seeing them. In the words of
literary critic Owen Barfield, the parable presents a conceptualization of the familiar that makes it stand out and
be apprehended in a new fashion.[5] So the literal or referential language can neither be ignored nor used merely as a
vehicle for stipulated meanings; it is central to the entire
parabolic meaning-effect.

Furthermore, the parable's referential function must
be seen in terms of the literary form in which it is placed
and presented. The parable is a text set within a broader
text. It possesses its own internal structure, composition
and logic which as a whole must be taken into account in
the task of speaking/hearing the parable. It is the parable
as a whole which is brought into metaphorical relationship
with the hearer.[6] Cadoux asserts:

> A parable is the work of a poor artist if
> the picture or story is a collection of
> items out of which we have to pick one and
> discard the rest...A good parable is an
> organic whole in which each point is vital
> to the rest; it is the story of a complex
> and sometimes unique situation or event,
> so told that the outstanding features of
> the story contribute to the indication and
> nature of the point.[7]

As a composition with integrity of its own, the possibility
for allegorical interpretation--something that violates
the integrity of the text as a whole--is precluded in so
far as we understand the words and sentences of the parable

to form an organic unity. If this is the case, two movements are necessary for understanding the meaning of the parable: (1) the parable must first be read for the parable's sake. That is to say, the reader/hearer's initial focus is upon the parable as an organic, structured whole.[8] It is the narrative structure at the deepest level that gives us access to this parabolic organization and its configuration. (2) Secondly, we are to understand that the parable's organic meaning is determined in part by its context, the most immediate of which is the Gospel. This is a two-way relationship: the parable's organic meaning influences the overall contextual significance, and conversely the context delimits the parable's absolute aesthetic autonomy.

Thus, the reading/hearing of the parable presents the convergence of two worlds and two onlooks: a "picture half" and a "real half" as Linnemann suggests. The references of the picture world are presented and understood in a certain shocking way, in a way that has its own structure and logic; nevertheless, the referential language is founded upon common, everyday experiences.[9] When the picture world comes into contact and metaphorical clash with real or ordinary ways of seeing things and the confronting onlooks and logics enter into tensive relationship, then interlock occurs and new meaning arises. The facts of the ordinary world are dislocated, as it were, in favor of the new way of seeing the world. The parable's referential language working on two "literal" levels has an indispensable role in communicating the meaning of the parable. We do not however have facts alone; they are presented within a certain interpretive framework.

This is essentially what Dodd means when he claims that
parables do more than give reference to matters of common
life: the parables arrest their hearers through their vividness and strangeness. The onlook function is then a presentation of a radically new way of seeing things and ordering
them. Parabolic language functions in this way by reinter-
preting the ordinary in terms of the strange and new in the
way of a clash between the worlds. Parable is a tensive
clash between the world and logic offered by the parable as
a whole and the world and logic referred to in literal, descriptive terms. Note that this is precisely what metaphor
accomplishes: it raises the possibility of creating new
meaning through the redirection of the hearer/reader's attention by means of imaginative shock. The metaphor shatters
the convention of predication--that is the meaning and
significance of referentially functioning discourse--by
presenting an alternate way of looking on things, a new way
of grasping things now seen in a different field (Black).
In so doing, metaphor offers a new way of seeing self in the
world.

Parables present a transformed comprehension of the
world. At its very core the parable as metaphor attempts
to shock the hearer by presentation of the new onlook in
such a way that the metaphorical twist or distortion of the
parable draws attention to the everyday, the ordinary, the
literal and concrete.[10] More than that, the parabolic onlook interprets the hearer (Fuchs).[11] We mean by this that
the world of the parable confronts the hearer and illuminates
him and, in the case of the Kingdom parables, gives an analogous word about God's transforming power in the world. In so
doing the parable calls for response. The parable's vividness

and arrest demand change of the hearer's way of looking on
the world and himself as a suitable response to the parable,
its world and most of all its speaker. Until the hearer
adopts the new way of seeing things, the parable goes un-
heard and the metaphorical process is stymied. The hearer's
response is imperative in order to complete the metaphor:
the hearer's way of looking on things stands as the second
element of the metaphor of which the first part is the
parable itself as an organic, logical whole. Just as the
onlook function has no content without references drawn from
everyday world and common life, and the references in turn
have no meaning apart from a perspective on them, even so
the onlook in order to be operational requires the hearer's
active participation and involvement. Parable becomes event
when the new perspective or onlook ushers in concommitantly
with the hearer's response. This clearly illustrates the
necessary interrelationship of parabolic language's multiple
functions.

The parable's performative function is more precisely
seen in the participation or self-involvement of the speaker/
hearer as a complement to the parabolic onlook. Upon hearing the parable the listener must decide whether the metaphor will be his own language, whether to unfold with the
story and be claimed by the power of the metaphor or to re-
ject the call and abide with the conventional. The hearer
must choose between worlds and logics and onlooks, and whichever way he decides he disposes himself to the concrete
reality as it is put forward by either the ordinary or the
new parabolic onlook. Such participation and decision involves the whole person. To be sure parable has an assertive function; but the catalyst that enables the new way of

seeing things as significant things to come to life is the
hearer's involvement in the parable set within the metaphorical process itself.

Because the hearer completes the parable by responding
in a self-involving way to the onlook, it is right to say
that the parable is per force open-ended, as Professor Wittig
has rightly argued. The comprehension of the parable then
becomes a very personal act and so precludes any simple definitive response. Such parabolic open-endedness undercuts the
reduction of the parable's meaning-effect to a simple point of
"widest possible application" whether it be moral (Jülicher)
or eschatological (Jeremias and Dodd) in nature. We must conclude with Funk that the parable's meaning is not exhausted
by its original import though this original import exerts some
controls over how the parable is to mean at any future time.
At this point we can distinguish between parable and allegory.
Whereas the parable has many possible completions and uses and
is not constrained by a one-point understanding for all time,
allegory in every detail is so closed and so constrained by
the one-point interpretation. Allegory is reducible to a
point; parable is not.[12]

In saying that the original import controls the present
parabolic meaning even in its open-endedness, we are guided
by the historical and cultural factors underlying the discourse of the parable to other dimensions of any structural
exegesis: for example, the Kingdom motif, the coming judgment
and the invitation to decision. The parabolic onlook of the
Kingdom parables provokes the hearer to face the metaphorical
word of the arrival of God's kingdom as a radical, shocking
reversal of the human situation. As Dodd suggests, "The
parable as metaphor (leaves) the mind in sufficient doubt

about its precise application to tease it into active thought."
Dodd underscores the open-ended nature of the necessary response to the parable.

The performative force of the parabolic language rests
in its power to bring about the new onlook by self-involvement
in the parabolic world. The parable's call for response and
the hearer's appropriation of the onlook are co-temporal. By
entering into the parabolic onlook the hearer opts for a new
ordering of things. The language performs in so far as it
announces that an event has transpired, that a judgment on
the reader's part has taken place, that interlock has occurred.
The parable induces and leads on to decision. When the parable
becomes event there is "discernment"--"the point hits home...
the subject matter concerns him". And whenever the parable is
heard in its organic whole and in its contextual application
both to the text in which it is placed and by way of its referents to the world two sorts of performative functions are set
into motion: on the one hand, the hearer steps into the parabolic world; on the other hand, the hearer looks on his world
in view of the parabolic onlook and his life patterns, behavior, and associations are transformed. Taken together both
aspects are part of the same process: the hearer/reader
creating new signification by his personal encounter with the
text.

With such a view of parabolic language functions we offer
an expansion of the model that attempts to account for the
complex relationship of the parabolic text (its language and
internal organization) to the speaker/hearer. At least this
is one possible way of meeting Professor Wittig's objection
to an analysis that is concerned only for the textual structures rather than with the text's con-textual situation.

Philosophical language analysis shows us, especially in the work of Wittgenstein, that meaning is manifold in nature and contextually delimited. This is in keeping with Wittig's initial observation. Seen in terms of our model, this series of functional constraints may be placed at the level of the enunciation: the speaker/hearer's language is constrained by referential, attitudinal and performative functions. That there are numerous textual and extra-textual structures which interrelate so as to produce the meaning-effect is readily seen. Hopefully our model as it continues to be worked out will provide the answer as to how exactly these factors relate to one another.

NOTES

1. John Searle, *Speech Acts*; Donald Evans, *The Logic of Self-Involvement: A Philosophical Study of Everyday Language with Special Reference to the Christian Use of Language about God as Creator* (London: SCM Press, 1967); J. L. Austin, *How to Do Things with Words*, edited by J. O. Usmsow (New York: Oxford University Press, 1973); Ludwig Wittgenstein, *Philosophical Investigations* (Oxford: Basil Balckwell, 1953).

2. Amos Wilder, *Early Christian Rhetoric* (London: SCM Press, 1964), p. 81.

3. Compare Dan Via, *The Parables: Their Literary and Existential Dimension* (Philadelphia: Fortress Press, 1967), pp. 61, 64.

4. Robert.Funk, *Language, Hermeneutic and Word of God* (New York: Harper & Row, 1968), pp. 59ff.

5. Owen Barfield, *Poetic Diction: A Study of Meaning* (Middleton, Conn.: Wesleyan University Press, 1973), p. 173; also see Funk, p. 159.

6. Funk, p. 147. Jülicher's treatment of the parable virtually ignored the parable as a whole by speaking of a single comparative point. It would be better to think of the metaphorical method of parable interpretation as supplying not only one point of comparison but also a number of subsidiary metaphorical points. Max Black, *Models and Metaphors: Studies in Language and Philosophy* (New York: Cornell University Press, 1962), especially pp. 27ff.

7. A. T. Cadoux, *The Parables of Jesus: Their Art and Use* (London: James Clarke and Company, 1930), p. 52.

8. Via, p. 48. It is the larger unit, the parable as a whole, which bears the meaning in the first instance.

9. This is not a new point of departure. Rudolph Bultmann makes the same claim in *History of the Synoptic Tradition*, translated by John Marsh (New York: Harper & Row, 1968), p. 174.

10. Funk, p. 158. Evans, p. 222.

11. Ernst Fuchs, *Studies in the Historical Jesus*, translated by A. Scobie (Napersville, Ill.: A. R. Allecson, 1964), pp. 206, 212.

12. This is also a position held by John Dominic Crossan, "Parable and Example in the Teaching of Jesus," *New Testament Studies*, 18 (1972), 305.

DISCUSSION

WITTIG: I want to thank you [Gary Phillips, John Plummer] for the sweeping and careful reading of this terribly abstract paper. Professor Plummer has pointed out two things I would like to comment on. First, I believe you are very right when you say that I have underestimated the reliance of the reader upon the structure of the text, and that is partly due to the way I felt coming to this conference. You say there must be scrupulous regard for the structure of the text in the reader especially of the indeterminate parabolic sign and you are right. However, I do not think I am doing what you charge me with doing when you say that my definition of parable leaks, because I did not try to make a definition of parable. I was interested in building a semantic definition of a parabolic sign which is very different from attempting to build a generic definition of a parabolic narrative. That is entirely another matter lying at the intermediate level of structure in a deep structure process. I am not completely clear how my attempts to build some semantic definition are related to the very basic deep structural analysis of the text. But I am sure that whatever generic transformations are used so as to define the nature of the parables of Jesus or the parables of Kafka or whatever narrative, it utilizes the parabolic sign. You are right in pointing out that those signs may occur in poetry, drama, epic, and so on. These are generic matters and it is to structure that I would look for a definition of whatever literary form(s) the sign might appear in. It may be that my definition is so overbroad that it doesn't mean anything. But what we need is to turn our attention to the nature of meaning, to a re-examination of the nature of metaphor from this point of view. I think metaphoric sign is different from parabolic sign, polysemic sign or homonymic sign. What we need is a fuller taxonomy.

CROSSAN: To pick up Gary's point, if you read the parables of Jesus either as the parables of Jesus or as you find them in the Gospel, you can say that parables portray everyday experience. Therefore, I heard Gary saying quite rightly that parables portray everyday experience. Now, if you go into the parables of Borges, you find that the world is capitalistic, irratic, god-ridden. Maybe the point is when you look at the parable not only across but generically, that if the mythical system you are attacking is god-ridden, then you go into everyday experience for shock. I don't think that whether it is everyday language or God language is the point.

WITTIG: You are talking about what we are accustomed to in the performative context of our normal exchange, right, and if we are accustomed to one sort of language we fall to another one to create shock and surprise. But I think that while you, Gary, were talking about performative language, I was talking about the paradox that Dom raised. You raised to me a moment ago a question about Dodd's use of parable in the historical context and I wanted to come back to that. The business about history and divine intervention in human time and the importance of knowing the historical context for that reason ought not to be overlooked. In literary history

a genuinely historical look at a literary text is not always
very productive but here what Dodd is grasping at is that
it is the whole focus, the whole center of the parable and
from that point of view given the performative context the
historical context cannot be overlooked.

VIA: Susan, could you specify more exactly what you mean
by the "denotatum". You use the example from the Vineyard
parable but you don't mean an actual reference to the world,
rather more a representation, an "as if" that "could be".

WITTIG: I say it could occur and I suppose I mean "as if".
But really I am concerned to try to pull the notion of referent back into our semiotic analysis. The European linguists
working out of the Saussurian, Hjelmslevian model have built
a semiotic analysis based on signifier and signified. Saussure when he wrote was concerned with syntactics and never
got around to doing semantics. The best discussion of this
is in Stephen Ullmann's two books on semantics. At any rate,
there is no proper referent in European semantics, no referential reality to which the sign refers. Language is really
circular and autotelic somehow. American linguists are very
impatient with this. Pike, for example, in *Language in Relation to the Unified Theory of Behavior* says he disregards
Saussure because there is no referent: language circles in-
ward always instead of outward to the world of human experience. Furthermore, he says Hjelmslev is absolutely silly to
build four levels, much less than two. I realize what a can
of philosophical worms I am getting into.

CROSSAN: Maybe you can explain the difference between in-
wards and outwards for me.

WITTIG: I am thinking of language just as signifier-signifie
so that there is no externalization of language and it is always circling back upon itself. That was the question you
[Marin] were addressing last night, I believe. Because you
used the term "referent" at one point I wasn't sure whether
you used it knowingly.

VIA: Susan, did you say at one point that you thought that
most parable interpreters have been primarily concerned with
the denotatum?

WITTIG: With the structure of the denotatum. I was talking
about structural analysis at that point, rather than concerning
themselves with structure of the unstated designatum which I
was saying was left up to the reader.

VIA: There is no way to get to the denotatum in the S_m except
through the S_1 and therefore I would be inclined to think that
most parable exegesis in practice has really been concerned
with the S_1 and the denotatum S_m as an inseparable unit. In
practice though, they probably have not read Saussure; they
are much closer to considering the parable as a sign in the
Saussurian sense. Then parable interpreters have gone on to
Jesus' historical situation. That is what we have in Dodd and
Jeremias. I am altogether in favor of your wanting some sort
of way out of the circularity of language but I think that in
considering the parable itself it probably has been considered
much more like a Saussurian sign, with the S_1 being the signifier and the denotatum or S_m being the signified.

WITTIG: It may be that I have redrawn in that little diagram the same signifier-signified relationship, just changing the letters around.   But I am still concerned that we build some notion of referent back into our semiotic model.   It is not quite so important here in what Barthes calls the connotative system.   And if you look in *Elements of Semiology* at the chapter on connotation and the semiotic you will find what looks like a pair of slipped boxes where he is describing connotative and metasemiotic systems--the metasemiotic is a complex word.   It is not so important in terms of connotation but when you move to a metasemiotic system where the sign refers to its own sign-ness then the Barthian model falls apart, or so it seems to me.

MARIN: A note of clarification first about Barthes.   You know that Barthes at the beginning of *Zero* questioned his own distinction derived from Hjelmslev about the notion of connotation, his own distinction between denotation and connotation.   He said finally denotation may in the analysis of literary texts mean nothing.   There is finally no denotation or true connotation where we try to reach the point where we can say, using your terms, that this sign denotes something.   So I think I would approach your problem from a completely opposite direction.   The need for a referent, and finally it is Barthes who has introduced this referential relation, is a goal that is difficult to realize.   Now I don't understand your response to one question where you say that Saussure was mainly interested in syntactics, on the contrary...

WITTIG: I'm sorry.   I was using that term rather loosely. I mean that he is interested in the way signs go together whether or not they may be syntagmatic or paradigmatic.   And of course he is interested in the relationship of the parole and the langue. But as for a theory of meaning, no.

ENGEL: But the whole thing has to do with meaning. It is the relation of the real world to the spoken word and this is a meaning relationship.

MARIN: It might be a matter of terminology.

WITTIG: It may be also the perspective I've gained. In fact that is precisely Ullmann's statement--namely, that Saussure apart from the relation of signifier to signified does not go into the theory of meaning at any length.

MARIN: But a more general question on your paper. I very much agree with basic statements in your paper, but I would ask you about the use of the term "energy"--the energy of the text or just energy. You make a distinction between energy of text and forces. Sometimes you use "forces" in the sense of that which from the outside constrains the reader to read the text in a certain way. In a certain sense we can consider these cultural constraints as powerful institutions constraining and prohibiting the way a reader thinks; it determines the limits of what is thinkable in a definite culture and society. But "energy" has another meaning. The text can be conceived as a productive machine that generates energy by itself and this energy seems to be generated by the emptiness of the text as if this power of the text appears in its holes, the empty place, because it is indeterminate. I have the same feeling that there is not only a problem of terminology but a real problem, maybe even philosophical, with the use of the term "force" in the Speech Acts theory. Illocutionary force—what does force mean in this sense?

WITTIG: You have given it a very rich reading. For me it was primarily metaphorical but it does refer to the indeterminacy of the text, to the gaps which force or seduce the reader to become involved in the text. Because it is non-redundant, because it lacks completed structure, the reader must then himself become a part of the text. Now I like Jim Crenshaw's phrase—the text reconstitutes me—and that is a bridge into further analysis. That was the strategy of the argument using the notion of the iconic sign.

PETERSEN: Susan, could you comment further on what you mean by material in the sign diagram?

WITTIG: That was the basis of Dan Via's question. Dan asked me if I saw that as an "as if" condition. And I said that I thought it was a scene, event or object imagined to occur in the world of human experience. I realize the philosophical problems associated with that and I suspect that is why semanticists have been inclined to avoid the question of referent in language.

ROTH: I would like to take off from the iconic meaning-making relationship that you find in your figure #5. You indicate that this is open ended and could be the case with the parable. There are two very extreme examples of this sort of meaning making. The one is from the Dead Sea Scrolls where the teacher of righteousness claims that he and he alone is the authentic interpreter of ancient works given to the

prophets; not even they understand. He and he alone understands and only in so far as they consent to his interpretation are they the in-group. Another extreme relates to the
modern Hindu interpretation of the Jesus of the Gospel. It
boggles the mind in terms of the possibilities that lay open
there. Now you have brought up the question in connection
with Wolfgang Iser's model of phenomenology of reading. I
wonder where you could place this in the range of possibilities open between the extremes I have sketched. It seems to
me that Iser's model is a voluntaristic, individualistic
model of reading and I am reminded of the protest of some
French Marxists critics of structuralism that this sort of
model is really nothing but the last gasp of the bourgeoisie.

WITTIG: Well, I remind you of another model where the
reader is completely passive and at the control of the structure of the text; for him the reader is only re-echoing the
text itself rather than incorporating, giving it life and
body in himself. As to your other question I think you are
commenting upon the performative context in a given culture:
that is, in a culture the need to look to the reader for
authority and to accept his authoritative reading of the
text. I am struck by what Dom Crossan said this morning
about the authority of the Church imposing itself upon the
text and saying "This is the reading." As far as the extremes, I am not sure as to what axis I should place this on.
I have just put it within a performative context.

ROTH: It seems to me we must raise the question of the
authoritative patterns of the social setting of the hearer
and while this is not the only question to be raised I think
one has to raise it too.

WITTIG: That is a good question. I am thinking now of a school of Medieval criticism which says that the four-fold allegorical reading of Medieval texts can be imposed on almost any Medieval text. If I belonged to that school, to that way of reading, it would be imposed upon me. You are right in pointing out that within the performative context in some social structures we are not as free to argue our own meaning from the text. But these are doctrinal constraints which limit the interpretation of the text.

SILBERMAN: Susan, you speak of the constraints of the language itself. If I read the Good Samaritan in English I am reading one thing; if I read the Good Samaritan in Greek I am reading something else. If I read the Good Samaritan in Hebrew I am reading something quite different. So I did that. I have Keil-Deilitzch in front of me and it is full of all the kinds of words which provide constraints not found if they are in Greek. Let me indicate what some of the possibilities are. Let us assume that Jesus spoke Hebrew or Aramaic or Hebrew-Aramaic interchangeably. You have interesting kinds of words which occur in the translation. You have *naphal*--and he fell; you have the verb Bob Culley called to our attention a number of times--he saw him; and another verb *wayigash*. Now all of these words suddenly begin to have resonances in my mind and I go to the twenty-third chapter of Exodus where you have "If your enemy's animal falls you must pick him up" but it doesn't have anything about a man; but then the reader has to remember movement of *Qal wahomer*--if your enemy's animal falls into the ditch how much more your enemy? And I begin to get a whole picture of a kind of dialectic going on then when I read the text in Hebrew that I don't get in English or Greek. You don't have one parable or one story--you have really three stories.

WITTIG: Let me start out at the other end and say that the text itself--the physical text on the page before you--may not be the only text which you are responding to at that moment. As you indicate, you are responding to your memories of earlier texts which provide often strange juxtapositions and you may come to a peculiar, strange understanding of a text just by virtue of the fact that you happen to remember something. The other comment refers to Professor Plummer's remark that the reader is really dependent upon the structure of the text. You respond to the physical structure of the words on the page. One word in one context though it may not appear in another, may have connotations; it may recall memories to you. Yes, I say, there is an example of the dependency of the reader on the structure, but not on the surface structure.

CROSSAN: To start again from your term "iconic relationship". I use the term "isomorphic structuration" and I use it for two reasons: first, I thought it had a nice lift to it; second was that I was trying to get to that constraint. Now, I don't see that as closed because if some strong player comes along he may give a transformation of structure that I wasn't expecting. But somebody may show me how this is isomorphic; it is a transformation. That is wide open as far as I am concerned. I don't get a connotation of its closing in. It is opening out into language; it is opening out into all of the possibilities of resonances. It is held together by

isomorphic structuration but in the transformation possibilities are always there in totally radical ways.

WITTIG: That is a kind of opening out energy where analogy
can allow you to pull strange things together that you hadn't
expected to find together. Here I simply meant it in the
sense that the concept we build on top of the text is constrained by the shape of the text. One of the best examples
of that is the highly determined allegory, *Pilgrim's Progress*,
where I am told what designatum to structure. It is highly
determined in that text and that is very unlike the parables
we have been studying this week, particularly the one that
was used last night and again today. They are highly indeterminate as compared with *Pilgrim's Progress*. So that there
are degrees, I suspect, of iconic structuring if indeed the
sign relationship I've posited has any validity at all. To
make a further point, indeterminacy is a quality of many
narratives, not just allegory, not just parable. These are
generic terms. But indeterminacy can be found in many,
many kinds of narrative forms. I think that what we need
here is help from an information theorist who can help us
out with the notion of redundancy. That can be measured
mathematically and has been.

MARIN: Take for example the model provided by the theory
of games. For instance, in listening to you I was imagining
a kind of chess play in which only a few of the rules of the
game are known by the receiver. And he has to guess in a
certain sense the complete truth. Paradoxically, I was again
thinking, what of the sender? If I completely interpret a
text giving a certain meaning to me, what about the sender?

SILBERMAN: The sender cannot really be saying all that he wants to say at that moment.

WITTIG: Yes, he is not in control of the structures that he uses and certainly not of their effects.   But I want to come back to the game analogy.   There is a book, *The Pragmatics of Human Communication*, and there is a chapter there on "Who is Afraid of Virginia Wolfe?" which approaches the text as a game which calls attention to the rules of the game and in the course of the drama alteration of those rules.   Here, that is really an example of Jakobson's metalinguistics where the code itself is called to our attention and the structuration of the code is changed in the middle of the drama.

MARIN: We can go on in this direction and define precisely the measure of the semantic freedom of the receiver.   There are some texts where the rules are already given explicitly and some in which we have to guess.   And that is my problem with Pascal's thoughts where I have only a few rules at hand. I have to guess.